Cross-cultural Challenges in International Management

The development of international business and of globalization in every field of activity requires the interaction of individuals and groups with diverse cultural, religious, ethnic and social characteristics in different institutional contexts. *Cross-cultural Challenges in International Management* addresses the various difficulties that may impede smooth communication and cooperation of those involved in such interactions. It examines what types of resources are mobilized to overcome such difficulties.

The cultural and societal challenges of international management must be considered at different levels: the one of strategy, which the first part of the book is devoted to, but also that of management and business practices, which are addressed in the third part of the book. Both strategic decisions and daily business practices, however, in the particularly fluctuating and incompletely defined international context, gain from being framed by ethical and corporate social responsibility, which the second part of this book is devoted to. *Cross-cultural Challenges in International Management* provides an analysis of specific situations revealing such cultural or societal challenges. Thus the reader will benefit not only from advanced theoretical knowledge in the field but also from practical applications in various professional contexts and various countries.

Practitioners, students in various fields of social sciences, particularly in management, communication and international relations, and researchers will widely benefit from this book.

Bruno Amann is Professor in Management Sciences at Paul Sabatier University in Toulouse, France. He is also Associate Professor in Tianjin Foreign Studies University (China).

Jacques Jaussaud is Professor in Management Sciences at the University of Pau (UPPA), Pau, France.

Routledge Frontiers in the Development of International Business, Management and Marketing
Series Editors: Marin Marinov and Svetla Marinova

Economic Transition and International Business
Managing Through Change and Crises in the Global Economy
Edited by Eric Milliot and Sophie Nivoix

Value in Marketing
Retrospective and Perspective Stance
Edited by Marin A. Marinov

Cross-cultural Challenges in International Management
Edited by Bruno Amann and Jacques Jaussaud

For more information about this series, please visit: www.routledge.com/business/series/RFDIBMM

Cross-cultural Challenges in International Management

Edited by Bruno Amann and
Jacques Jaussaud

NEW YORK AND LONDON

First published 2021
by Routledge
52 Vanderbilt Avenue, New York, NY 10017

and by Routledge
2 Park Square, Milton Park, Abingdon, Oxon, OX14 4RN

Routledge is an imprint of the Taylor & Francis Group, an informa business

© 2021 Taylor & Francis

The right of Bruno Amann and Jacques Jaussaud to be identified as the authors of the editorial material, and of the authors for their individual chapters, has been asserted in accordance with sections 77 and 78 of the Copyright, Designs and Patents Act 1988.

All rights reserved. No part of this book may be reprinted or reproduced or utilised in any form or by any electronic, mechanical, or other means, now known or hereafter invented, including photocopying and recording, or in any information storage or retrieval system, without permission in writing from the publishers.

Trademark notice: Product or corporate names may be trademarks or registered trademarks, and are used only for identification and explanation without intent to infringe.

Library of Congress Cataloging-in-Publication Data
Names: Amann, Bruno, 1961– editor. | Jaussaud, Jacques, 1957– editor.
Title: Cross-cultural challenges in international management / edited by
 Bruno Amann and Jacques Jaussaud.
Description: New York : Routledge, 2020. | Series: Routledge frontiers in
 the development of international business, management and marketing |
 Includes bibliographical references and index.
Identifiers: LCCN 2020018490 | ISBN 9780367457907 (hardback) |
 ISBN 9781003025337 (ebook)
Subjects: LCSH: International business enterprises—Management. |
 Multinational work teams. | Intercultural communication. | Social
 responsibility of business.
Classification: LCC HD62.4 .C756 2020 | DDC 658/.049—dc23
LC record available at https://lccn.loc.gov/2020018490

ISBN: 978-0-367-45790-7 (hbk)
ISBN: 978-1-003-02533-7 (ebk)

Typeset in Sabon
by Apex CoVantage, LLC

Printed in the United Kingdom
by Henry Ling Limited

Contents

List of Figures and Tables	viii
Acknowledgements	x
List of Abbreviations	xi
List of Contributors	xiii

1 Introduction and Overview   1
BRUNO AMANN AND JACQUES JAUSSAUD

PART I
Cultural and Societal Challenges in Strategic
Decision-Making   9

2 How to Survive in an Unstable Environment for a Long
Time to Come: A Study of Firms Operating in Tunisia
During the Democratic Transition   11
ALYA CHARFI AND JAMIL CHAABOUNI

3 Asymmetric Alliances and SMEs' Internationalization   35
ZOUBEYDA MAHAMADOU

4 Autonomy or Abandonment? An Analysis of Authority
Figures in the Context of International Post-Acquisition
Integration   60
YASMINE SALEH AND EMNA MOALLA

5 Cultural Challenges and Quality Management Practices
of a German Multinational in Brazil   74
MADELEINE BAUSCH, CHRISTOPH BARMEYER AND ULRIKE
MAYRHOFER

vi *Contents*

PART II
Ethical and Social Responsibility Issues in International Management

95

6 CSR Action Mechanisms of International Companies:
An Analysis in the Light of African Realities 97
SUZANNE M. APITSA

7 The Ethical Tools of Multinationals: A Proof of Cultural
Diversity 118
HAMZA ASSHIDI

8 The Long March of the CSR in China: From Confucius
to the Teachings of Business Schools 137
GILDAS LUSTEAU AND ISABELLE BARTH

9 "Islamic Ethics and the Spirit of Capitalism": The Case of
MÜSİAD in Turkey 156
LAURE DIKMEN

PART III
The Challenges of Cross-Cultural Issues in International Management

173

10 The Limits of Managerialism for International Enterprise
in India 175
JOHN EUSTICE O'BRIEN AND JOSIANE MARTIN-O'BRIEN

11 Environmental Considerations When Purchasing Transport
Services: A Comparison of Management Approaches
Between Swedish and French Shippers 193
NATHALIE TOURATIER-MULLER AND DAN ANDERSSON

12 Does International Mobility Really Increase Students'
Intercultural Competence? 209
ANNE BARTEL-RADIC AND MARIE-ESTELLE BINET

13 Are Intercultural Competences at the Center of Job-Market
Demands? 227
SOPHIE WODOCIAG, AXELLE LUTZ AND CHIARA GHISLIERI

Contents vii

14 Conclusion 248
BRUNO AMANN AND JACQUES JAUSSAUD

Index 249

Figures and Tables

Figures

3.1	An internationalization model for SMEs	48
5.1	A multi-level analysis of quality management transfer in a multinational	79
7.1	Coding scheme (extract)	123
9.1	Conceptual model	159
10.1	Five domain (PETOS) enterprise model (O'Brien, 2014a)	181
10.2	Managerial tension within Indian enterprise	182
12.1	Impact of international experience on intercultural competence: theoretical model	215
13.1	Expectation of the parties in the international job market	232

Tables

2.1	Firm bankruptcies (staff > 10)	17
2.2	Synthetic business climate perception indicator, IPCA, 2013	17
2.3	Cases description	20
2.4	Comparison of performing and less performing firms	29
2.5	Factors associated with exploiting opportunities	29
3.1	Identification of the interviewed SMEs	40
3.2	Cross-sectional analysis of the empirical data	44
3.3	Presentation of the "Pacte PME" sample	50
4.1	Data collection	65
5.1	Three levels of analysis and associated characteristics	76
5.2	A multi-level analysis of major challenges in Germany and Brazil	87
6.1	Sample description	105
7.1	Presentation of the multinationals interviewed	122
7.2	Key elements related to the ethics of the multinationals studied	128
8.1	Theoretical model of relationships between the ten basic values	147

Figures and Tables ix

8.2	Questionnaire of values by portraits	149
8.3	Average scores of Chinese students for the ten motivational areas	151
8.4	Average scores of French students for the ten motivational areas	152
9.1	Sample description	162
9.2	Dependent variable	163
9.3	Independent variables	165
9.4	Multiple linear regression analysis (dependent variable: performance)	167
10.1	Popular models of management	177
11.1	List of the Swedish shippers interviewed	198
11.2	List of the French shippers interviewed	199
11.3	Some of the criteria used when selecting carrier/ transport provider	201
11.4	Transportation purchasing organization characteristics	203
12.1	Cultures concerned by the critical incidents used in the survey	216
12.2	International experiences measurement	218
13.1	Profile of participants by category	235
13.2	Convergent and divergent representations of the expected competences	238
13.3	Parallel between competences and intercultural competences	240

Acknowledgements

This book brings together, in part, a selection of the best papers that were presented at the 7th annual Atlas AFMI conference that took place in Antananarivo, Madagascar, May 2–4, 2017. The remainder of the book comprises contributions requested by the editors from authors with expertise in their chosen subject matter.

Abbreviations

ACAL	Alsace-Champagne-Ardenne-Lorraine
AD	anno domini
ANOVA	analysis of the variance
APII	Agency for the Promotion of Industry and Innovation
ARA	activity-resource-actor
BC	before Christ
BOP	bottom of the pyramid
BtoB	business to business
CEO	chief executive officer
COP	Conference of Parties
CSR	corporate social responsibilities
DITC	Division of Labour Inspection and Conciliation
ERPG	ethnocentric, regiocentric, polycentric and geocentric
ESI	European Stability Initiative
FDI	foreign direct investment
FIEA	Financial Instruments and Exchange Act
GHG	greenhouse gas emissions
HRM	human resources management
HRMI	international human resources management
ILO	International Labour Organization
IMF	International Monetary Fund
IMP	Group International Marketing and Purchasing Group
INS	National Register of Firms
IPCA	Synthetic indicator of perception of the business climate
ISO	International Organization for Standardization
ITCEQ	Tunisian Institute of Competitiveness and Economic Studies
LOE	liability of emergingness
LOF	liability of foreignness
LON	liability of newness
LOO	liability of outsidership
M&A	mergers and acquisitions
MNC	multinational corporation

xii *Abbreviations*

NGO	non-governmental organization
OHASAS	Occupational Health and Safety Assessment Series
PVQ	Portrait Values Questionnaire
SAP	structural adjustment programs
SEBI	Security Exchange Board of India
SEM	structural equation modeling
SENAI	National Service for Industrial Learning
SME	small and medium-sized enterprise
SOX	Sarbanes-Oxley Act
TQM	total quality management
TÜV	Technischer Überwachungsverein
UNCTAD	United Nations Conference on Trade and Development
UNFCCC	United Nations Framework Convention on Climate Change
VAT	Value Added Tax
WTO	World Trade Organization

Contributors

Dan Andersson is an Associate Professor in Logistics and Transport, and Head of Unit at the Division of Service Management and Logistics at Chalmers University of Technology in Sweden. His research focuses on purchasing transport services and he has substantial academic and practical experience in outsourcing. For the last ten years his work has been related to different aspects of management of sustainable transport, and he has most recently been involved in a number of urban freight projects.

Suzanne M. Apitsa is Doctor-HDR (accreditation to supervise research) in Management Sciences, researcher and member of the research facility (Management Research Centre) (EA-1722), IEA, University of Poitiers, France. Her research revolves around several axes: intercultural and diversity management, CSR, international HRM, internationalization of SMEs and management of African organizations and business networks in Africa. She has published in diverse domains. Her teaching duties at IEA, Poitiers, at ESCE Business International School (Paris) and at INSA-Rouen cover the international management of human resources, international business and intercultural management.

Hamza Asshidi is a young researcher in management sciences at the University of Grenoble Alpes, Grenoble, France. His thesis focuses on multinational companies and how they deploy their CSR and ethics systems internationally in a context of cultural diversity. He previously studied humanities (history) and social sciences (sociology, public law, international relations). He specializes in strategic management and international and intercultural management, which he teaches as part of his doctorate in Grenoble.

Christoph Barmeyer is Professor of Intercultural Communication and Management and co-Director of the Master of International Cultural and Business Studies at the University of Passau (Germany). He holds a doctorate in intercultural management and learning styles from the Saarbrücken University (Germany) and was for eight years Maître de Conférences at the Ecole de Management, Université Strasbourg (France).

xiv *Contributors*

His areas of research and teaching are constructive intercultural management and the co-creation of new working cultures, intercultural transfer of management practices and French-German management. He has published books (e.g., *Intercultural Management: A Case-Based Approach to Achieving Complementarity and Synergy.* Palgrave, 2016) and articles in journals like *Gérer & Comprendre, Gestion, International Business Review, International Studies of Management and Organization, International Journal of Intercultural Relations, International Journal of Cross-Cultural Management, Management International* and *Revue Sciences de Gestion.*

Dr. Anne Bartel-Radic is a full Professor in Management at Sciences Po Grenoble, University of Grenoble Alpes, Grenoble, France, and researcher at CERAG. Her research focuses on the management of cultural diversity, on intercultural competence of people and organizations, and strategic management. She is the director of the research cluster in Social Sciences of the University of Grenoble Alpes, president of the scientific commission of Sciences Po Grenoble and board member of the francophone association in international management, Atlas-AFMI.

Isabelle Barth is Dean of Research at INSEEC U. and Dean of INSEEC School of Business and Economics. For 20 years she has been a full Professor in Management at four French universities. She has conducted research in diversity management and CSR for two decades. She supervised 11 doctoral research studies in this field with an international approach.

Madeleine Bausch is a doctoral student and research associate at the Chair for Intercultural Communication at the University of Passau (Germany). In research and teaching in the area of intercultural management, she is primarily interested in the transfer of organizational practices (quality management), particularly between Germany and Latin American countries, as well as in creativity and innovation in multicultural workplaces. She holds a master's degree in international cultural and business studies from the University of Passau, and she specialized in Romanic languages and business studies during her bachelor's degree at the University of Mannheim (Germany). During and between her studies, she spent several years abroad in Latin America, mainly in Brazil, Chile and Ecuador. She has published in the *International Journal of Cross-Cultural Management* and has co-authored several book chapters.

Dr. Marie-Estelle Binet is a full Professor in Economics at Sciences Po Grenoble, University of Grenoble Alpes, Grenoble, France, and researcher at GAEL in the field of applied public economics. Originally enrolled in the local public economy, she now extends her research to environment and natural resources economy and regional economy. Her empirical work uses the tools of applied econometrics, survey techniques and more

Contributors xv

recently experimental economics. She is the Director of Research of Sciences Po Grenoble.

Jamil Chaabouni is Professor in Management Studies. He has taught at the University of Sfax, Tunisia, and has undertaken many consultancy assignments on behalf of firms and national and international organizations. He is tenured Doctor in Management Science at the University Philippe of Marbourg, Germany, and holds an HDR from the University of Tunis. His research work covers strategy, the organization of firms, international management and information systems management.

Alya Charfi is Doctor of Management and Junior Lecturer at Ecole Supérieure de Commerce of the University of Sfax, Tunisia. She is also Ambassadress of Francophonie for the Agence Universitaire de la Francophonie in Central and Eastern Europe. Her research revolves around three axes: knowledge management, participative democracy and human capital in creative and cultural industries.

Laure Dikmen is Lecturer in Management Science at IAE, Poitiers, France, where she directs the Master's 1 in Management and International Commerce and also sabbaticals. Member of the International Strategy Intelligence (ISI) axis of the CEREGE research facility, she is co-responsible for the doctoral workshops. A member of the board of directors of l'Association Francophone de Management International (Atlas/AFMI), she co-directs the SAFARI (Fusion & Acquisition, International Alliances and Networks) workshop. Her research work revolves around the determinants of the performance of strategic alliances in emerging countries and the link between business and management.

Chiara Ghislieri is Lecturer, HDR, in the Psychology of Work and Organizations at the University of Turin, Italy. Her research focuses on work-family balance, on well-being linked to work and job insecurity, on leadership, followership, entrepreneurship and on the professional orientation and formation of adults. The study of gender differences is a transversal approach in her research axes.

Gildas Lusteau is Director of the *Alliance Française* in Chengdu, China. A Doctor in Management Sciences (Strasbourg University, EM Strasbourg, Humanis EA 7308), he has spent more than ten years in China. His research focuses on different areas: corporate social responsibility, values, Chinese youth, interculturality.

Axelle Lutz is in the second year of her doctorate in Management Sciences in the Organizations Management Research Centre (CREGO) at the University of Bourgogne, Franche-Comté, France. She is the coordinator of the Interreg Rhin Supérieur projects at the University of Haute-Alsace. Her research is concentrated on employability and the needs of the labor

xvi *Contributors*

market as well as on career management. In particular, in her thesis she examines the specifics of career management in a cross-border context.

Zoubeyda Mahamadou holds a PhD in Management Sciences and is Assistant Professor at the European Business School Paris (EBS Paris)/INSEEC U. She is member of INSEEC U. Research Center. Her research focuses on asymmetric strategic alliances of SMEs and the aeronautical industry, the internationalization process of SMEs, the relationship between companies' organizational culture, and employees' performance.

Josiane Martin-O'Brien, PhD, is Professor of Management at the International University of Monaco and member of IUM-INSEEC U. Research Center. With long professional experience in the development of international academic projects, she completed her PhD in management at Paris Dauphine (2016). Focusing on India and the internationalization of Indian managers, her research interests include the use of ethnographic fieldwork to study the local embedding of universal management principles in non-western countries. She has lectured in management programs from CNAM Paris, ESCP Europe Paris, IIM Raipur India, Bellarmine University, USA, and Purdue University, USA. She is a regular contributor to conferences in France and internationally.

Ulrike Mayrhofer is Professor of International Business at IAE Nice Graduate School of Management, Université Côte d'Azur. She is Program Director of the Executive MBA (master of business administration) and co-responsible for the "Digital Marketing & International Business" team of the GRM-lab (Groupe de Recherche en Management). Her teaching and research interests concern international and intercultural management, corporate strategy, and marketing. She has published numerous books, book chapters, and articles in scientific and professional journals. She is associate editor of *Management International,* senior editor of *European Journal of International Management,* board member (representative France) of EIBA (European International Business Academy) and honorary president of Atlas AFMI (Association Francophone de Management International).

Emna Moalla is Professor of International Business at ESSCA School of Management, Angers, France. She holds a PhD in management sciences from IAE Lyon, Université Lyon 3, Lyon, France. Her research focuses on the internationalization process of firms and cross-cultural management. She has published several articles in scientific journals and has participated in various conferences.

John Eustice O'Brien is an independent researcher in Monaco following a career in the United States as professor of sociology, director of an institute of research, and consultant for public and private agencies and enterprises. In addition to journal publications and contributions to

Contributors xvii

professional conferences on the global political economy and critical management studies, with special interest in India, he was invited as visiting scholar at the Indian Institute of Management, Lucknow. He is working on a third book in a series exploring the problem of rationality for critical social sciences.

Yasmine Saleh is a researcher in management and innovation at Frog–Altran, a strategy and design consulting company. She holds a PhD in management science from the University of Nantes, France. Her research focuses on the influence of national culture in the business context and on managerial innovation and new collaborative spaces. After several years of teaching and research in these fields, she oriented her career for more applied research with a cross-cultural perspective.

Nathalie Touratier-Muller is an associate professor in logistics and purchasing management at ESC PAU Business School, France. Her current research focuses on freight transport sustainability as well as sustainable outsourcing practices. She worked previously in France and abroad as a supply chain project manager and as a purchasing manager in the electronic industry. Her PhD thesis explored the impact of French public policies identifying levers that encourage shippers (client companies) to take the environmental footprint of products being transported into greater account. Since then, she has been particularly interested in the future of the purchasing function, integrating environmental and social considerations.

Sophie Wodociag is tenured Doctor in Management Science and the Psychology of Work, Lecturer in Management Science and directs the master's in intercultural management and international business at the University of Haute-Alsace (UHA), Alsace, France. Researcher at the Organization Management Research Centre (CREGO) of the University of Franche-Comté, UHA Antenna and member of the Chair Management and Health at Work (MANSAT) of the University of Grenoble Alpes, her research themes are mainly focused on international and cross-border mobility, the development of intercultural and transversal competencies with a view to better employability, and well-being at work.

1 Introduction and Overview

Bruno Amann and Jacques Jaussaud

International management involves considerable cultural and societal challenges, and this book aims to highlight and analyze the principal issues arising therefrom. The development of international activities requires the interaction of individuals and groups with diverse cultural, religious, ethnic and social characteristics in different institutional contexts. Therefore, the development of international activities will be susceptible to misunderstandings, to incomprehension between these individuals and groups and to rejection by collaborators, consumers or other local actors; it will also be susceptible to judicial sanctions for the non-respect of incorrectly identified or misunderstood legal rules (Bosche, 1993; Davel et al., 2008). As stated by Chanlat and Pierre (2018, p. 14), this international development is (in its intercultural meaning) fundamentally a source of tension, synonymous with resistance to change, with openness to the other and uncertainty; it is rarely euphoric, delightful or neutral.

The temptation is, however, considerable to imitate some competitors who take advantage of lesser institutional development in certain developing countries to exploit, without great consequential concern, human or natural resources. The extreme case of the tragedy that occurred in Bangladesh in April 2013, caused by the collapse of the unsafe Rana Plaza buildings, which housed numerous garment factories with workers toiling for famous brands in developed countries (1,127 deaths according to the official account), should not allow us to overlook the long list of other similar tragic cases that have resulted from such activities. Such incidents frequently cause irreparable damage, which is sometimes given significant media coverage, damaging the image and even the performance of the implicated international firms. Conversely, media coverage of such tragedies sometimes leads to the implementation of improved practices: the questioning of the operations methodology of Foxconn or Petragon in China under NGO pressure, for example; the introduction of social audits at sub-contractors' production facilities—one can thus observe in certain sectors the existence of "best practices" benchmarking in which mimetic tendencies direct participants toward the best social protection practices.

2   Bruno Amann and Jacques Jaussaud

In addition, in the case of uncertainty as to which standards to apply, which is quite prevalent in international undertakings, organizations have a tendency to resemble each other (Bodet and Lamarche, 2007), at least in the construction of norms and practices, such as in CSR. We are now in the domain of *soft law*. In addition to soft law, this tendency will sometimes have legislative consequences like, for example, law no. 2017–399 of March 27, 2017 in France on the control obligations of parent companies and of order placing firms. As emphasized by Pereira (2018, p. 71), *"between judicial and managerial rules one can see interactions relating to competition trends but also relating to coordination trends."*

Personnel in charge of the development of firms' internationalization, whether home based or foreign based, thus have to be extremely careful. The intensification of international exchanges and the growing interpenetration of economies during the recent decades are leading to an increasing number of executives and operational personnel, in firms of all sizes, to be involved in firms' internationalization. An increasing number of personnel from an increasing number of firms are thus becoming involved in intercultural interactions, dealing with different types of institutional frameworks that are unevenly developed and difficult to fully understand.

The cultural and societal challenges of international management need to be considered at different levels: naturally, from a strategic perspective, which the first part of the book addresses, but also from a management and business perspective, which the third part of the book addresses. The second part of this book addresses strategic choices relating to issues, such as daily management practices, which, in the constantly changing and not fully defined international context, benefit by being shaped by the ethical decision-making and corporate social responsibility of firms; otherwise, serious managerial mistakes may occur.

If by strategy one understands a set of choices and decisions that enable firms to integrate into their environment and to take advantage of it, one readily perceives the cultural and societal challenges that arise at this primary level. The environment in its international dimension is extremely diverse and complex and thus the source of considerable risk. The first problem that arises is to identify the pertinent information in respect of the relevant environment. A certain French industrial group, which transferred to China at the beginning of the 2000s some activities in respect of which European environmental regulation had become too "restrictive," found itself a few years later—when it had already started production in China—subject to local Chinese regulations directly inspired by the regulations applicable in Europe. Therefore, what was pertinent were not the gaps between regulatory frameworks at the time of the transfer of production, but the future direction of Chinese regulations in this area. Furthermore, the problem of the acceptability of such goods in particular markets occurs. Equally, the issue arises of the acceptability of firms' practices that firms plan to develop in the host country in respect of sales, advertising or human resources management, even in respect of industrial site location, firms' alliances or competitive strategies. Broadly speaking, a certain number of "liabilities" (handicaps, difficulties) identified in the academic literature is indicative of the variety of difficulties that can occur in terms of acceptability. Studies on international management have for a long time underlined that the international development of firms is confronted by different costs from multiple sources (Hymer, 1976; Kindleberger, 1969). These costs can arise, for example, from unfamiliarity with the local host environment, from economic and political differences, from the lack of longevity and level of experience associated with the firms, from being outside the host countries' networks, from the size of the firm or even from the level of distrust felt by the host country. These "liabilities" exist for all firms that internationalize, but have particular characteristics when the internationalizing firm is from an emerging country. According to Chittoor et al. (2015), international expansion by acquisition gives rise to significant risks in general, but particularly where the acquiring party is from an emerging country that is exposed to numerous problems that may hamper their international expansion. They are confronted with the difficulty of being a foreign firm (liability of foreignness (LOF)), with the handicap of being a new firm on the international market (liability of newness (LON)), with the potential difficulty of not being part of a host country network (liability of outsidership (LOO)) and with the disadvantage that they are from an emerging country (liability of emergingness (LOE)).

All fields of management are involved, as all imply interactions with local individuals and groups, with local institutions, or even with international or third party country institutions. Third country firms, as epitomized by the firms engaged in Iran in 2018, attracted the anger of the president of the United States and the threat of penalties because they were using US dollars in transactions. Furthermore, we can see the difficulties posed for the French company Alstom in the United States in respect of corruption allegations in Indonesia (Pierucci and Aron, 2019). The arrest in Canada of Meng Wanzhou, Huawei's chief director of finance, on charges of violation of Iran embargo sanctions, is another example of the extraterritoriality of some US legislation. All possible reactions, positive but especially negative, by individuals, groups and established bodies need to be planned for and incorporated into strategic thinking; otherwise, it gives rise to grave risks and even further, it gives rise to the risk of terminal failure.

Beyond making strategic choices, it is at application and even more so at operational level that the various challenges to be confronted need to be considered. It is, in effect, at application level, in the concrete realization of activities that the interactions multiply in extremely varied local situations. Beyond the strategic choices, these interactions may suffer from mutual incomprehension or conscious or unconscious inappropriate behaviors, which at best are merely a source of inefficiency but which frequently are the source of conflict, failure, blockages or accidents. This, of course,

4   Bruno Amann and Jacques Jaussaud

this gives rise to the delicate question of the adequacy of the preparation of the executives and other personnel responsible for working in an international context, both from the intercultural dimension and from the perspective of institutional otherness. In relation to the intercultural dimension, two often opposing approaches can be undertaken (Davel et al., 2008; Chanlat and Pierre, 2018): one aims at increasing awareness of the differences in respect to the culture of the country concerned, with the risk of incompleteness of such awareness and the reinforcing of stereotypes that such an approach implies; the other approach aims to develop the competence of the personnel involved in these intercultural interactions (i.e., with people of other cultures and in unexpected situations).

Preparing personnel to work in foreign countries or in an international context is essential. It is equally essential to develop adequate systems of control (Schaan, 1983, 1988; Geringer and Hebert, 1989). This consists of ensuring that the processes and the behavior they engage in will remain controlled and that the results are in line with expectations. Deploying international control systems requires the considerable expansion of the types of control and the linkage of all available resources, due to the diversity of the contexts and situations where the personnel will work in different parts of the world (Schaan, 1983, 1988; Geringer and Hebert, 1989; Ghoshal and Nohria, 1989; Jaussaud and Schaaper, 2006). This might equally give rise to a rethinking of the organizational structure of the multinational firm, with the creation of regional offices in response, in particular (but not solely) to control requirements (Enright, 2005; Ambos and Schlegelmilch, 2010; Amann et al., 2014).

For Geringer and Hebert (1989, p. 236) control can be defined as "the process by which one entity influences, to varying degrees, the behaviour and output of another entity through the use of power, authority and a wide range of bureaucratic, cultural and informal mechanisms."

If one accepts this definition, particularly in relation to international management, then ethical decision-making and corporate social responsibility, when they are strongly embedded and widespread in a multinational firm, become part of the system of control, in the sense that they aim to influence the behavior of personnel. In international management, the question of social responsibility is particularly sensitive due to the multiplicity of stakeholders, countries and different cultural perspectives (Cournac, 2015). What might be regarded as innocuous behavior in the home territory of a multinational could be regarded as unacceptable in another country. Multinationals need to address this difficulty with pragmatism and their own political rationale; otherwise, they may be held to account sooner or later.

We also ascertain at this stage the challenges facing multinationals. Employees can only take ownership of the ethical behavior of firms on the basis of shared values. Yet, the most significant cultural differences, it should be recalled, are the differences in values, or more precisely, the

Introduction and Overview 5

differences in the distribution and hierarchy of values (Schwartz, 1992, 2006; Schaaper and Zhen, 2013). How, then, to decide on ethical values, in particular, in a framework of the requirement of social responsibility, capable of gaining the support of all, across cultures and borders? Before even posing the problem in such global terms, numerous firms are confronted with the difficulty of transmitting their values or even engaging with the issue and are constrained by the requirement of obtaining the agreement of all, to adapt rather than to transmit values (D'Iribarne, 2012; Barmeyer and Davoine, 2013). Besides, a global, universalist approach, even if it seems necessary to impose grand ethical principles at an abstract level, is confronted by such practical difficulties that the nature of the social responsibility of multinational firms is frequently differentiated according to geographic zones (Arthaud-Day, 2005), and more precisely according to territories (Cournac and Gatignon-Turnaud, 2013; Cournac, 2015).

Cross-cultural Challenges in International Management offers in its various chapters an analysis of specific situations containing such cultural and societal challenges. It studies what sort of responses are harnessed to overcome these challenges. Among these situations, we highlight the following:

- Strategic decision-making in an unstable environment and in a specific cultural environment, and where appropriate, in an interorganizational context.
- The contribution and the limitations in a Muslim or Indian context, for example, of ethical input in management in general and in international management.
- The management of local or multicultural employees, in particular, in difficult situations.

The list of cases highlighted allows analysis of the cultural and societal challenges facing international management. The chapters in the first part of the book analyze these challenges from the perspective of strategic decision-making, be it in a particularly volatile context (Tunisia after the Jasmine revolution, for example, in Chapter 2 by Alya Charfi and Jamil Chaabouni); in the context of alliances (Chapter 3 by Zoubeyda Mahamadou); or in international acquisitions (Chapter 4 by Yasmine Saleh and Emna Moalla); Chapter 5 by Madeleine Bausch, Christoph Barmeyer and Ulrike Mayrhofer considers the cultural challenges and quality management practices of a German multinational company in Brazil. Other chapters in the second and third parts of the book analyze, from a completely different perspective, the impact on management of ethical dimensions in given cultural contexts: African (Chapter 6 by Suzanne M. Apitsa), Chinese (Chapter 8 by Gildas Lusteau and Isabelle Barth), Muslim (Chapter 9 by Laure Dikmen) or more generally (Chapter 7 by Hamza Asshidi and Chapter 11

6 Bruno Amann and Jacques Jaussaud

by Nathalie Touratier-Muller and Dan Andersson). The issue of ethics and corporate social responsibility of firms in international management is therefore studied in depth. In Chapter 10, John Eustice O'Brien and Josiane Martin-O'Brien examine the limits of classical managerial approaches in the Indian context; Chapter 12 by Anne Bartel-Radic and Marie-Estelle Binet addresses the issue of international student mobility; whereas in Chapter 13, Sophie Wodociag, Axelle Lutz and Chiara Ghislieri research (from a completely different perspective) to what extent intercultural competencies can be at the heart of success in the labor market. Each contributor is solely (or together with co-contributors) responsible for structuring the research and the development of ideas in their chapters, which sometimes address sensitive issues.

Overall, the sequencing of the book is as follows:

- The cultural and societal challenges in strategic decision-making (Part I)
- Ethical and societal responsibility issues in international management (Part II)
- The challenges that interculturalism poses in international management (Part III).

This sequencing does not preclude confronting intercultural, ethical and societal problems, which are covered throughout the chapters. Each part and each chapter individually provide clear answers to the question of cultural and societal challenges that firms and other organizations are confronted with in their processes of international development.

References

Amann B., Jaussaud J., Schaaper J. (2014). "Clusters and regional management structures by Western MNCs in Asia: overcoming the distance challenge." *Management International Review*, 54(6), pp. 879–906.

Ambos, B., Schlegelmilch, B. D. (2010). *The New Role of Regional Management.* Basingstoke: Palgrave Macmillan.

Arthaud-Day, M. L. (2005). "Transnational corporate social responsibility: a tridimensional approach to international CSR research." *Business Ethics Quarterly*, 15(1), pp. 25–40.

Barmeyer, C. I., Davoine, E. (2013). "'Traduttore, Traditore'? La réception contextualisée des valeurs d'entreprise dans les filiales françaises et allemandes d'une entreprise multinationale américaine." *Management International/International Management/Gestión Internacional*, 18(1), pp. 26–39.

Bodet, C., Lamarche, T. (2007). "La responsabilité sociale des entreprises comme innovation institutionnelle. Une lecture régulationniste." *Revue de la régulation. Capitalisme, institutions, pouvoirs*, 1.

Bosche, M. (sous la direction de). (1993). *Le management interculturel.* Paris: Nathan.

Chanlat J.-F., Pierre, P. (2018). *Le management interculturel, Evolution, tendances, critiques*. Caen: Editions EMS Management et Société, Collection Les Essentiels de la Gestion.

Chittoor, R., Aulakh, P. S., Ray, S. (2015). "What drives overseas acquisitions by Indian firms? A behavioral risk-taking perspective." *Management International Review*, 55(2), pp. 255–275.

Cournac, A. (2015). "De la différenciation des pratiques de RSE de l'entreprise multinationale à l'égard de ses territoires d'implantation." *Management International*, 19(4), pp. 155–167.

Cournac, A., Gatignon-Turnau, A.-L. (2013). "Quand l'entreprise se dit 'responsable vis-à-vis des territoires où elle est implantée'—Décryptage à partir de l'analyse des rapports de développement durable." In U. Mayrrhofer and P. Very, *Le management à l'écoute du local*, Ed. Gualino, collection Management international, pp. 172–187.

Davel, E., Dupuis, J.-P., Chanlat, J.-F. (sous la direction de). (2008). *Gestion en contexte interculturel, Approches, problématiques, pratiques et plongées*. Quebec: Les Presses de l'Université de Laval, avec la collaboration de Télé-Université (UQAM).

D'Iribarne, P. (2012). *Managing Corporate Values in Diverse National Cultures, the Challenge of Differences*. London: Routledge.

Enright, M. J. (2005). "The role of regional management centers." *Management International Review*, 45(1), pp. 83–102.

Geringer, J. M., Hebert, L. (1989). "Control and performance of international joint ventures." *Journal of International Business Studies*, 20(2), pp. 235–254.

Ghoshal, S., Nohria, N. (1989). "Internal differentiation within multinational corporations." *Strategic Management Journal*, 10(4), pp. 323–337.

Hymer, S. H. (1960 [publ. 1976]). *The International Operations of National Firms: A Study of Direct Foreign Investment*. Cambridge, MA: MIT Press.

Jaussaud, J., Schaaper J. (2006). "Control mechanisms of their subsidiaries by multinational firms: a multidimensional perspective." *Journal of International Management*, 12(1), pp. 23–45.

Kindleberger, C. (1969). *American Business Abroad*, New Haven, CT: Yale University Press.

Pereira, B. (2018). "L'entreprise et les droits de l'Homme: de la confusion et concurrence des règles à l'intelligence normative." *RIMHE: Revue Interdisciplinaire Management, Homme & Entreprise*, 32(3), pp. 71–84.

Pierucci, F., Aron, M. (2019). *Le piège américain, l'otage de la plus grande opération de déstabilisation économique témoigne*. Paris: JC Lattès.

Schaan, J. L. (1983). *Parent Control and Joint Venture Success: The Case of Mexico*. PhD thesis, University of Western Ontario.

Schaan, J. L. (1988). "How to control a joint venture even as a minority partner." *Journal of General Management*, 14(1), pp. 4–16.

Schaaper, J., Zhen, J. (2013). "Valeurs Confucéennes en Chine mesurées par les valeurs personnelles et domaines motivationnels de Schwartz." *Management International*, 17(4), pp. 58–82.

Schwartz, S. H. (1992). "Universals in the content and structure of values: theoretical advances and empirical tests in 20 countries." *Advances in Experimental Social Psychology*, 25, pp. 1–65.

Schwartz, S. H. (2006), "Les valeurs de base de la personne: théorie, mesures et applications." *Revue française de sociologie*, 47(4), pp. 929–968.

Part I

Cultural and Societal Challenges in Strategic Decision-Making

The four chapters in Part I of the book analyze the cultural and societal challenges of international management through strategic decision-making, whereas those of Part II deal with questions of ethics and societal responsibility in international management and those of Part III with the challenges posed by interculturality.

In Chapter 2, Alya Charfi and Jamil Chaabouni explore how some companies manage to get through troubled periods, such as the Jasmine revolution in Tunisia, whereas others do not and more often than not end up disappearing. The chapter seeks to identify the factors that make companies resilient in such a context.

In Chapter 3, Zoubeyda Mahamadou examines the objectives, determinants and strategic issues of asymmetrical alliances between SMEs and large multinationals. This type of alliance has to date been rarely studied. Yet they constitute a means for SMEs to develop and internationalize. This chapter is based on in-depth interviews with French SMEs involved in such asymmetric alliances.

In Chapter 4, Yasmine Saleh and Emna Moalla examine the processes of collaboration and integration in the context of international acquisitions. They explore the case of an Egyptian cement company acquired by a French group in 2008. The tumultuous integration process in this case offers a rich field of lessons.

In Chapter 5, Madeleine Bausch, Christoph Barmeyer and Ulrike Mayrhofer examine some major challenges faced by a German multinational company when transferring quality management practices from a German to a Brazilian plant. Their case study of a German "hidden champion" reveals how difficulties arise due to cultural and institutional differences as well as organizational micro-political and power struggles.

2 How to Survive in an Unstable Environment for a Long Time to Come
A Study of Firms Operating in Tunisia During the Democratic Transition

Alya Charfi and Jamil Chaabouni

Introduction

Firms are evolving in a world that has become unstable and violent, going through democratic revolutions and the rise of extremism and terrorism. This instability affects the development of businesses or the maintenance of their operations in countries with an uncertain future. Sometimes the survival of the firm becomes the issue, when the institutions of their country of origin collapse, the economy is crippled or war rages.

This research aims to understand how certain firms manage to get through troubled periods whereas others struggle to emerge from them or even collapse. More particularly, we are interested in the factors associated with firms' resilience. Crisis management requires improvisation (Weick et al., 1999), shock absorption ability and renewal ability (Wildavsky, 1991). The shock absorption ability consists in mobilizing internal or external resources to resist the disruptive event. The renewal ability consists in finding new solutions: launching new businesses or revising business models. It therefore supposes seizing or building opportunities to emerge from the crisis.

In this research, we analyze managers' responses concerning the encountered difficulties and the seizing/building of opportunities that contributed to their firm's resilience. We conducted this study in a Tunisian context characterized by the "democratic revolution" that began at the end of 2010—a popular uprising to end dictatorship and establish a democratic transition. Locally based firms have experienced difficulties, but some have navigated the difficulties better than others. We have attempted to identify, through managers' responses to our questions, the factors contributing to explain these differences in socioeconomic performance. Our approach is inductive, with existing studies mainly focused on sudden shocks and not on long-term crises.

Our results show that the better-performing firms could seize business opportunities whereas those experiencing more economic difficulties

12 Alya Charfi and Jamil Chaabouni

simply attempted to absorb the shock with the existing scope of their business. Some opportunities are seized; others are built. Beyond the actions taken, performing firms' managers demonstrate entrepreneurial behavior: some have the chance to identify an increased demand for their products; others rely primarily on themselves and their networks to find solutions. This ability to seize or build opportunities therefore influences their firms' resilience during long periods of sociopolitical and economic unrest.

The chapter presents this research by successively reviewing the literature on resilience to crises, the knowledge acquired about opportunities seizing/building, the empirical research process, the results obtained, the discussion on the results and the conclusion.

Literature Review

Organization's Resilience

Multiple definitions of resilience have been elaborated (Kendra and Wachtendorf, 2003). Wildavsky's definition (1991: 77) will be retained: "Resilience is the ability to cope with unanticipated dangers after they have become manifest, learning to bounce back." The concept, therefore, contains several facets: dealing with an unexpected event, learning from it and emerging stronger. Organizational resilience was introduced into management sciences within the crisis research framework.

Researchers recognize the difficulty of measuring a priori a firm's resilience. They have generally analyzed a posteriori firms' actions, having or not having survived unpredictable shocks (Begin and Chabaud, 2010; Lengnick-Hall and Beck, 2005). According to Kendra and Wachtendorf (2003), organizational resilience seems associated with the possession of certain resources and abilities favorable to crisis resolution: financial surplus, good decision-making systems and so forth. In addition, resilience assumes the development of specific abilities facilitating dealing with the unpredictable. Researchers have notably identified the importance of improvisational ability. Improvisation is defined as "the deliberate and substantial amalgamation of the development and execution of a new production" (Miner et al., 2001: 314). Improvisation is a spontaneous creative ability. For Weick et al. (1999), improvisation is about finding new ways to combine resources or actions that already belong to the organizational repertoire. Resilience therefore combines assets and actions: overcoming a crisis depends on the initial possession of resources and on the ability to spontaneously combine them in a new way.

Resilience and Long-Term Crisis

Most studies of resilience focus on shock occurrences (Hollnagel et al., 2009). Hence, the Mann Gulch fire (Weick, 1993), the Three Mile Island

How to Survive in an Unstable Environment 13

nuclear accident (La Porte, 1982) and the space shuttle Challenger explosion (Vaughan, 1996) were analyzed. Nevertheless, some works are devoted to long-term crises resilience in respect of family-owned firms.

Begin and Chabaud (2010) traced the path of a family-owned firm created in 1826 which successively had to face war and decolonization, expropriation and nationalization, and furthermore, its main market decline. The authors identify three resilience components:

- Shock-absorption ability: consists of mobilizing surplus internal resources or external resources. This enables resistance to occur to the disruptive event.
- Renewal ability: enables the finding of new diverse solutions—organizational change, new businesses launching and business model review. This ability is an action form to emerge stronger from the shock, according to Wildavsky's (1991) definition.
- Appropriation ability: consists of learning from previous shocks to better anticipate or respond to future crises. According to Begin and Chabaud (2010), this learning ability, identified by Wildavsky (1991), is difficult to observe.

Other works have been devoted to long-term crises, particularly in the Tunisian context following the late 2010 "democratic revolution" that ousted the incumbent president to move toward a democratic transition. This was followed by a long period of instability, characterized by economic paralysis, high political uncertainty and numerous social movements. Several studies attempted to comprehend how firms operating in Tunisia managed to get through this troubled period, particularly the first year of transition. Based on Begin and Chabaud's (2010) reflections, Chaabouni et al. (2015) studied six firms that survived the Tunisian crisis while focusing on the abilities held before the crisis and those activated by the crisis (shock absorption ability and renewal ability). They found that the surviving firms' managers had activated at least one ability held before the crisis. They initially had either financial prudence or organizational social capital or both. Improvisation theories based on held abilities, therefore, seem to apply to long-term sociopolitical crises contexts interspersed with unexpected shocks. Managers' emphasis on social capital and/or financial prudence corresponds to the possession of organizational backgrounds, from which the firm improvises within a short-term shock context (Weick et al., 1999; Miner et al., 2001; Kendra and Wachtendorf, 2003).

Chaabouni et al. (2015) found that all firms activated a shock-absorbing ability whatever the nature and range. Nonetheless, not all of them developed renewal ability. Renewal ability development seems linked to the possession of one of the two held abilities cited by the respondents. When the firms could initially rely on their social capital and financial prudence, they

14   *Alya Charfi and Jamil Chaabouni*

simply absorbed the shocks. In other research, Marouane and Chtrourou (2015) and Mzid (2015) also identified this absorption ability.

This research on survival over a long-term crisis period has mostly aimed at identifying resources and resource combinations that could contribute to firm resilience. In a long-term crisis context, with firms' markets permanently collapsed, it is unlikely that the mere shock absorption ability would be sufficient to maintain businesses' levels. There is therefore a need to seize new business opportunities. These issues have seldom been studied in a crisis context. Conversely, they are the research object in an entrepreneurial context. The following is a review of the literature on seizing opportunities by entrepreneurs.

Seizing or Building Opportunities

Seizing opportunities is studied within the entrepreneurship framework— more particularly, firm setup. Economists and management researchers have explored how entrepreneurs identify a market opportunity to establish a firm. Entrepreneurship is even defined by managers as "the understanding of how opportunities to bring new goods and services to market are discovered, created and exploited, by whom and with what consequences" (Venkataraman, 1997: 120).

Three conceptions of the relationship between the opportunity and the entrepreneur have emerged over time. Initially, Austrian economists described the entrepreneur as a vigilant person, ready to seize market opportunities existing in his environment. Thanks to his vigilance, the entrepreneur knows how to recognize business opportunities (Kirzner, 1973). This economistic conception of a stock of opportunities existing independently of entrepreneurs was taken up in management sciences by Venkataraman (1997). The opportunity is presented as having an existence of its own. Two distinct and clearly identified objects coexist: the entrepreneur and the business opportunity.

This economistic conception has been criticized. Whereas Kirzner assumed the immediacy of the opportunity discovery, several researchers have identified maturation and learning process as necessary to recognize opportunities (Hills et al., 1997). This recognition frequently comes from the entrepreneur's contacts network that helps him learn and identify opportunities. These researchers' perspective is more subjective (Gaglio, 1997): they evoke a cognitive process of identifying opportunities depending simultaneously on the entrepreneur's personality, his human capital (information, knowledge, experience) and his favorite modes of thinking. It is by giving meaning to the environment that the entrepreneur can recognize opportunities that others cannot see.

A third group of researchers envisions the emergence of opportunities from a constructivist perspective (Sarasvathy, 2001; Smith and Di Gregorio, 2003). For them, opportunity has no existence in itself. It is

How to Survive in an Unstable Environment   15

developed, shaped and built by the entrepreneur through learning and creative processes. For Sarasvathy (2001), firm setup follows an implementation process, the business opportunity being built by all resource providers as the entrepreneur's project matures. This approach, therefore, highlights the entrepreneur's social capital: his contacts networks that contribute to forging the opportunity.

Research Question

The accumulated knowledge, on the one hand on organizational resilience to shocks, and on the other hand on seizing entrepreneurial opportunities, can be combined to study the survival of firms over a long period of social, political and economic upheaval.

Resilience to shock and the few works studying long-term crises have identified the necessity of absorbing shock and developing renewal ability. These works have focused on the resources rallied to get by and the improvisational ability of the management team.

The renewal ability is based on the recognition of opportunities to be seized or built. Research on opportunities identification has been conducted within the entrepreneurship framework and includes some factors specific to the manager in the identification process, namely vigilance, human capital and social capital.

Nonetheless, a long-term crisis context is different from a firm setup context. Hence, we can question the factors associated with seizing/building opportunities in the framework of a long-term crisis.

* First, do the factors associated with seizing opportunities in the entrepreneurial framework also emerge in the long-term crisis framework?
* Second, is there any specificity related to the firm's markets that contributes to opportunities seizing? We know, for example, that a crisis creates novel businesses, as evidenced by the US security market after the terrorist attack of September 11, 2001 (Spich and Grosse, 2005).

Hence our research question: which factors specific to the firm management and its markets contribute to new market opportunities seizing during a long period of economic turmoil?

Empirical Study

Research Methodology

The foundations of organizational resilience in a long-term crisis context have rarely been studied; that is why, following Eisenhardt and Graebner (2007) and Yin's (1994) recommendations, we have implemented an

16 Alya Charfi and Jamil Chaabouni

inductive research approach, dedicated to the study of an important phenomenon, in respect of which theory is almost non-existent. We have opted for a multiple case study aimed at building a theory. Let us first present the studied context before explaining how we selected the firms' cases.

The Tunisian Context

On December 17, 2010, Mohamed Bouazizi, a young fruit and vegetables street vendor, set himself alight outside the prefecture in Sidi Bouzid, a city in the center of the country, because the municipal police had once again confiscated his merchandise. Unemployed like many Tunisian youth, the merchant becomes a symbol for an entire people who take to the streets. The "revolution" is underway, President Ben Ali is ousted from power and a provisional government is formed to organize future elections and establish a constitution. Tunisians talk about their "democratic transition"; foreigners evoke the "Jasmine revolution." For a year, a lot of social unrest generated a climate of insecurity in the country and created a high degree of power instability, which led to several successive reshufflings in the interim government. Consequently, the national economy suffered. Foreign firms avoided the country: in the first semester of 2011, foreign investment projects declined by 40% and partnership requests collapsed by 50%. The National Agency for the Promotion of Industry and Innovation (APII) identified 172 fully or partially owned foreign firms that left the country in 2011 (Tounsi, 2012). As for domestic firms, many were unable to withstand the economic collapse. In November 2011, the APII estimated TND 173 million as the amount of firms' losses directly or indirectly caused by social unrest. These losses resulted in the loss of 10,000 jobs (Ayari, 2012). Fully or partially exporting firms in the subcontracting sector were the most damaged.

Over the period 2012–2015, firm closures continued. Table 2.1 shows the number of firms with more than ten employees that went bankrupt.

The Tunisian Institute of Competitiveness and Economic Studies (ITCEQ) notes in its survey report on the business climate (2013) that the latter deteriorated compared to 2012, particularly because of security problems.

At the social level, the number of strikes recorded by the Ministry of Social Affairs reached its peak in 2011 and 2012 with 527 and 524 strikes, respectively; it then dropped in 2013 to 399 and rebounded in 2014 to 451 (Ministry of Social Affairs, 2014).

For firms, all this resulted in the emergence of a new context essentially characterized by the sudden occurrence of unusual events for which they were not prepared. In addition to economic disruptions, these events were also social, with uprisings and collective protest movements marking that period. The social actors' protest repertoire was enriched with new forms of collective action and their content evolution, moving toward more unexpected conflict and violence within the firms. New actors came into

How to Survive in an Unstable Environment 17

Table 2.1 Firm bankruptcies (staff > 10)

Bankruptcies	2012	2013	2014	2015
10 to 19 employees	35	23	23	32
20 to 49 employees	33	17	28	15
50 or more employees	21	17	21	11
TOTAL	89	57	72	58

Source: INS *National Register of Firms*, 2016.

Table 2.2 Synthetic business climate perception indicator, IPCA, 2013

IPCA 2013	*0.6235*
Insecurity	0.475
Bank financing	0.562
Taxation and social charges	0.589
Corruption	0.644
Macro and regulatory framework	0.645
Market practices	0.646
Administrative procedures and judicial system	0.68
Human resources	0.724
Infrastructure	0.775

Source: IPCA: Synthetic business climate perception indicator calculated from nine domains assessed by firms' managers. (The closer to 1 the IPCA is, the more favorable the business climate).

ITCEQ: Tunisian Institute of Competitiveness and Quantitative Studies: main results of the 2013 annual competitiveness survey.

action: the unemployed, the marginalized and even neighboring residents of firms' sites. Other traditional stakeholders, such as banks, clients, trade unions or competitors partially modified their behavior (Chaabouni and Very, 2015). The loss of internal and external actors' benchmarks made firms' business more difficult. The crisis has therefore created a series of new problems to which the firms did not have a given response.

During the study period, Tunisia's corruption ranking fell according to the Corruption Perception Index published by *Transparency International*, and it was ranked 76th in 2015. In its 2014 report, the World Bank notes that the privileges and rents associated with crony capitalism in the current system in Tunisia are widespread, and that the associated interest groups would apply their full weight against any change that might take away their privileges (World Bank Annual Report 2014, p. 22).

State authority has continued to deteriorate during this period and the functioning of public services has not improved. Unemployment is almost unchanged at 15%, and despite the promises of different successive

18   *Alya Charfi and Jamil Chaabouni*

governments, economic policies have not met expectations. De facto, the balance of payments deficit has worsened, foreign exchange reserves have fallen, external debt has risen and the Tunisian currency has significantly devalued. Despite political advances with the consensual adoption of the constitution and the organization of democratic elections in 2014, the economic and social situation remains very fragile. The World Bank concludes its report on the unfinished revolution by noting that prosperity in Tunisia is hampered by policies that have reduced the country's overall economic performance. This poor performance is the result of various obstacles that have hindered the functioning of the market and of distortions introduced by erroneous, albeit often well-intentioned, economic policies (World Bank Annual Report 2014, p. 17).

Case Selection and Data Collection

For the multiple case study, we have selected cases in accordance with certain parameters and a confidentiality constraint: a theoretical sampling combined with possible access to the field. Theoretical sampling consists in choosing cases of firms that seem particularly suitable for studying a particular phenomenon: we thus focus our selection on medium-sized firms (4 to 50 employees) operating in industry or services (we have eliminated banks and credit agencies that can play a particular role in the context of a national crisis).

To study the role of factors specific to the manager, we wanted to compare cases of economic success and failure. Contact has been made with the Courts of First Instance to identify firms that ceased business during the transition (2011–2015). We were informed that the firms that have ceased business leave no contact details, neither telephone, nor postal, nor other; the manager is no longer contactable and the firm file is almost empty. We subsequently obtained from the companies' directory the phone contact details of a few firms that closed and attempted to contact them, but without success. Therefore, we concluded that failure does not refer to the permanent cessation of business but rather to the existence of deep economic difficulties. We then turned to the Labour Inspectorate, which receives the files of firms in difficulty.

When firms face increasing economic and social problems and are unable to manage them independently, they resort to the Division of Labour Inspection and Conciliation (DITC). The DITC is a division of the Regional Directorate of the Labour Inspectorate. It is responsible for monitoring the application of social legislation, promoting social dialogue, following up professional relations and resolving collective labor conflicts (Decree 2001–441 of February 13, 2001, establishing the organization and the responsibilities of the regional social affairs directorates). In case of difficulties leading to technical unemployment and staff dismissal, the firm refers to the DITC and a file is submitted to it. A procedure is then

How to Survive in an Unstable Environment 19

initiated, in which the firm's management, trade union and the DITC participate to reach an agreement that aims to protect the different parties' interests. In some cases, the firm in difficulty may reach a bilateral arrangement with its employees even after appealing to the DITC. Once an agreement has been reached or the firm has declared bankruptcy, the file is permanently closed. As long as a settlement has not been found, the case remains pending. Between 2011 and 2013, 179 cases (47 in 2011, 68 in 2012 and 64 in 2013) were filed with the DITC in the Sfax region. About 30 of the submitted files between 2010 and 2013 remained outstanding.

We have reviewed with the DITC head in the Sfax region all the files that have been outstanding since 2010. Only 13 firms could be extracted for use from the outstanding files because all the others faced insolvency without a judgment having being pronounced. We contacted the 13 by phone; eight were unreachable even at their headquarters, which was interpreted as the permanent closure of the firm. Among the remaining five, we identified two firms in difficulty that worked with the DITC in the Sfax region between 2010 and 2015 (ED1, ED2). The third enterprise in difficulty, ED3, was identified through personal contacts in Tunis. The other three firms (ER1, ER2, ER3) used DITC services prior to the crisis (2010), but had not resorted to it since then. We considered that these latter firms had recovered prior to the crisis, and had managed to make it through the 2010–2015 period better than those two that used the DITC during that period. If they had experienced serious difficulties, they would have resorted to the DITC. As property access is complicated in the Maghreb countries (Zahra, 2011), we availed of the contact opportunity to obtain the firms' agreement to participate in the survey. These six firms are outlined in Table 2.3.

Data were collected by interview with the firm's managing director, financial director or manager based on open-ended questions about the context, the encountered problems and the seized business opportunities. The interviews lasted on average two hours; the responses were recorded and transcribed on paper. Multiple interviews per firm were not possible. In addition, the anonymity of respondents and their firms was guaranteed. These constraints are characteristic of the Maghreb and Middle East countries (Zahra, 2011)

The interviews took place in 2015 covering the entire period from the end of 2010 to the interview date. We considered that this is a long enough time frame to capture the events encountered during a long-term crisis, compared to a traditionally studied short-term shock. We also considered this time frame to be sufficiently short from a methodological rigor perspective: given the nature of the subject (emergence of unexpected events and implemented solutions), it is unlikely that the collection method would suffer from a historical bias, linked to the lapse of respondents' memories. Encountered problems and attempted solutions to the problems are unlikely to be forgotten, or on the contrary to be distorted in such a short period of time.

Table 2.3 Cases description

Firm	Success or failure?	Sector	Head office	Workforce 2014	Creation	Number of establishments	Share holding	CA 2011 (K DT)	Interviewee
ED3	failure	Trade in audiovisual equipment	Tunis	4	1949	1	Group	150	Managing director
ER1	success	Painting	Sfax	42	1971	1	Family run	6,121	Financial director
ED1	failure	Textile clothing	Sfax	40	1987	1	Family run	134	Manager
ER2	success	Engineering and metallurgical industries	Sfax	50	1969	3	Family run	6,700	Financial director
ED2	failure	Treatment and regeneration of used oils recyclable materials recovery	Sfax	15	1998	1	Group	200	Manager
ER3	success	Plasturgia	Sfax	40	1970	2	Family run	4,000	Managing director

The content of the written transcripts has been analyzed on a case-by-case basis by highlighting the encountered difficulties, any opportunities that may have been seized or built, and the manager-specific factors that were associated by respondents with opportunity seizing. An analysis of the response tone of the respondents was also conducted. Back-and-forth literature reviews were regularly made.

Results

The responses of the managers are first analyzed by focusing on the difficulties and opportunities encountered in each case. The cross-case analysis raises the following questions: Do businesses face the same difficulties? Which companies recognize opportunities? Are opportunities seized or built?

Firms, Difficulties, Opportunities

Let us start with the three failure cases.

ED3, an audiovisual equipment trading firm, experienced significant difficulties during the democratic transition, with losses at the end of 2011 equal to the previous year's profits and revenues having fallen by half during the year. It then approached the DITC to lay off some of its staff. According to its manager, the most important problem it faced is the political instability since early 2011, with successive governmental changes, inter-party struggles and trade union activism. The manager says:

> Then there were several temporary governments and the situation was unclear because we didn't know if there would be an election. Therefore, the state's demand for our equipment . . . has dropped significantly because the successive temporary governments were just managing day-to-day.

This instability led to a freeze in public projects representing 70% of the firm's turnover. It also led to the shutdown of certain projects between Tunisia and some Gulf countries on which ED3 was positioned to play a role. Personnel changes in the administration created inertia, particularly increasing customs delays. The second difficulty was associated with the location of the firm, in Bourguiba Avenue in Tunis, where many more or less violent demonstrations and clashes took place. Unfavorable exchange rate changes, particularly in 2012, resulted in extra costs on equipment purchases. The decline in purchasing power, noticeable in 2013, reduced private investment, contributing to reduce ED3 turnover. Employee claims, from 2011 to 2014, reduced productivity: "We also face social problems in the form of challenges and demands. Our employees encouraged by the rebellious atmosphere in the country, claim higher wages, shorter working hours: this leads to a drop in the performance of the firm." The lack of long-term visibility precluded any attempt to develop a clear investment plan and a clear budget strategy. Finally, strikes within customs, and air and sea transport firms paralyzed the firm's business and logistics.

In respect of most of these difficulties, the manager felt powerless, unable to find solutions on his own. Nevertheless, in response to the slow-down in orders, he developed in 2013 a new event sound business that proved to be profitable. He also sought new market opportunities abroad, particularly in Algeria, yet without achieving success. He deplored the lack of financial resources and good cash flow that would have enabled him to get better through the crisis.

ED1 is a textile and clothing manufacturer whose economic situation has deteriorated significantly since 2011. The main encountered problem is linked to rising costs (personnel costs, raw materials, spare parts, electricity) which have led to a loss of competitiveness and profitability, delays of nearly ten days in salary payments, inability to pay incentives, and finally raised concerns for the firm's survival. The exchange rate of the dinar also contributed to the firm's problems. Furthermore, the firm experienced internal social problems. These internal upheavals in 2012 and 2013 resulted in a high rate of unjustified absenteeism, workers' resistance to absenteeism regulations, unlimited freedom of expression, theft, and increasing demands on the part of workers (e.g., unearned bonuses). This led to a weakening in performance and production, non-compliance with the production schedule and even reluctance to participate in training sessions.

The situation remains tense, as the manager explains:

> Even today, there was a 25% absenteeism rate which disrupts the team leader's work. . . . We feel helpless with respect to this phenomenon. The absent female workers even refuse to provide us with the necessary supporting documents for their absence. They do not even appreciate being sent a telegram or questionnaire following unjustified absence.

The firm closed for a week and the DITC intervened. Customs in 2013 contributed to delays in imports and blocked exports; there was equipment storage insecurity, difficulties in meeting commitments to third parties, and a deterioration in cash flow. The firm also suffered from the obsolescence of its production equipment while being unable to change it to satisfy customers' needs and optimize production. The firm has had to be shut down periodically, causing delivery delays and contributing to its possible closure. The Tunisian economic crisis combined with the global crisis has led to a reduction by customers of ED1 of their sourcing of material in Tunisia. Finally, local public transit difficulties have led to delays and worker absenteeism.

The manager has not identified any market opportunities and relies on state financial support to maintain his business. He is happy that some foreign countries continue to source product from the firm. He regrets the initial lack of financial resources that would have enabled the firm to better get through the crisis.

ED2 was created to reprocess the residues of olive oil production, namely *margine*. This enterprise had already accumulated losses before the uprisings, but the situation worsened afterwards. Several factors have contributed to this, starting with social problems. The firm found itself faced with neighboring residents of their margine reprocessing basins demanding employment or accusing them of causing pollution. These neighbors have blocked the firm's sites several times by organizing sit-ins, even attacking employees and blocking potential Korean customers who came especially to meet the managers. As the manager says:

> It is true that we have had some problems such as employees' strikes and sit-ins. We found ourselves faced with violence at the workplace, and also found ourselves in the courts. We had only 12 employees and we had to recruit three more because the neighbours of our margine basins were demanding to be employed. Other neighbours have benefited from the situation to complain about bad odours, mosquitoes and sanitary problems caused by our basins. We were obliged to pay them an indemnity of 300dt per shareholder."

These blockages have led oil producers to dispense with the firms services, preferring to discharge the toxic untreated margine in nature or into channels. The sit-ins were only solved after court intervention. It was necessary to recruit three to sit-in, pay an indemnity of TND 300 to the neighbors per shareholder (total of TND 30,000); resort to the sanitary authorities to deny the validity of the neighbors' pollution claims; and pay private firms to clean up the margine basin environment (disposing of mosquitoes, mice). At the same time, the firm experienced a rise in its expenses due to the employees' internal claims concerning their salaries and improvements in their working conditions. As the oil producers were both shareholders and customers of the firm, they refused to raise prices to offset the increased costs.

> The problem is that when it is considered necessary to increase the price of our service to oil producers (1,2 dt or 1,3 dt instead of 1 dt per m³ of margine), my associates, who are our main customers, are reluctant to pay.

Instability has also led to the emergence of competitors using unfair methods of competition in a state with little competition control. Public-private partnership undertakings have been frozen, and a high degree of inertia developed within the administration in terms of decision-making. Successive transitional governments no longer supported the reprocessing of margine as before. Moreover, the years 2011 to 2014 were marked by a severe drought, limiting olive oil production and margine reprocessing

24 Alya Charfi and Jamil Chaabouni

needs. All these combined events reduced cash flow to zero, preventing wages from being paid, creating technical unemployment and prompting DITC intervention.

In terms of opportunities, the manager relies on obtaining a loan from ANGET (national waste management organization) and a grant from the German government to get rid of pollution. He would like the price of electricity to fall. He also expects improved weather conditions to help him get by.

Let us now describe the firms that were better off during the crisis (without using the DITC services).

ER1 is a painting firm that operates autonomously despite having been acquired by a large foreign group in the 2000s. This group invested in a modern and efficient production system. Since 2011 the firm has witnessed social movements especially among young employees, which have been reflected in absenteeism:

> During the revolution, we found ourselves with new young recruits, with their advantages and disadvantages. They were productive and performing well. But they lacked discipline, unlike employees with 20 or 30 years of service. For example, they had high rates of absenteeism. I think their rebellious attitude is the result of the revolution (2012/2013).

The payment of an extraordinary bonus also created internal unrest and even a daylong strike by some of the employees. It was necessary to push through early retirement for 18 employees in 2011 and nine in 2012. The firm has also undergone roadblocks by the unemployed, who have paralyzed its business and delayed its supplies and deliveries. Finally, strikes in 2013 at the port of Radès and among suppliers also complicated the smooth running of business: it was impossible to have access to local and imported raw material and to finished product stock. Production had to be halted and the firm shut down for three days. The manager refers to this situation:

> We have been blocked by the strikes carried out at our Sfaxian suppliers and at all the firms located on Gabes road. The latter was blocked, preventing suppliers and carriers from delivering the raw material to us. We didn't even have access to our finished goods warehouse.

Regarding opportunities, the manager cites that the revolution itself was beneficial to his business. The democratic transition and the lack of state control led to anarchic construction development: the buildings damaged by popular uprisings had to be repainted. "The whole country had been burned and it was an excellent opportunity for us to sell our paint to the affected Tunisians. In addition, there have been many clandestine constructions that contributed to an increase in our sales." De facto, the firm has

How to Survive in an Unstable Environment   25

expanded into these growth markets, managing to increase its turnover by 50% yearly between 2011 and 2014. Retirements were compensated for by the recruitment of motivated and competent employees who contributed to improving the firm's productivity and economic margins.

ER2 produces hardware, such as nails and screws. Before the crisis, it had experienced difficulties related to smuggling from Libya, leading to DITC intervention and layoffs in 2008. The sociopolitical events since the end of 2010 have created many difficulties. First, the customs blockade of raw material imports led to high-priced raw materials supply on the local market: "Raw material was blocked at customs level which blocked our imports. We were then forced to buy the raw material from Fouledh. This causes a 30% rise in the cost of raw materials." Furthermore, this blockade concerned spare parts that the firm imported from France and Italy. There followed a 20-day stoppage of screw production, and then the technical unemployment of a few workers in the spring of 2011. Exports to Algeria and Morocco were suspended that year, also due to strikes in ports, but resumed in 2012. By the end of 2011, turnover fell by 25% and profits by 10%. Strikes by transport firms have led to a review of the organization's logistics, and the transport function is now carried out by the firm itself. Finally, the firm has reacted to the promptings of external stakeholders, including the unemployed in 2011, and had to recruit six people from the demonstrators. These young unemployed encouraged employees to strike.

The manager cites two major opportunities that his firm has been able to seize. First, the Libya insurgency that followed the Tunisian revolution stopped the smuggling of competing products, shielding the firm from unfair competition and giving it access to a new clientele: "The Libyan revolution was in favour of the firm, because it was at the source of the suspension of imports from Libya." On the other hand, given the political instability, wealthy Tunisians sought to invest in buildings during the crisis, leading to numerous real estate developments. Yet, construction is ER2's main market.

ER3, a manufacturer of plastic parts and tubes, had to overcome several problems. First, the Libyan revolution led to a fall in demand in the local market in 2011, which was a large outlet for the firm: "In the aftermath of the revolution, my money was blocked because these Tunisian promoters could not, in turn, get reimbursed by the Libyans. This decrease in turnover was about 30%. The balance sheet for 2011 was in deficit." At the same time, the decline in public demand was combined with the saturation of the Tunisian market. The fall in public demand is associated with the inability of the public administration to make decisions during a period of chaotic government: "The decline in demand is also justified by the suspension of public markets. The government is in a chaotic situation and public officials are unable to make decisions." These events have led to an increase in receivables collection time and in unpaid drafts in 2011. An important French customer halted a partnership project that it relaunched two years later. Losses at the end of 2011 amounted to between 3% and 5% of turnover. The firm has also experienced internal and external social problems. Internally, the firm's technical equipment was sabotaged and daily requests for salary increases were made in 2011. Externally, the firm was unable to deliver goods to Kasserine and Gafsa due to sit-in roadblocks. The strike at the Port of Radès in 2013 created supply problems from Europe, Qatar and Saudi Arabia, forcing the use of more expensive local supplies and weakening cash flow.

The manager of ER3 regrets the lack of technical skills available on the Tunisian market that would enable him to increase his competitiveness. Nevertheless, he has exploited various opportunities. Since 2012, on the advice of exporting partners, ER3 has been developing a direct export business to African countries without going through intermediaries, a business that provides it with significant margins. It has embarked, with the support of the Chamber of Commerce that plays a facilitating role and the use of Tunisian and Ivorian consultants, on a project to rent a production site in the Ivory Coast to install the firm's old machinery and produce for that country and other sub-Saharan African countries. This project was to be launched in 2015:

> For this purpose, I plan to rent a firm in the Ivory Coast in which I will install a technician and two of my old machines which I decided not to throw away. This production unit will be the direct counterpart of my African customers. My low prices will be competitive.

The firm is negotiating with its French partner the possibility of ensuring the marketing of the partner's products on the Tunisian market. The manager also studies business opportunities in Malaysia. He envisages future diversification in the iron processing market thanks to his contacts within the professional network formed by iron producers. Finally, in 2014, he approached the Public Revenue Administration to negotiate the possibility of making purchases with recovered suspended value added tax (VAT; recovery of the cumulative amount of rebates not having been reimbursed to the firm in the period of the transitional governments).

The examination of these cases shows that all the firms have encountered difficulties, some of the same nature (port and transport strikes, import blockades, unemployed agitation and sit-ins), others unique (ED3 and its offices located on the troubled Bourguiba Avenue; ED2 and its shareholders-clients refusing to agree to increased prices, etc.). It also shows that not all of them have taken advantage of business opportunities during the 2011–2014 period. Let us examine these results by means of comparative analysis of the studied cases.

Inter-case Analysis

This analysis will deal successively with the following questions: Do firms confront the same difficulties? Which firms recognize opportunities? Are opportunities seized or built? What factors specific to markets or to business management are associated with seizing or building opportunities?

Difficulties Encountered

All firms have faced difficulties related to the crisis and 2011 appeared to be a black year for all, but the unstable political and social situation created further difficulties in the following years. Firms faced external problems: political instability and the unemployed actions are cited by all. Importing and exporting firms (ED1, ED3, ER1, ER2, and ER3) froze their foreign operations. All of them also experienced difficulties with their employees, which initially took the form of claims for better conditions following the revolution. Firms that have used the DITC during the crisis period are not different from others in these respects.

On the other hand, the industry and ecosystem in which the firm operates influence the emergence of certain difficulties. It should be noted that the markets of two firms considered as performing (ER2 and ER1) have developed over the entire period (hardware and painting, respectively). The other four firms, conversely, experienced a more or less significant fall in their sales in Tunisia. In the ecosystem specific to each firm, particularities are noteworthy. For example, the successful firm ER3 saw its main French partner reduce its commitment at the beginning of the crisis. Another example worked in both directions: the Libyan revolution favored ER2 (halted smuggling) and penalized ER3 (market collapse). In summary, the nature of firms' activities and the geographical location of its operations influence the emergence of difficulties specific to firms in our sample. But many of the encountered problems are similar in all the firms, regardless of their level of performance.

Recognition of Business Opportunities

The recognition of business opportunities distinguishes between less and better performing firms. Among those less performing firms, ED1 has not identified any business opportunities and relies on the government to get by. ED2 relies on subsidies to ensure its sustainability. It tried to seize an opportunity (Korean market), but this was negated by the sit-in. ED3 is the only less performing firm to have seized an opportunity (sound systems) that enabled it to survive, but it failed to maintain its pre-crisis employment and level of business.

As for performing firms, two have benefited from industry-related factors: the growth of the paint market for ER1 and the growth of the

28 Alya Charfi and Jamil Chaabouni

hardware market for ER2. As for ER3, it has seized several opportunities while its traditional market was in trouble: direct sales in Burkina Faso and Cameroon, establishment of a production facility in the Ivory Coast, and sales of foreign partners' products on the Tunisian market.

Note as well the absence of complaints about both the lack of financial resources of performing firms and their non-demands for subsidies. Each enterprise relies mainly on itself to get through periods of turmoil, whereas the less performing firms would first like financial support from the state.

To sum up, all performing firms have seized business opportunities without seeking financial support. Less performing ones seek financial support; only one of them leveraged a small opportunity that saved it from shutting down.

Opportunities Seized or Built

The literature is shared between "old school" researchers who see the entrepreneur drawing on a stock of opportunities that exist independently of him, and "new school" researchers who speak of the entrepreneur as a builder of opportunities. While examining our cases, contrasting situations are revealed. Let us take the three performing firms of which ER2 and ER1 essentially saw an influx of demand for their traditional products. De facto, their managers only had to deploy commercial resources and adapt production to this phenomenon emerging in their environment. We can therefore say that they seized the opportunity that presented itself to them. Conversely, ER3 has undertaken many steps to develop new markets in other countries. It invested a great deal to come up with projects that took time to develop: its approach is more in line with opportunity building. In fact, our cases tell two stories about opportunities recognition: a story of opportunities seized without much effort and a story of opportunities built with a lot of effort.

Factors Associated With Seizing/Building Opportunities

Some factors associated by respondents with the exploitation of opportunities differentiate between seized and built opportunities. Seizing opportunities can be associated with a market factor. ER2 and ER1 witnessed a demand increase during the crisis period and managed to meet it. However, this market factor is not reflected in the ER3 manager's response. This one highlights his networks that contributed to recognize and exploit the opportunities: the advice of external partners for sales in Cameroon and Burkina Faso; the assistance of consultants and the chamber of commerce for the establishment of a production facility in the Ivory Coast; an industrial partner for the new market in Tunisia. These are therefore the personal networks—the manager's social capital—reflected in the response.

Additional Differences

Finally, the review of the responses shows similarities between all managers in performing firms. First, a response that we would describe as positive about the crisis period: yes, the crisis creates difficulties, but we will successfully emerge from them. Conversely, the responses are more pessimistic from the less performing firms: the responses are of a similar type—our firms will survive, provided that the crisis ends. It should be noted, however, that the tone of the response may be the consequence, not the cause, of the achieved performance. It makes more sense to be positive when the firm is performing positively.

Subsequently, there are references in performing firms' responses to entrepreneurial behavior, to being on the lookout for opportunities, which recalls the vigilance concept identified by Kirzner (1973) characterizing entrepreneurs. This entrepreneurial behavior does not appear in less performing firms. For example, the ED1 manager studied a development opportunity in Algeria but never acted on it.

Tables 2.4 and 2.5 summarize the main conclusions of the inter-case analysis.

Table 2.4 Comparison of performing and less performing firms

	Less performing firms	*Better performing firms*
	ED1, ED2, ED3	*ER1, ER2, ER3*
Difficulties encountered	high	high
Leveraging opportunities	weak (one sole opportunity for this group)	systematic
Vigilance toward opportunities	low	high
Subsidy expectations	yes, in two out of three cases	no
Tone of response to crisis	pessimistic	positive

Table 2.5 Factors associated with exploiting opportunities

	Seized opportunities	*Built opportunities*
The enterprises' common factors	Entrepreneurial behavior: vigilance	
Specific factors	Market growth of the enterprise	Manager's relationships network

30 Alya Charfi and Jamil Chaabouni

Discussion of Results

This research, based on a comparison of managers' responses in relation to the 2011–2014 crisis and the exploitation of opportunities, makes a contribution to the understanding of the survival of firms in times of crisis. We have compared firms having resorted to the DITC during that period and having to reduce their business, with firms having managed to maintain or expand their business.

This comparison helped identify the ability to exploit opportunities as a factor that could explain why particular firms belong to one group and not another. We then studied the factors associated with the exploitation of opportunities, showing that some firms differ according to whether the opportunity is seized or built. Let us examine these results in detail.

Seizing Business Opportunities and Business Performance

Our investigations tend to show that performing firms have systematically seized business opportunities while being affected by difficulties arising from social, political and economic instability. Conversely, less performing firms have not, with one exception, exploited any opportunity. The only opportunity leveraged (ED3) was not sufficient to maintain its business level.

Our initial reasoning is that seizing business opportunities corresponds to the implementation of renewal ability. Performing firms have therefore developed a renewal ability considered necessary by researchers working on crises (Begin and Chabaud, 2010; Wildavsky, 1991). The ER3 manager bears witness to this: "I would like to launch a diversification strategy with new products such as iron." It should be noted that this result partially contradicts the conclusions of Chaabouni et al. (2015), which identified Tunisian firms capable of withstanding the crisis as simply firms capable of actuating a shock absorption ability. The study period may explain this result. The study of these authors was conducted over the year 2011, whereas ours considered a much longer period, from 2011 to 2014. It can therefore, be assumed that shock absorption ability ensures survival over a relatively short period of time but is not sufficient to ensure survival over several years. This explanation is reinforced by our research: most of the less performing firms in our sample seem focused on shock absorption.

Therefore, we formulate the following research proposition:

> *P1.* The economic performance of the firm in a long-term social, political and economic crisis is associated with its ability to exploit business opportunities during the period.

Factors Associated With the Exploitation of Opportunities

There is still a debate in the entrepreneurship field about exploiting opportunities: are opportunities seized or built by the entrepreneur? On the one hand, opportunities seized are considered to have their own existence independent of the entrepreneur (Venkataraman, 1997); on the other hand, opportunities are built by the entrepreneur through the maturation and learning associated with projects (Sarasvathy, 2001). This debate on firm setup takes a different form in the context of SMEs: we can talk about opportunities seized when demand comes to the firm and opportunities built when the manager decides to launch into new markets.

The opportunities exploited in a long-term crisis period are of two types. Some firms had to adapt to an increase in demand for their products; another developed foreign projects to externally deploy its operations. Somehow it can be said that some firms are lucky whereas others need to redouble their efforts to recognize these opportunities. Our research shows that the built opportunities have benefited from the resources provided by the manager's networks. This is what the ER3 manager explains: "it is my relationships within my professional network and the feedback I get about the attractiveness of the iron market that give me that desire."

Hence our research propositions concerning the factors specific to each type of operation:

> P2. In times of long-term social, political and economic crises, some factors associated with opportunities exploitation depend on the nature of the exploitation.
>
> - *P2.1.* The market characteristics (demand) are associated with opportunity seizing.
> - *P2.2.* The managers' ability to mobilize their networks is associated with opportunity building.

Finally, our data exploration has highlighted the entrepreneurial character of performing firms' managers: they are looking for opportunities, demonstrating what Kirzner (1973) calls vigilance to characterize the entrepreneurs he studied. Hence our third research proposition:

> P3. In times of long-term social, political and economic crises, the manager's entrepreneurial (vigilance) character is associated with opportunity exploitation.

Our research thus contributes to deciphering why some firms manage better than others to overcome periods of long-term sociopolitical crisis. By identifying opportunity exploitation as an explanatory factor, we are paving the way for researchers interested in the subject.

32 Alya Charfi and Jamil Chaabouni

Nevertheless, our research suffers from several limitations. The inductive qualitative approach, based on discourse analysis, allows concepts and constructs to emerge but not to be precisely measured. Future research should focus on defining more precisely opportunity building and seizing to be able to test our proposals.

Our reduced sample matched our willingness to exploit the managers' responses in depth so as to explore an almost empty field of knowledge research, but it limits the possibility of generalizing the results obtained. This is why we have made our further research proposals. These proposals could be transposed and tested in a country, such as Egypt, which experienced the same socioeconomic upheaval as Tunisia.

Our analysis on seizing opportunities also deserves field testing in other African countries, which are negotiating a deep and comprehensive free trade agreement with the EU (ALECA), as these agreements create new situations for local firms by confronting them in their traditional markets with competition from European firms without having sufficiently prepared for such competition. Also, future research could attempt to validate these proposals by using quantitative methods, knowing, however, that this type of study is difficult to implement in Tunisia and that tracking firms' performance is complicated.

In terms of managerial involvement, our findings point out that resilience in times of crisis is not simply comparable to shock absorption ability. Surviving firms stand out from those in difficulty by their ability to track down opportunities to redeploy their business. Instinctively, the emergence of a national revolution can lead to introversion, a desire to safeguard what can be safeguarded. Our research suggests a different approach. The manager confronted with such a socioeconomic crisis has an incentive to focus his attention on seeking business opportunities, by mobilizing his networks, studying in depth the structural evolution of the markets in his country and beyond. Survival and prosperity seem to be linked to firms' ability to renew themselves.

Conclusion

Political, economic and social upheavals around the world influence the functioning of firms and sometimes question their very survival. Development planning is becoming difficult, and some economic environments are so deteriorated that locally based firms are struggling to survive. Our research aims to understand why some firms are doing better than others facing the same problems. We chose Tunisia as a field study because it has experienced a long-lasting social, political and economic crisis beginning in late 2010 with the "Democratic Revolution." We compared firms' business practices according to their level of performance and identified the exploitation of business opportunities as a factor differentiating better performing from less performing firms. We then analyzed the factors

How to Survive in an Unstable Environment 33

associated with the two forms of opportunities exploitation: seizing and building.

The research highlights the need for questioning and for renewal ability to overcome such long-term crises. If the firm can absorb a short-term shock, this absorption ability seems insufficient when the crisis persists. Our work opens the curtain on a little-explored research field. And yet, it deserves to be researched. The rise in popular protests, populist movements and terrorist acts is creating an environment that firms should become accustomed to. It is likely that the liberal economy developed in a relatively calm social environment could quickly become but a memory, and the new economic "normality" has not yet been designed.

References

Ayari, C. (2012). "Situation économique et sociale: Un cri d'alarme," January 19. www.leaders.com.tn/article/situation-economique-et-sociale-un-cri-d-alarme?id=7484.

Begin, L., Chabaud, D. (2010). "La résilience des organisations: le cas d'une entreprise familiale." *Revue Française de Gestion*, 200, pp. 127–142.

Chaabouni, J., Very, P. (2015). *Crise, transition: comment les entreprises tunisiennes s'en sortent-elles?* Tunis: Editions C.L.E.

Eisenhardt, K. M., Graebner, M. E. (2007). "Theory building from cases: opportunities and challenges." *Academy of Management Journal*, 50, pp. 25–32.

Gaglio, C. M. (1997). "Opportunity identification: Review, critique, and suggested research." In J. A. Katz (ed.), *Advances in Entrepreneurship, Firm Emergence, and Growth*. Greenwich, CT: JAI Press.

Hills, G. E., Lumpkin, G.T., Singh, R.P. (1997). "Opportunity recognition: perceptions and behaviors of entrepreneurs." In *Frontiers of Entrepreneurship Research*. Wellesley, MA: Babson College, pp. 168–182.

Hollnagel, E., Journé, B., Laroche, H. (2009). "La fiabilité et la résilience comme dimensions de la performance organisationnelle." *M@n@gement*, 12(4), pp. 224–229.

INS (Institut National de la Statistique). (2016). "Statistiques Issues du Répertoire National des Entreprises." www.ins.tn/sites/default/files/publication/pdf/RNE-2016-1-web.pdf.

ITCEQ (Institut Tunisien de la Compétitivité et des Etudes Quantitatives). (2013). "Principaux résultats de l'enquête annuelle sur la compétitivité." www.itceq.tn/fr/index.php?rub=283&srub=433.

Kendra, M. J., Wachtendorf, T. (2003). "Elements of resilience after the World Trade Center disaster: reconstructing New York City's emergency operation center." *Disasters*, 27(1), pp. 37–53.

Kirzner, I. (1973). *Competition and Entrepreneurship*. Chicago: University of Chicago Press.

La Porte, T. R. (1982). "Design and management of nearly error-free organizational control systems." In D. L. Sills (ed.), *Accident at Three Mile Island: The Human Dimensions*. Routledge, London, pp. 238–252.

Lengnick-Hall, C., Beck, T. E. (2005). "Adaptive fit versus robust transformation: how organizations respond to environmental change." *Journal of Management*, 31, pp. 738–757.

34 *Alya Charfi and Jamil Chaabouni*

Marouane, S., Chtrourou, W. (2015). "Les entreprises apprennent-elles des crises passées?" In J. Chaabouni and P. Very (eds.), *Crise, transition: comment les entreprises tunisiennes s'en sortent-elles?* Tunis: Editions C.L.E. pp. 95–134.

Miner, A. S., Bassoff, P., Moorman, C. (2001). "Organizational improvisation and learning: a field study." *Administrative Science Quarterly*, 46, pp. 304–337.

Ministère des Affaires Sociales. (2014). "Guide des Statistiques Sociales (en langue arabe) (دليل الإحصائيات الاجتماعية)." www.social.tn/fileadmin/user1/doc/annuaire_2014_version_final.pdf.

Mzid, I. (2015). "La résilience organisationnelle de l'entreprise familiale: l'impact du capital familial." In J. Chaabouni and P. Very (eds.), *Crise, transition: comment les entreprises tunisiennes s'en sortent-elles?* Tunis: Editions C.L.E., pp. 25–55.

Sarasvathy, S. D. (2001). "Causation and effectuation: toward a theoretical shift from economic inevitability to entrepreneurial contingency." *Academy of Management Review*, 26(2), pp. 243–288.

Smith, K. G., Di Gregorio, D. (2003). "Bisociation, discovery, and the role of entrepreneurial action." In M. A. Hitt, R. D. Ireland, S. M. Camp, and D. L. Sexton (eds.), *Strategic Entrepreneurship, Creating a New Mindset*. Oxford: Blackwell, pp. 129–150.

Spich, R., Grosse, R. (2005). "How does homeland security affect U.S. firms' international competitiveness?" *Journal of International Management*, 11, pp. 457–478.

Tounsi, F. (2012). "Conférence de Presse du Directeur général de l'Agence de Promotion de l'Industrie et de l'Innovation Tounsi F.," January 24. www.tap.info.tn/fr/fr/economie/commerce-et-industrie/17412-rassurer-les-investisseurs-nest-pas-seulement-la-responsabilite-de-lapii-.html.

Vaughan, D. (1996). *The Challenger Launch Decision*. Chicago: University of Chicago Press.

Venkataraman, S. (1997). "The distinctive domain of entrepreneurship research." *Advances in Entrepreneurship, Firm Emergence and Growth*, 3, pp. 119–138.

Weick, K. E. (1993). "The collapse of sense making in organizations: the Mann Gulch Disaster." *Administrative Science Quarterly*, 38, pp. 628–652.

Weick, K. E., Sutcliffe, K. M., Obstfeld, D. (1999). "Organizing for high reliability: processes of collective mindfulness." In R. S. Sutton and B. M. Staw (eds.), *Research in Organization Behavior*, vol. 21. Stanford: JAI Press, pp. 81–124.

Wildavsky, A. (1991). *The Rise of Radical Egalitarianism*. Washington, DC: American University Press.

World Bank (2014). "The World Bank Annual Report 2014. Washington, DC: World Bank. © World Bank." https://openknowledge.worldbank.org/handle/10986/20093 License: CC BY-NC-ND 3.0 IGO.

Yin, R. K. (1994). *Case Study Research: Design and Methods* (2nd ed.). Newbury Park, CA: Sage.

Zahra, S. A. (2011). "Doing research in the (New) Middle-East: sailing with the wind." *Academy of Management Perspectives*, 25, pp. 6–21.

3 Asymmetric Alliances and SMEs' Internationalization

Zoubeyda Mahamadou

Introduction

Internationalization is currently an imperative, key factor in all companies' development, whether in developed or developing countries. As Lu and Beamish (2006) noted, many companies will eventually expand their geographic reach from domestic to foreign markets. This is particularly the case for small and medium-sized enterprises (SMEs), which are traditionally perceived as organizations with limited financial resources and geographic reach. Internationalization is then an obvious path for them, and even a prerequisite for survival (Mercuri and Rais, 2010). This also represents an important opportunity for them to grow and enhance their key competencies across a range of markets (Lu and Beamish, 2001).

All SMEs pursuing internationalization have several options, including exports, licenses and direct investments; and all types of strategic alliances, such as equity and non-equity alliances, joint ventures, competition and asymmetric alliances. Each of these entry modes has its own advantages and disadvantages (Anderson and Gatignon, 1986; Pan and Tse, 2000); however, the most notable of these approaches focus on relational capital, which these companies establish to seize growth opportunities beyond their domestic markets (Prashantham and Dhanaraj, 2010).

This research is particularly interested in asymmetric alliances, which are generally considered as alliances between MNCs and SMEs (Mouline, 2005). According to Cherbib and Assens (2015), asymmetric alliances involve companies at different stages in not only their technological mastery and learning of industrial and technical skills and knowledge, but also in their access to financial and commercial resources. Scholars have rarely focused on this type of alliance; despite their growing popularity, researchers have seldom paid particular attention to asymmetrical alliances as a means of internationalization. Currently, many SMEs have used this strategic model in their expansion as they perceive asymmetrical alliances as a means of handling the constraints and challenges facing them in their internationalization processes.

This research is prompted by the scarcity of empirical works on this subject and their subsequent contrasting results, and it is based on the following question: "What determines SMEs' choices of asymmetric alliances in their internationalization processes?"

We use exploratory, qualitative research to answer this question. We are particularly interested in the case of French SMEs, which have increasingly used asymmetric partnerships to develop internationally so as to improve their performance. This chapter begins with a literature review of SMEs' internationalization, as well as strategic alliances in general and asymmetrical alliances in particular. We then describe our methodology, followed by the results of the research. The chapter concludes by discussing our results and highlighting the implications of our research findings, the limitations of the research, and possible extensions of the research area for future studies.

Internationalization of SMEs

This section will discuss the main constraints SMEs face in their internationalization processes, as well as the role of inter-organizational relationships—and particularly asymmetric alliances—in addressing these constraints.

The Constraints to the Internationalization of SMEs

Clearly, internationalization is currently one of the most important means to consider in promoting SMEs' growth. Although expanding their operations to new markets allows SMEs to achieve higher returns and growth, and geographic expansion provides attractive opportunities for growth and value creation, implementing such a strategy can involve many challenges.

First, structurally defined small enterprises (Jaouen, 2006) are characterized by limited critical resources and capabilities compared to larger firms. This implies a lack of financial resources, human capital, and other internal capacities needed to act effectively at the international level (Stoian et al., 2016). Similarly, Cazabat (2014) argued that SMEs have an inadequate financial structure and an internal structure unsuitable or difficult to "internationalize"; this is more of a disadvantage in the international market compared to large groups. When venturing into international markets, SMEs also face various additional obstacles and risks related to their lack of experience and knowledge of foreign markets (Lee et al., 2012). In respect of their external environment, SMEs are characterized as having a reduced quantity and quality of information. This translates into insufficient knowledge among management teams and distribution channels, and heightened risk for financiers and lenders (Beamish and Jung, 2005; Puthod and Ganassali, 1996). This also increases SMEs' vulnerability to change and their difficulties in accessing new markets. Moreover, it should be noted that regarding internationalization efforts in particular, the knowledge developed locally may not be

Asymmetric Alliances and SMEs 37

relevant in new foreign markets (Lu and Beamish, 2001; Lee et al., 2012). Thus, internationalization poses a major challenge for SMEs.

Consequently, the central hypothesis that emerges here involves SMEs' international development, which can be hampered by not only their insufficient structural means and resources but also by a lack of information and experience (Puthod and Ganassali, 1996; Mercuri and Rais, 2010; Stoian et al., 2016). These intrinsic and extrinsic deficiencies all constitute obstacles for SMEs, whether in producing new opportunities, commercializing their innovations or developing their competitive advantage in unknown markets (Lu and Beamish, 2001; Lee et al., 2012). Considering these constraints and specifications, SMEs face a crucial dilemma in determining the best strategy or option for internationalization (Mercuri and Rais, 2010).

Asymmetric Alliances and Internationalization of SMEs

Among the internationalization options available to SMEs, interorganizational relationships are widely recognized as essential, as they provide SMEs with the necessary information and resources to access new markets (Johanson and Vahlne, 2009; Ramadan and Levratto, 2011; Stoain et al., 2016). However, it should be noted that despite researchers' growing interest in SMEs' internationalization, they have rarely studied strategic alliances' general role in the process of recognizing international business opportunities. This is even more pronounced when one considers the particular case of asymmetric alliances.

Asymmetric alliances are generally considered as cooperative operations between companies of different sizes, and especially between SMEs and MNCs (Mouline, 2005). However, Harrigan (1988) refines this reductive, asymmetric formulation—which focuses a priori on the size differential— to adopt a multidimensional approach to partners' asymmetries. This author observed that in addition to differences in size and national or geographical origins, such criteria as experience in cooperation, cultural homogeneity, and the size of the assets involved in the relationship should be considered in defining asymmetric alliances. (Other authors have also reviewed the asymmetries between partners, such as Cherbib and Assens, 2015; Mahamadou, 2016; and Pérez et al., 2012). These alliances increasingly allow each partner to cope with rapid environmental turbulence by exploiting their complementarities; this is particularly the case for SMEs that can benefit from such partnerships to cope with the constraints related to their internationalization processes.

Among the few works integrating the issue of asymmetric alliances in SMEs' internationalization processes, we can count, inter alia, the conceptual work by Acs et al. (1997), which emphasized that given the challenges of globalization—such as the protection of property rights and barriers to entry—and all their related costs, innovative SMEs must abandon direct international expansion. Further, these SMEs must adopt an "intermediated" expansion, or an indirect, international expansion, which involves relying on certain resources and skills among major partners, including global affiliate networks and marketing skills. Consequently, MNCs act as catalysts and/or facilitators of SMEs' international development. From the same perspective, Etemad et al. (2001) developed a conceptual model highlighting the notion of indirect internationalization through asymmetric partnerships. They noted SMEs' interest in collaborating with MNCs to increase their international competitiveness. Ulubaşoğlu et al. (2009) then indicated that partnerships with large foreign accounts allow SMEs to increase their production capacity and more easily access new markets. Such partnerships are an understandable necessity for SMEs given their low capital and their desire for internationalization.

In summary, SMEs' partnerships provide them with access to large companies' capital, production capacity, powerful distribution networks and customers. These alliances also give SMEs the opportunity to access scarce resources and complementary capabilities, such as management skills, expertise in management or marketing, information on new markets, and advice. This can enable them to cope with some of their limitations (Acs et al., 1997; Jaouen, 2006; Chen and Chen, 2002; Beamish and Jung, 2005; Alvarez and Barney, 2001; Mercuri and Rais, 2010).

In addition to accessing MNCs' resources and skills, asymmetric alliances allow SMEs to rapidly internationalize. Integrating SMEs in large companies' value chains enables the former to reduce the risks, costs, and time associated with internationalizing their products. They can also quickly access global markets without having to build their own infrastructures or negotiate complex contracts with many agents (Kalaignaman et al., 2006; Puthod and Ganassali, 1996; Mercuri and Rais, 2010; Etemad et al., 2001). More importantly, SMEs will gradually accumulate new market information and internally develop new organizational capabilities (Lu and Beamish, 2001; Etemad et al., 2001).

Asymmetric alliances also allow SMEs to benefit from their large corporate partners' credibility and brand identity (Venkataraman et al., 1990; Alvarez and Barney, 2001; Nguyen, 2007). Moreover, SMEs' partnerships with major players can signal the quality of their activities and products, which consequently brings them external recognition and an initial reputation (Chetty and Wilson, 2003; Ramadan and Levratto, 2011; Zain and Ng, 2006). Furthermore, Chen and Chen (2002) confirm this approach in an empirical study of 1,597 Taiwanese small business partnerships with large foreign accounts. These authors demonstrate that asymmetric alliances with partners having well-established reputations provide SMEs with a certain legitimacy in new markets and thus promote their internationalization.

Overall, the literature indicates that in addition to alliances' general benefits, asymmetric alliances allow SMEs to create growth potential and improve their competitive advantage (Etemad et al., 2001). As Kalaig-nanam et al. (2006) stated, small businesses have an interest in forging alliances with large firms to benefit from their critical size and increase their sales growth. Therefore, this is one way for SMEs to successfully commercialize their innovations and products by taking advantage of, for example, large companies' national and international distribution networks (Alvarez and Barney, 2001).

In practice, this type of alliance has gained popularity among the strategic choices available to entrepreneurial companies. Therefore, their role in SMEs' internationalization process must be examined to enrich the current literature. We also highlight several pitfalls and gaps on this subject, whether theoretical or empirical.

Methodology

The research methodology selected is a qualitative, multiple case study (Yin, 1984), a methodological choice guided by our goal of understanding and explaining how asymmetric strategic alliances impact SMEs' internationalization processes.

We consider two data samples for our exploratory study. First, we consider asymmetric alliances established in the "Pacte PME"[1] framework: this is a joint association created in 2010 that brings together 53 major private and public companies, 20 competitiveness clusters and 21 professional organizations. This association aims to strengthen relationships between major international companies and French SMEs to reveal new leaders among mid-size companies. Moreover, this field has been favored because it enables researchers to address concrete examples of asymmetrical partnerships. Although academic publications addressing asymmetric alliances have indicated that researchers have not yet consistently studied this theme, one exception is the work by Mercuri and Rais (2010). From this perspective, we conduct a comparative study of 60 asymmetric alliances' cases presented in the "Pacte PME" from 2010 to 2016 (see the Appendix, Table 3.3). Our study sample considers the following criteria: first, our cases only involve partnerships between SMEs and MNCs, with SMEs defined as companies with workforces between 10 and 250 employees (European Commission). This definition does not consider turnover and/or balance sheet data, as this is more complex information. Second, we choose not to consider SMEs with less than 20 employees to avoid excessive differences in the sample companies' management policies and objectives. Finally, we only consider cases of alliances with complete information available in respect of our research variables.

In addition to data derived from our first sample—and to allow a more complete approach to the subject—we conducted ten recorded, semi-structured interviews with French SMEs involved in asymmetric alliances. Each interview lasted 60 to 90 minutes, and each respondent

40 Zoubeyda Mahamadou

was closely involved in the conduct of their company's asymmetric alliances. The alliances from our second sample are non-equity asymmetric alliances, which are typically contractual and do not involve the creation of a separate legal entity for the project's coordination and management. Table 3.1 describes the ten asymmetric alliances studied in this research. Each of our interviews results in a thematic coding according to items identified in our theoretical model and transcripts (King, 1998).

Table 3.1 Identification of the interviewed SMEs

	Numbers of Employees in the SME	Respondents	Purpose of the Asymmetric Alliance
Case 1	44	Director general	Joint project for technological development + commercial relationship (original equipment manufacturing contracts)
Case 2	30	CEO	Commercial relationship (original equipment manufacturing contracts)
Case 3	35	Director general	Commercial relationship (original equipment manufacturing contracts)
Case 4	25	Director general	Joint research programs + commercial relationship (original equipment manufacturing contracts)
Case 5	86	Sales manager/ Commercial director	Commercial relationship (original equipment manufacturing contracts) + technology transfer relationship + joint R&D project
Case 6	138	Operations director	Commercial relationship (original equipment manufacturing contracts)
Case 7	130	Director general	Commercial relationship (original equipment manufacturing contracts)
Case 8	250	Director general	Commercial relationship (original equipment manufacturing contracts) + joint product development project
Case 9	40	CEO	Commercial relationship (manufacturing) + research project
Case 10	100	Sales manager/ Commercial director	Commercial relationship (maintenance + repair)

Source: For reasons of anonymity, we consider a threshold value for the MNCs' workforces in France.

These alliances' relationships will be analyzed only from the SME's side of the alliance, as the extent to which all partners' perceptions would converge is unknown. The choice of SMEs as a study object is justified by the near absence of theoretical and empirical research analyzing asymmetric alliances' advantages in SMEs' internationalization processes. Similarly, SMEs' current pace of innovation can be considered as fundamental for larger players given SMEs' role in manufacturing their components. Many MNCs—such as those in the aeronautics or automotive industries—have integrated organizational models that include their final products' different components being manufactured by many subcontracting partner SMEs.

Analysis of Results: Asymmetric Alliances and Internationalization of SMEs

The data collected from the "Pacte PME" allowed us to define the following basic characteristics for each of our 60 asymmetric alliances: the type of partnership, partners' motivations and the partnerships' benefits for each of their stakeholders. This first analysis reveals that all the studied asymmetric alliances can be considered as additive, complementary alliances according to Mitchell et al. (2002) configuration. These alliances enable MNCs to seek benefits from the knowledge of their partner SMEs: their capability to innovate; their organizational characteristics, such as responsiveness, agility and flexibility; and commercial advantages, such as their attractive value for money. This translates into the following objectives for MNCs: to achieve real commercial innovation, to face competitors by developing competitive advantage and to ensure financial progress and optimization.

Alternatively, these partnerships help SMEs to leverage their national and international development, as SMEs can not only improve their turnover and achieve dynamic growth in terms of their employee workforce and financial resources, but they can also invest in development operations: specifically, research and development, knowledge acquisition and diversification, extending their product ranges and markets, acquiring new qualifications and standards, and product promotions. Stakeholders generally perceive these partnerships as mutually beneficial; although these relationships are initially characterized by their considerable imbalance in terms of size, resources, competencies, qualifications, and management methods, both partners jointly act to achieve their desired goals.

Our analysis of the "Pacte PME" empirical data also allows us to clearly distinguish 31 of 60 cases—or approximately 52% of the cases studied—that highlight the importance of asymmetric partnerships in SMEs' internationalization processes. These results clearly define two internationalization modes: (1) direct internationalization and (2) indirect or assisted internationalization.

42 *Zoubeyda Mahamadou*

Direct Internationalization

In this case, the SME internationalizes without the accompaniment and the support of its MNC partner (10 of 31 cases). The SME relies solely on the benefits from their asymmetrical alliances to internationalize. Furthermore, the SME acquires financial credibility and stability through the following:

- Major contracts and important business volumes with their MNC partners
- The acquisition of new contracts and business in the MNC's network, which includes the MNC's local suppliers and customers.

This result is also corroborated among the ten cases considered during our interviews. Each of these respondents indicated that asymmetrical relationships allow SMEs to market their technologies and products and acquire larger market shares. For example, the CEO of Case 4 SME noted:

> If they are not there, we have no money, [and] we close. It's simple. . . . The reasons for these agreements for our SME are recurring revenues that are difficult to get with an SME, and especially the capacity to sell projects with larger financial envelopes than with an SME. . . . If you work with X, for example, you are sure to be paid, you limit financial risk, and you are more attractive to other customers, and therefore you can gain market share.

This was also confirmed by the commercial director of Case 10 SME. Once financial credibility has been established, the SME can more easily conduct development and investment activities to realize its international ambitions.

Asymmetrical alliances also benefit from the MNCs' references, as this first promotes the SME's credibility, reputation, and brand image and then subsequently develops its relationship with external and international actors. The SME becomes more reliable and attractive to potential customers due to this new visibility and credibility.

All the SMEs interviewed in our study (ten out of ten cases) corroborate this result; they emphasized that they want to take advantage of these partnerships to acquire references and achieve their growth objectives. For example, the sales manager of Case 5 SME noted:

> These relationships give us access to the multinational's resources in terms of international representation and showcasing of our goods, which will somehow replace the financial investments we would have to make to expand internationally.

The CEO of Case 9 SME also indicated that

> It's always credibility, but branding is also important. Suppose that I work with X and we call Y; well, they'll say that a priori if I work with

X, it's a good thing. . . . What interests me in working with a large group is especially the accompaniment they can give us, [and] they can also keep us going. Indeed, our developments are quite expensive and if we work closely with these people, it can make us perennial, it allows us to access their credibility.

In summary, in 10 of 31 cases in the "Pacte PME" sample and in 10 out of 10 cases in the interview sample, asymmetric alliances serve as a catalyst for SMEs' internationalization due to the benefits they provide. This is reflected for these SMEs through either (1) the creation of branches and subsidiaries abroad or (2) the conclusion of contracts with foreign customers or new large-account customers.

Indirect or Assisted Internationalization

Beyond the financial benefits and references these asymmetric partnerships provide, SMEs can rely on their MNC partners' assistance and support to internationalize (21 of 31 cases). The SME in this instance benefits from the following:

- MNCs' directions and advice to facilitate opportunities, whether administrative or in human resources: negotiation methods, payment terms, guarantees, deadlines and penalties, among others.

  - Certification methods can be used to reinforce qualifications or internal quality systems.

- Access to the MNCs' networks can create new customers and help in acquiring financing.
- The MNC can recommend the SME and promote its reputation. These recommendations also act as a guarantee from the MNC regarding the SME's knowledge and product quality.
- Other benefits, including the following:

  - Joint international projects with MNCs
  - The MNC assigning technological property and licenses to the SME
  - Risk-sharing, such as financial risks
  - The MNCs initiating lesser knowledge transfers to the SME, such as international business volunteering
  - Temporary access to the MNC's facilities.

The international development of SMEs through the support and accompaniment of their partners, the MNCs, is thus better than direct international development. This trend can be explained by the partnerships registered on the "Pacte PME," as the latter are part of a governmental approach in which the French state has encouraged SMEs' international development. Thus, MNCs in the "Pacte PME" context are primarily solicited for advice and

44 Zoubeyda Mahamadou

Table 3.2 Cross-sectional analysis of the empirical data

Benefits of Asymmetric Alliances			
"Pacte PME" data (60 cases)	For 29 of 60 cases	For 31 of 60 cases	
	National growth (critical size, turnover evolution: significant business volume + extension of the customer portfolio + acquisition of market shares)	10 of 31 cases: 1. Financial credibility 2. Reference: credibility (branding) and market recognition	21 of 31 cases: 1. Financial credibility 2. Reference: credibility (branding) and market recognition 3. The MNCs' support and assistance —The MNC's orientation toward opportunities —Advice: Administrative and HR (negotiation methods, payment terms, warranties, deadlines and penalties, and order taking, among others) • On certifications and enhancing qualifications; the internal quality system —Access to the MNC's networks (creating contacts with new customers or help in the acquisition of financing) —Recommending the SME and promoting its reputation —The MNC also uses these recommendations to guarantee the SME's knowledge and product quality —International joint projects with the MNC —Transferring technological property and licenses from the MNC to the SME —Risk-sharing, such as financial risks, or the euro/dollar exchange rate —The MNC's transfer of knowledge, such as international volunteering in business —The SME's access to the MNC's facilities, including temporary access to their premises

Benefits of Asymmetric Alliances

Interview data (10 cases)	For 10 of 10 cases National growth (critical size, turnover evolution: significant business volume + extension of the customer portfolio + acquisition of market shares)	For 10 of 10 cases 1. Financial credibility 2. Reference: credibility (branding) and market recognition	For 5 of 10 cases 1. The MNCs' support and assistance —Administrative and HR (negotiation methods, payment terms, warranties, deadlines and penalties, and order taking, among others); these differ among countries —Strategic recommendations —Access to the MNC's networks —Promoting the SME's activities —International joint projects with the MNC
Internationalization	–	Direct internationalization	Indirect or assisted internationalization

support. In other words, the MNC is particularly committed to support the SME's internationalization and to help it profit from its network and contacts.

This result is also corroborated by our interviews with SME representatives. Our investigation revealed that MNCs' international support is one reason that SMEs establish asymmetric alliances (5 of 10 cases). These partnerships allow MNCs to support SMEs and provide them with their expertise in terms of their knowledge of international markets and their management of technical issues. This point is illustrated through comments from our respondents; first, the director general from Case 1 SME notes the following:

> The MNC puts us in touch with new customers. The MNC helps us in the evaluation of the negotiation cycles, [and] in the order-taking and payment processes, which differ from one country to another. Not only did the MNC's recommendations enable the SME to refine its strategy, but it also allowed the SME to consolidate its know-how and become credible internationally to acquire references.

The CEO from Case 3 SME also indicated that "international support saves administrative and human resources time; we won months."

In summary, a cross-sectional analysis of our empirical data allows us to propose the following in Table 3.3, which describes the determinants of SMEs' choices of asymmetric alliances.

Discussion and Conclusion

This chapter primarily aimed to explore the determinants of SMEs' choices of asymmetric alliances in their internationalization processes. Ultimately, we considered a research framework developed from a literature review of SMEs' internationalization, and asymmetric alliances in particular. This study's results were derived from a qualitative analysis of 70 cases, including data from "Pacte PME" and interviews, regarding French SMEs' asymmetric alliances. Some of our results both confirm and illustrate the theoretical foundations presented in our analytical framework, whereas others delineate new knowledge. These results may also provide a noteworthy theoretical basis for future research given the exploratory nature of the existing work.

First, we determined that asymmetrical alliances allow SMEs to develop their financial resources, including their attaining a critical size, increased business volume, and sales growth. This gives them a certain credibility and indicates their increased reliability in the eyes of other companies, such as better relationships with banks to facilitate access to financing. This result corroborates previous theoretical and exploratory results—including those by Etemad et al. (2001)—that asymmetric alliances constitute a means of growth for SMEs and improve their competitive advantage. We also corroborate the empirical results of Ulubaşoğlu et al. (2009), which indicate that SMEs can use asymmetric partnerships to increase their production capacity and more easily access new markets. Moreover, contrary to previous studies, we specify that these partnerships' financial credibility can be perceived as a means of promoting the SME's attractiveness, whether nationally or internationally. This lessens major firms' reluctance to build closer relationships with smaller, riskier businesses. Moreover, SMEs with sufficient financial resources can engage in activities similar to those engaged in by larger MNCs, including research and development investments, the employing of necessary human resources and establishing sufficient distribution networks to handle foreign market constraints (Kalaignanam et al., 2006). Financial credibility enhances the SME's chances of survival and mitigates the risks and uncertainty associated with a new environment or host country.

Our results also corroborate work by Alvarez and Barney (2001), Venkataraman et al. (1990), and Nguyen (2007), who argue that asymmetric alliances allow SMEs to benefit from their MNC partners' credibility and branding. These factors give SMEs some external market recognition and signal the quality of their activities (Chetty and Wilson, 2003; Ramadan and Levratto, 2011; Zain and Ng, 2006). These results also corroborate Chen and Chen's (2002) findings, which highlight that asymmetric alliances with partners with well-established reputations give SMEs a certain legitimacy in new markets to promote their internationalization. Therefore, an SME in a partnership with a large company indicates to local

Asymmetric Alliances and SMEs 47

actors that the SME has met its larger MNC partner's rigorous qualifications criteria.

The literature also emphasizes the importance of MNCs' assistance and support in SMEs' internationalization processes; specifically, asymmetric alliances allow SMEs to benefit from certain resources, augment any skills they may lack, and improve their likelihood of accessing foreign markets (Chetty and Wilson, 2003; Zain and Ng, 2006). Other resources include, for example, access to their MNC partners' distribution networks; general skills or expertise in management and marketing; and information on new markets and internationalization processes (Acs et al., 1997; Etemad et al., 2001; Alvarez and Barney, 2001; Chen and Chen, 2002; Beamish and Jung, 2005; Mercuri and Rais, 2010; Johanson and Vahlne, 2009; Ramadan and Levratto, 2011; Stoain et al., 2016). Our results corroborate these findings in the extant literature.

Additionally, it should be noted that previous works have failed to reach a consensus regarding the types of support that may be available to SMEs, as their research fields and approaches substantially differ. The current research allows us to clearly define the different forms of support that a French SME can deploy to benefit from asymmetric alliances in the internationalization process (Table 3.3). We can also observe that MNCs' support for SMEs predominantly include the SME's access to MNCs' networks, recommendations, promotions, and advice. However, previous works do not emphasize the importance of recommendations and promotions among the possible supports MNCs can provide to SMEs. Overall, our results are similar to those of Kalaignaman et al. (2006), Puthod and Ganassali (1996), and Etemad et al. (2001), in that asymmetric alliances allow SMEs to rapidly internationalize. They also decrease SMEs' difficulties, costs and time—such as administrative costs, negotiations and market uncertainty—associated with internationalizing their products or services.

Subsequently, this research reveals two key points. First, the SME's internationalization framework is characterized by its choice of asymmetric alliances, which is ultimately determined by the SME's acquisition of financial credibility; the benefit from the MNC's references, including credibility and brand image; and the MNC's assistance and support. The advantages of asymmetric alliances allow SMEs to overcome their constraints to internationalization, specifically their small size and limited internal resources.

Second, these research results define two modes of internationalization for SMEs through asymmetric alliances: direct and indirect (or assisted) internationalization. In the first case, SMEs primarily internationalize using their own resources, namely, relying on their newly acquired financial reliability and references due to their multinational partnerships. This approach contrasts with the results from Acs et al. (1997) and Etémad et al. (2001), which support a single internationalization mode, indirect internationalization, in the context of asymmetric alliances. These authors posit that direct internationalization does not imply any rapprochement between SMEs and MNCs. In the second case, SMEs indirectly internationalize by taking advantage of the support from their multinational partners. Figure 3.1 summarizes our results.

This research provides several theoretical and managerial implications, particularly given the limited attention paid to analyzing asymmetric alliances in general, and their role in SMEs' internationalization processes in

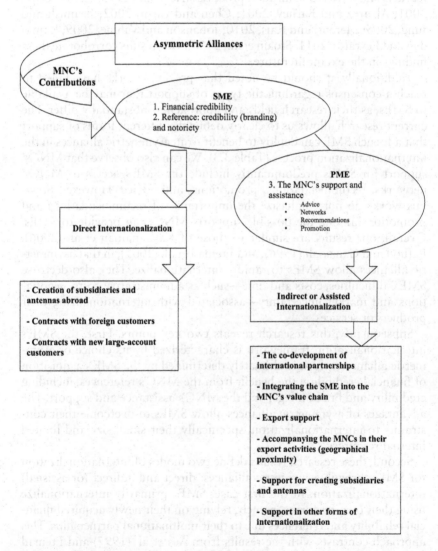

Figure 3.1 An internationalization model for SMEs

particular. We believe that this study could provide small business managers with insights regarding the factors to consider in respect of their firms' internationalization.

While this study significantly contributes to literature on asymmetric alliances, its potential limitations should also be highlighted. First, given our sample's multi-sectoral nature, our results should not be generalized without caveats. We should also note that the asymmetric alliances considered for our study were those as presented under the "Pacte PME" framework, which is a rather particular context as it only notates successful asymmetric alliances. Additionally, this research only considered one side of the alliance: the SME's perspective. Future research avenues can be empirically proposed; specifically, this study should be extended to larger samples and analyze both the contrasting MNC and SME perspectives. Other future studies should also examine the reasons for choosing asymmetric alliances in SMEs' internationalization processes among developing countries and compare them with those in developed countries.

Appendix

Table 3.3 Presentation of the "Pacte PME" sample

SME	Year Created	Number of Employees in the SME	SME's Activity	MNC	MNC's Activity	Asymmetric Alliance's Purpose	Year the Relationship was Created
SME1	1969	44	Manufacturing printed circuits	MNC1	Aerospace	Subcontracting	2007
SME2	2002	80	Consulting and software development	MNC2	Public sector purchases	Software development and training MNC's staff	2007
SME3	1978	120	Equipment manufacturing	MNC3	Energy	Commercial relationship: equipment designed and produced by SME	1997
SME4	1986	50 to 99	Electronics, electricity	MNC4	Electrical distribution, automation and industrial controls	Co-development of technological solutions	2009
SME5	2007	250	Delivery of maintenance services	MNC5	Hospital sector purchases	Service delivery	2012
SME6	1983	100	Consulting and software development	MNC6	Helicopter design and manufacture	Software development	1988

Asymmetric Alliances and SMEs 51

SME7	1980	93	Electronics	MNC7	Meteorology and energy	Development and manufacturing of advanced technological equipment	2011
SME8	1985	190	Micro-electronics	MNC8	Micro-electronics	Service provision by SME; R&D projects	1987
SME9	1996	110	Electronics	MNC9	Aerospace	Co-development of electronic components	2011
SME10	2007	22	Software development	MNC10	Banking	Software development	2011
SME11	2006	81	Energy and the environment	MNC11	Food	Service provision by SME	2009
SME12	1912	100	Climatic engineering	MNC12	Public sector purchases	Commercial contracts (single party agreement)	2011
SME13	1979	70	Sheet metal workshop	MNC13	Manufacturing scientific and technical instruments	Subcontracting	1982
SME14	1988	50	Boiler-making and mechanical assembly	MNC14	Energy	Design and production by SME (national agreement)	2007

(Continued)

Table 3.3 (Continued)

SME	Year Created	Number of Employees in the SME	SME's Activity	MNC	MNC's Activity	Asymmetric Alliance's Purpose	Year the Relationship was Created
SME15	1999	24	Computer editing	MNC15	Hospital sector purchases	Single party agreement	2011
SME16	2003	53	Data processing	MNC16	Energy	Co-sales partnership	2003
SME17	1979	60	Software editing and electronic equipment manufacturing	MNC17	Space studies	Agreement to develop and manufacture advanced technological equipment	2005
SME18	1980	65	Supplier of belt conveyors	MNC18	Transport	Outsourcing of MNCs' activities, maintenance	2005
SME19	2005	190	Engineering	MNC19	Electrical distribution, automation and industrial controls	Co-development of technological solutions	2009
SME20	1986	39	Mechanical	MNC20	Research and innovation in alternative and atomic energies	Subcontracting	1989
SME21	1985	50	Electronic systems design	MNC21	Electronics	Subcontracting	2001

SME22	1936	110	Marketing of garlic, onions, etc.	MNC22	Retail	Marketing, commercial and innovation research	2008
SME23	2003	100	Data processing	MNC23	Electronics	Service provision by the SME	2009
SME24	1996	100	Management software editing	MNC24	Multiple activities: postal services, banking, etc.	Outsourcing of MNC's publishing activities; subcontracting	2004
SME25	1987	155	Pultrusion of carbon fiber profiles	MNC25	Aeronautics and space	Subcontracting	2010
SME26	2003	35	European software editing	MNC26	Innovation and advanced engineering consulting	SME accompanies MNC for advice, consulting and commercial relations	2009
SME27	2008	200 to 299	Design and manufacturing of kinematic equipment	MNC27	Rail transport infrastructure	Co-development of equipment and innovative projects	2009
SME28	2004	25	Manufacturing of technical solutions	MNC28	Aeronautics and space	Equipment development	2010
SME29	1993	240	Studies, engineering, production and consulting	MNC29	Electrical distribution, automation and industrial controls	Manufacturing of advanced technology products	2010

(Continued)

Table 3.3 (Continued)

SME	Year Created	Number of Employees in the SME	SME's Activity	MNC	MNC's Activity	Asymmetric Alliance's Purpose	Year the Relationship was Created
SME30	1994	200	High-precision mechanics and aerospace consulting	MNC30	Helicopter design and manufacturing	Subcontracting	2003
SME31	1987	40	Design and manufacturing of light fixtures	MNC31	Energy, telecommunications, transportation	Subcontracting	2012
SME32	1986	160	Training and implementation of remote monitoring	MNC32	Banking	Service provision by SME	2010
SME33	1988	200 to 249	Systems infrastructure specialists	MNC33	Banking	SME develops services and innovative solutions	2010
SME34	2011	35	Design and manufacturing of radio communications equipment and geolocation systems	MNC34	Space studies	Creation and development of advanced products	2011
SME35	2009	26	Design, prototyping, production and commercialization of electric-powered urban delivery vehicles	MNC35	Multiple activities: postal services, banking, etc.	Product development (design)	2009

SME36	2003	160	Electronic equipment design	MNC36	Space studies	Development of advanced technological tools	2003
SME37	1982	50	Design and development of technical systems	MNC37	Aerospace	Co-development of technological solutions	1999
SME38	1986	28	Coatings/paints for the space industry, other industry and high technologies	MNC38	Space studies	Product development/co-development	1986
SME39	2001	48	Electrical assembly and wiring	MNC39	Air transport	Service provision by SME	2007
SME40	1977	65	Space industry	MNC40	Aeronautics and space	Co-developing "LYRE" project; development of state-of-the-art equipment for the MNC	2011
SME41	1947	105	Engineering	MNC41	Technological research and innovation in alternative and atomic energies	Process development	2011
SME42	1988	48	Services	MNC42	Banking	Service provision by SME	2009
SME43	1980	52	Clinical trials	MNC43	Pharmaceutical group	Service provision by SME	2009

(Continued)

Table 3.3 (Continued)

SME	Year Created	Number of Employees in the SME	SME's Activity	MNC	MNC's Activity	Asymmetric Alliance's Purpose	Year the Relationship was Created
SME44	1991	25	Furniture design	MNC44	Public sector purchases	Commercial contract	1997
SME45	1998	90	IT consulting	MNC45	Aeronautics and space	Development of a tool for the MNC, with intellectual property sharing and licensing to SME	2000
SME46	2000	44	Quality control	MNC46	Pharmaceuticals	Subcontracting; development of advanced scientific solutions	2006–2007
SME47	1978	19	Manufacturer of high-precision parts	MNC47	Aeronautics and the space industry	Manufacture of parts for MNC	1990
SME48	2008	40	Software editing	MNC48	Multiple activities: postal services, banking, etc.	Development of software, co-branding (filing patent in common)	2009
SME49	2005	92	General and precision mechanics	MNC49	Missile development and manufacturing	Development of technological tools	2013
SME50	1992	35	Computer systems development	MNC50	Air transportation	Development of software and transfer of knowledge to MNC	1992
SME51	2007	60	Independent IT consulting firm	MNC51	Luxury services	Service provision by SME	2010

SME52	1923	20	Manufacturer of workwear for industry, the construction sector and communities	MNC52	Electricity transmission	Product manufacturing	2007
SME53	1989	60	Publishing	MNC53	Banking	Commercial contracting	2011
SME54	2004	20 to 49	Engineering, technical studies	MNC54	Services for industry and health	Co-development of technological solutions	2007
SME55	1961	220	Equipment manufacturer in the railway industry	MNC55	Rail transport infrastructure	Co-development of special processes	2005
SME56	1962	220	Manufacturer and integrator of innovative technologies	MNC56	Technological research and innovation in alternative and atomic energies	Subcontracting	1980
SME57	2003	23	Software editing	MNC57	Missile development and manufacturing	SME's development of decision support solutions	2010
SME58	1980	20	IT services	MNC58	Data processing	Service provision by SME	2005
SME59	1983	100	Consulting and software packages editing	MNC59	Aeronautics and the space industry	MNC assists SME with provision of advice	2009
SME60	1996	100	Electric vehicle manufacturing	MNC60	Public sector purchases	Commercial contracting	2004

Source: For confidentiality reasons, we have not retained the real names of the companies in our database. Furthermore, the subject MNCs all have a workforce of more than 500 employees.

58 Zoubeyda Mahamadou

Note

1. www.pactepme.org/.

References

Acs, Z., Morck, R., Shaver J. M., Yeung, B. (1997). "The internationalization of small and medium-sized enterprises: A policy perspective." *Small Business Economics*, 9, pp. 7–19.

Anderson, E., Gatignon, H. (1986). "Modes of foreign entry: A transaction cost analysis and propositions." *Journal of International Business Studies*, 17(3), pp. 1–26.

Alvarez, S. A., Barney, J. B. (2001). "How entrepreneurial firms can benefit from alliances with large partners." *Academy of Management Executive*, 15(1), pp. 139–148.

Beamish, P. W., Jung, J. C. (2005). "The performance and survival of joint ventures with asymmetric parents." *International Business Review*, 10(1), pp. 1–16.

Cazabat, G. (2014). *L'internationalisation des Petites Entreprises: Une Nouvelle Représentation, la Facilitation D'internationalisation*. Thèse Gestion Et Management. Conservatoire National des Arts et Métiers—CNAM.

Chen, H., Chen, T.-J. (2002). "Asymmetric strategic alliances: A network view." *Journal of Business Research*, 55(12), pp. 1007–1013.

Cherbib, J., Assens, C. (2015). "Les Alliances Asymétriques. Une Étude de Cas Comparative en Tunisie." *La Revue Des Sciences De Gestion*, 5(275–276), pp. 165–172.

Chetty, S. K., Wilson, H.I.M. (2003). "Collaborating with competitors to acquire resources." *International Business Review*, 12(1), pp. 61–81.

Etemad, H., Wright, R., Dana, L.-F. (2001). "Symbiotic international business networks: Collaboration between small and large firms." *Thunderbird International Business Review*, 43(4), pp. 481–500.

Harrigan, K. R. (1988). "Strategic alliances and partner asymmetries." In Farok J. Contractor and Peter Lorange (eds.), *Cooperative Strategies in International Business: Joint Ventures and Technology Partnerships Between Firms*. Boston: Lexington Books, pp. 205–226.

Jaouen, A. (2006). "Typologie D'alliances Stratégiques en Très Petite Entreprise." *XVème Conférence Internationale De Management Stratégique*, Annecy, pp. 1–27.

Johanson, J., Vahlne, J.-E. (2009). "The Uppsala internationalization process model revisited: From liability of foreignness to liability of outsidership." *Journal of International Business Studies*, 40(9), pp. 1411–1431.

Kalaignanam, K., Shankar, V., Varadarajan, R. P. (2006). "Asymmetric new product development alliances: Win-win or win-lose partnerships?" Working Paper, Institute for the Study of Business Markets, 2, pp. 1–36.

King, N. (1998). "Template analysis." In G. Symon and C. Cassel (eds.), *Qualitative Methods and Analysis in Organizational Research: A Practical Guide*. Thousand Oaks, CA: Sage, pp. 118–134.

Lee, H., Kelley, D., Lee, J., Lee, S. (2012). "SME survival: The impact of internationalization, technology resources, and alliances." *Journal of Small Business Management*, 50(1), pp. 1–19.

Lu, J. W., Beamish, P. W. (2001). "The internationalization and performance of SMEs." *Strategic Management Journal*, 22(6–7), pp. 565–586.

Lu, J. W., Beamish, P. W. (2006). "SME internationalization and performance: Growth vs. profitability." *Journal of International Entrepreneurship*, 4(1), pp. 27–48.

Mahamadou, Z. (2016). "PME et Firmes Multinationales: Performance des Alliances Asymétriques." *Revue Management International*, 20(4), pp. 158–175.

Mercuri, S., Rais, M. (2010). "Alliance Stratégique Entre PME et Grande Firme Internationale!" *Quel Rôle Pour Le Middle Manager!?* Congrès Internationalisation des PME, pp. 1–27.

Mitchell, W., Dussauge, P., Garrette, B. (2002). "Formation et gouvernance des alliances entre concurrents : une approche par les ressources." Paris: Conférence de l'AIMS, pp. 1–25.

Mouline, A. (2005). "Symétrie et Asymétrie des Alliances dans une Industrie en Mutation! Le Cas des Télécommunications." *Management International*, 10(1), pp. 75–87.

Nguyen, C. T. (2007). *Objectifs et Difficultés du Partenaire Local Coopérant avec les Firmes Multinationales Étrangères! Le Cas du Vietnam*. Thèse de Doctorat, Tours.

Pan Y., Tse, D. K. (2000). "The hierarchical model of market entry modes." *Journal of International Business Studies*, 31(4), pp. 535–554.

Perez, L., Florin, J., Whitelock, J. (2012). "Dancing with elephants: The challenges of managing asymmetric technology alliances." *Journal of High Technology Management Research*, 23(2), pp. 142–154.

Prashantham, S., Dhanaraj, C. (2010). "The dynamic influence of social capital on the international growth of new ventures." *Journal of Management Studies*, 47(6), pp. 967–994.

Puthod, D., Ganassali, S. (1996). "L'alliance, Une Option Permettant de Contourner les Dilemmes Classiques de la PME." *Congrès International Francophone de la PME*, pp. 1–10.

Ramadan, M., Levratto, N. (2011). "Conceptualisation de L'internationalisation des PME: Une Application au Cas du Liban." *Revue Internationale Des PME (RIPME)*, 24(2).

Stoian, M.-C., Rialp, J., Dimitratos, P. (2016). "SME networks and international performance: Unveiling the significance of foreign market entry mode." *Journal of Small Business Management*, pp. 1–21.

Ulubaşoğlu, M. A., Akdis, M., Sabahat, B. K. (2009). "Internationalization and alliance formation: Evidence from Turkish SMEs." *International Small Business Journal*, 27(3), pp. 337–361.

Venkataraman, S., Van De Ven, A. H., Buckeye, J., Hudson, R. (1990). "Starting up in a turbulent environment: A process model of failure among firms with high customer dependence." *Journal of Business Venturing*, 5(5), pp. 277–295.

Yin R. (1984). *Case Study Research*. Beverly Hills, CA: Sage.

Zain, M., Ng, S. I. (2006). "The impacts of network relationships on SMEs' internationalization process." *Thunderbird International Business Review*, 48(2), pp. 183–205.

4 Autonomy or Abandonment?
An Analysis of Authority
Figures in the Context of
International Post-Acquisition
Integration

Yasmine Saleh and Emna Moalla

Introduction

Inter-organizational relationships are continuously growing on a global scale. These international transactions take various forms, such as mergers and acquisitions (M&As), joint ventures or contractual agreements. The year 2015 was notably characterized by a substantial increase in international M&As (CNUCED, 2016). Nevertheless, these transactions have a high failure rate (Barmeyer and Mayrhofer, 2002), and dealing with cultural differences is especially challenging (Denison et al., 2011). Indeed, national culture remains a difficult phenomenon to manage due to its complexity. This challenge makes the integration phase more difficult and increases the risk of failure of international M&As. It is therefore important to give serious consideration to this phase by taking into account cultural differences.

In the literature, national culture is a central concept in the field of international business (Harzing and Pudelko, 2016). It involves various approaches. Researchers (e.g., Hofstede, 1980; House et al., 2002, 2004) developed cultural frameworks to better understand this concept and its influence on the integration phases. However, these tools seem to be insufficient to overcome cultural challenges, and it is acknowledged that a qualitative approach is necessary (Shenkar, 2001, 2012).

This research focuses on the influence of cultural differences in international M&As, with a focus on the hierarchical relationship between the acquiring and the acquired company. Thus this chapter attempts to enrich the literature, which has demonstrated the importance of cultural differences in hierarchical relationships (Hofstede, 1980; House et al., 2002, 2004; Hofstede et al., 2010) and to provide a new perspective of authority figures based on an ethnographic approach. For this purpose, we analyzed the case of an Egyptian cement manufacturer acquired by a French group in 2008. A few years after the acquisition, the new subsidiary experienced an unprecedented crisis: a production shutdown and change of personnel in the executive committee. This crisis marked a turning point in relations between the new local management and the acquiring company. This particular context reveals the expectations of the subsidiary personnel in respect to the acquiring company and allows identifying the differences in authority figure conceptions from a cultural perspective.

We have structured this chapter in three parts. The first part outlines the extant literature on cultural difficulties during the post-acquisition integration phase. In the second part, we present the methodology deployed and the case study. We then detail the main results relating to the authority figures, both in the subsidiary and in the acquiring company, and the way they are embedded into their cultural contexts. Finally, we discuss the main results and then outline the conclusions.

The Cultural Challenges Throughout the Post-Acquisition Integration

In order to access new markets, a company must select the appropriate entry mode. Several alternatives are possible, such as through exports, cooperation with foreign partners or acquiring a wholly owned subsidiary through an M&A (Mayrhofer and Urban, 2011). We focused this research on the latter entry mode.

The Complexity of International Acquisitions

Mayrhofer and Urban (2011, p. 145) define an international M&A as "a relationship between companies from different countries that leads to the integration of involved companies; one of the M&A consequences is the loss of independence for at least one of them." In the case of mergers, at least two existing companies come together either by absorption or by the creation of a new entity that absorbs them both (Blanchot, 2009). In the case of acquisition, the acquiring company takes 100% control or a majority share of the acquired company. These types of foreign entry modes involve risks, especially during the integration phase when conflicts may emerge. The phase of post-acquisition integration begins as soon as the M&A is officially announced to the employees of the concerned companies (Samuel, 2003). New relationships between the two companies start to develop at this time. We can describe this phase as the gradual process by which employees in both companies learn to work together and to cooperate (Haspeslagh and Jemison, 1991). In an international context and beyond differences on the level of organizational cultures, this first phase often brings together widely different national cultures. Therefore, managing these cultural differences during the integration phase is crucial for the success of the deal (Barmeyer and Mayrhofer, 2002). In most cases, the main objective of the acquiring company is to optimize existing capacities (Datta, 1991). This optimization objective is fundamentally achieved by seeking synergies between the two companies in order to reduce costs and increase profits. However, these objectives are difficult to meet if the differences in practices and cultures of the two companies are not properly addressed. In this sense, Datta (1991, p. 283) explains that "the barriers related to the integration phase may cause the acquiring company to be unable to effectively manage the integration of the acquired company." Hence, the cultural integration phase should have a central place throughout the management of the acquisition. The success of an acquisition depends on the success of the post-acquisition integration, according to Haspeslagh and Jemison (1991). During this phase, the risk of critical incidents related, for example, to a miscommunication or an incompatible management style threaten the success of the deal. Barmeyer and Mayrhofer (2002) highlighted this phenomenon by studying the incompatibility of the approaches to teamwork between German and French personnel. Both cultures usually share a common goal to achieve, but the way to respond to it is different. Whereas the former considers it as a collaborative work, the latter perceives it more as a set of individual contributions. The possible misunderstandings linked with the divergence of players' expectations can lead to cultural conflicts (Barmeyer and Mayrhofer, 2002). Slangen (2006) also presents another goal of international acquisitions, other than the search for synergies. He points out that these deals often aim to increase sales or to reduce foreign market risks. In these cases, the relationship between the two companies is limited to few interactions with a high degree of autonomy for the acquired company. In this context, culture seems to be less problematic due to the limited contacts between the various actors and the low level of post-acquisition integration. The empirical investigation performed by Slangen (2006) shows that a high level of post-acquisition integration is likely to reduce the performance of the international acquisition. According to the author, a high level of integration implies daily contact between the respective teams and thus increases the risk of cultural incidents. Based on national culture, Huang et al. (2016) suggest that a big difference in the power distance between the acquiring and the acquired company is likely to weaken the value creation of international acquisition. Therefore, the acquiring company faces the following dilemma: on the one hand, the desire to develop synergies by emphasizing a close relationship with the target company; on the other hand, the success of the deal, which implies greater autonomy. Faced with this dilemma, multinationals adopt different approaches to manage their relationships with their foreign subsidiaries. Widely used in the literature, Perlmutter's (1969) EPG model identifies three main different approaches. The first approach, known as ethnocentric approach, is characterized by strong control carried out by the headquarters over the subsidiary's activity, with a centralization of the decision-making process. In this case, the number of expatriates is usually high in order to transfer expertise from headquarters to foreign subsidiaries. Under the second approach, called the polycentric approach, headquarters grants a high degree of autonomy to subsidiaries and takes into account the values and practices of the foreign country. The majority of management and executive positions in the

Autonomy or Abandonment? 63

subsidiaries are held by local people who are familiar with national culture. Under the third approach, the geocentric approach, there is a high degree of collaboration between headquarters and subsidiaries around the world with strong interdependence. A more comprehensive model, EPRG, was developed by Wind et al. (1973), where a regiocentric approach was added. It focuses on the regional interdependence with strong power given to regional headquarters. These last two approaches, geocentric and regiocentric, respond to the desire to generate economies of scale and illustrate a more advanced stage in the company's internationalization process.

National Culture and Authority Figure

National culture refers to the culture of a country or nation. Describing a country's culture is a complex task. This complexity has been of great interest for researchers who have made national culture a central concept in the field of international business (Harzing and Pudelko, 2016). They analyzed this concept and its impact on entry modes (Morschett et al., 2010) or on company performance (Slangen, 2006; Huang et al., 2016). To this end, these empirical studies have used the cultural frameworks developed by comparative management research.

Two approaches have essentially contributed to a better understanding of the influence of national culture in intercultural situations. The first approach is based, at the origin, on social psychology research. This quantitative approach aims to develop attitude scales in order to characterize national cultures (Hofstede, 1980; Hampden-Turner and Trompenaars, 1993; Trompenaars and Hampden-Turner, 1998; Schwartz, 1999, 2004; House et al., 2002, 2004; Hofstede et al., 2010). The second approach, qualitative, draws inspiration from ethnology and anthropology (Hall, 1976; Chapman, 1996; D'Iribarne, 2000, 2004). It attempts to capture the subtlety of different cultures.

Although these two approaches have different epistemological foundations, they provide, each in their own way, a better understanding of the underlying cultural values and their influences on companies.

The question of authority figures has been addressed by researchers adopting either the quantitative or the qualitative approach. Numerous studies have shown the diversity of conceptions of authority figures according to national cultures. The cultural framework proposed by Hofstede et al. (2010) contributes to this issue through the so-called power distance dimension. By referring to authority, this dimension describes how a nation approaches inequality. It is defined by Hofstede et al. (2010, p. 83) as "the degree of expectation and acceptance of an unequal distribution of power by those individuals who have the least power within a country's institutions and organizations." The choice of the adopted power distance depends on the culture of who has the power. Societies with a high power distance are characterized by a more centralized power and a more autocratic leadership style. In a company, this may take the form of power given to a small number of people. Subordinates then report to their superiors who monitor their work.

As a result, according to Hofstede et al. (2010, p. 96), subordinates prefer "a benevolent autocrat, a 'good father'" whom they respect. It seems important to emphasize the emotional relationship that may be perceived in this superior-subordinate relationship. Conversely, power is decentralized, and the organization is rather flat in societies where power distance is lower. In these societies, the relationship between superior-subordinate is among peers where subordinates are more autonomous with a limited degree of supervision.

According to the second, qualitative approach, D'Iribarne (1989) suggests different forms of social regulation that are specific to the French context, such as hierarchical relations. This leads back to the centralization of power and to the large distance between superior and subordinate. According to the author, power is considered acceptable in the hands of a superior when he does not hinder the area of competence of his subordinates. In addition, the superior has almost full power to act and to provide the necessary resources for his subordinates when they encounter difficulties, or when their level of competence is insufficient to deal with the situation. In line with Hofstede, D'Iribarne highlights the emotional aspect of the relationship between superior and subordinate in the French context.

Therefore, in the context of international acquisitions, the issue of power and hierarchical relationships deserves the greatest attention in order to ensure the success of these transactions.

The Case of the Acquisition of an Egyptian Cement Company by a French Group

In order to understand the influence of cultural differences in the international post-acquisition integration process, we study the case of an Egyptian cement manufacturer acquired by a French group. The crisis in the new subsidiary crystallizes employee frustrations since the acquisition four years earlier. In accordance with deductive logic, we were able to characterize these relationships and portray the authority figures for each of the entities.

Presentation of the Case

The French group is one of the world leaders in building materials. It is a major player in cement, concrete and aggregate activities. By 2015, it is present in 90 countries and has 100,000 employees worldwide. Its presence on the Egyptian market dates to 2007 following the acquisition of the cement company in question.

The Egyptian entity was created in 1996 and has 2,500 employees, half of whom are associated with the cement activity. The headquarters

Autonomy or Abandonment? 65

are located in Cairo and the cement plant is about 100 km away in the governorate of Suez. With production starting in 1999, the plant has five production lines with a maximum capacity of 10.6 Mt/year, making it the second largest plant in the world. In 2008, the vast majority of employees were local. The founder, a graduate in economics from the University of Chicago, is a member of a famous Coptic family. This family business is well known and established in the Egyptian economy since the 1950s. The youngest son in the family founded his company to diversify the family business. Taking advantage of a positive economic environment in emerging markets, the company expanded rapidly on a regional scale and became a major player in the cement market before its acquisition.

Four years after the acquisition, the subsidiary experienced an unprecedented crisis: the workers stopped production and went on strike. In a deteriorating social context, they put pressure on and asked for a change in the management, which was composed of locals.

Methodology

The research is a case study (Yin, 2003) with a focus on "a contemporary phenomenon in [its] real context" (p. 25). It has an ethnographic dimension (Villette, 2014) with a long-term immersion and a qualitative data collection in order to capture the logic behind the hierarchical relationships on the inter-organizational level. We conducted semi-directive interviews, observations, a documentary data collection and informal exchanges (see Table 4.1). This data collection took place over a nine-month period, from December 2012 to September 2013. More specifically, we conducted 30 interviews with managers and operational staff in the Egyptian subsidiary. We also interviewed directors from the headquarters in France. Each of these interviews lasted between 60 and 90 minutes. For the subsidiary, we

Table 4.1 Data collection

	Semi-directive interviews	Informal discussions	Observations	Documentary collection
Headquarters – French group				• Code of conduct
				• Press releases
Directors	5	no	no	• Various documents (organizational charts, flyers, etc.)
Egyptian subsidiary				
Directors and managers	11	yes	2 days/week in a nine-	
Operational staff	14	yes	month period	
Total	30	–	58 days	

66 Yasmine Saleh and Emna Moalla

structured the interviews with the three following topics: the presentation of the interviewee, the changes perceived after the acquisition and the reasons for the strike in their view. For the headquarters, we structured the interviews with different topics: the management of post-acquisition integration in general and then in the specific case of the Egyptian subsidiary. We conducted and recorded all interviews in the interviewee's mother tongue. As for the rest of the data collection, we transcribed the observations and the informal exchanges within the subsidiary in a "logbook" (Wacheux, 2009). Finally, we collected documentary data such as the French group's code of conduct and press releases.

Thereafter, we undertook a manual coding and decoding using the Miles and Huberman analysis method (2003). We first identified the way in which the headquarters sees its role as a new figure of authority toward the subsidiary through five categories: the management philosophy of the headquarters, the management of the international mergers and acquisitions, the management of the acquisition of the Egyptian subsidiary, crisis management and hierarchical relationships. We then traced the expectations of the subsidiary in respect of the headquarters. These expectations crystallize how a "good authority figure" should look in Egypt, in particular by reflecting the management style of the former owner. We identified three categories: the owner's management style, scenes from the cement manufacturer's daily life before the acquisition and organizational culture.

Different Perceptions of Authority

A Headquarters That Is Respectful of Local Teams

The French cement group is a century-old company with a humanist tradition. It has a strong culture drawn from the convictions of its leaders that has passed down through the generations. From the 1980s, the group experienced a strong internationalization of its activity, which led the top management to formalize its values in a code of conduct in 1978. In this document, the group describes and defends its management style with a *subsidiary authority*. It is this authority figure that the group had during the management of the post-acquisition integration of the Egyptian subsidiary. This authority figure knows two fundamental principles: it must not prevent people from conducting their own actions, and its mission is to interfere in its subsidiary's affairs by directing and supporting these people only if the situation they face is difficult or if it exceeds their power to resolve. Therefore, in the context of an acquisition, the subsidiary has a great deal of autonomy and the headquarters intervenes only if necessary. We will describe here the main features of this authority by recalling the actions taken during the post-acquisition integration period.

Autonomy or Abandonment? 67

An Authority Figure That Empowers Local Management

Local management, through delegation and participation, is one of the fundamentals of the management philosophy of the headquarters. In the Egyptian subsidiary, after the acquisition, management remained in the hands of the locals and there were no French expats. A director of the headquarters explained,

> We don't come up saying: here it is, the group model, and you sweep up the rest. No. . . . We come up saying: we will bring you our values, our ways of functioning, but we will try to develop local teams.

In addition to maintaining local management, Egyptian employees say "nothing has changed" in terms of work processes. They say that what is new after the acquisition is the introduction of reporting, audit procedures and more scrupulous safety measures.

Indeed, the French company explains its philosophy of letting the locals manage their entities through the concept of "multi-local management" in its code of conduct. At the same time, it specifies that local management must have an open and international mind to enable synergies to take place at group level. As an example, the term *local* (and its derivatives *multi-local, locally,* etc.) is used 20 times in the document compared to nine times for the term *global*. Local management is one of the most important fundamentals of the management philosophy, as displayed by the group.

An Authority Figure That Guides Without Constraining

The French group described the code of conduct as its "backbone," its key success factor. It has a strong symbolic value because it conveys the personal convictions of the leaders who have led the group to become the world leader in its sector. To disseminate this *supplément d'âme*, the code of conduct is translated into nearly 20 languages and is communicated to all subsidiaries around the world. Moreover, it was not designed in a contractual logic and each subsidiary decides whether to use the document or not. A director of the headquarters explains: "Unlike an Anglo-Saxon way, which is more mechanistic, more roll compressor, where there is one way with a single procedural way of doing things . . . the [code of conduct] is trying to capture the spirits."

In the Egyptian subsidiary, the managers and local directors obtained access to the code of conduct after the acquisition. The group organized get-together sessions called "Meet the Group" in order to explain its culture. It described the code of conduct "as a star to follow." Here again, the headquarters played the role of support without imposing its reference values.

68 Yasmine Saleh and Emna Moalla

An Authority Figure That Supports Its Subsidiaries in Difficult Situations

The first time the headquarters interfered in the subsidiary's business was during the plant strike. In the difficult context where local management could no longer manage the situation, the group sent a delegation of directors who decided to respond to employee demands. Local management was changed. An English director with 25 years' experience within the group then took the reins. The headquarters has thus fulfilled its role, according to its philosophy, by helping the subsidiary solve its problems at the local level. Employees were satisfied with this change of management and the arrival of an expatriate director.

A Subsidiary Looking for a New "White Knight"

After the acquisition, two distinct hierarchies replaced the CEO and owner of the Egyptian cement company: the former industrial director, now general manager, for overall management; and the group's headquarters, for the property management. This change in governance disrupted the employees especially because, for them, the former owner embodied a "good authority figure."

At the same time, their expectations in respect of the new hierarchies remained unsatisfied, which is one of the elements explaining the crisis. We call this authority figure a "white knight," as it embodies the figure of a savior with the qualities that go with it: strong, selfless and resourceful. This portrait of the white knight does not counter the company's more financial objectives. We will describe the main features of this authority figure by recalling some scenes from the daily life of the company before contextualizing and explaining them in the Egyptian shared meanings.

An Authority Figure That Is Close and Humble

Employees describe the former owner as a manager who was close because of his regular presence at the local headquarters and at the cement plant. They appreciated his presence especially as he was not skilled in the field and because the working conditions were difficult due to the location of the plant in a desert area. A maintenance engineer says, "we are not a biscuit factory where it smells vanilla. It smells [like] dust and sweat here." He always had his lunch break at the same canteen as the employees, which contrasts with the actions of more classical, and less appreciated, hierarchical superiors in Egypt.

In terms of communication, the CEO used rather popular language to the point that his interlocutors almost forgot his Anglo-Saxon background. For example, he would greet employees by using expressions such as "*Sabah el Fol*" (A white rice like jasmine) instead of the regular *Sabah el kheir* ("Good morning"). He used to know employees by their names and for those who were having financial difficulties, he used to call them by referencing the quality of their father or mother (*Abu* or *Om Ali* for Ali's father or mother), as popular habit dictates. In return, the employees used to call him according to the popular and respectful formula *ya basha* ("Oh Pasha"). In the local context, an immediate superior who belongs to a wealthy class and who shares the ways of doing and being of his subordinates is considered a good authority figure.

An Authority Figure as a Fair Donor

The former CEO used to act as a financial guarantor for his employees by providing support to employees in need. Gifting/counter-gifting dominated the interpersonal relationships. For example, the donation of money for the arrival of a newborn or for funeral expenses was a common practice in the company. At a time when the industry was not very cost-sensitive, employees used to describe the CEO as generous. In return for high salaries, the employees had a strong sense of belonging to the company: "We used to feel that it was our company, our money and our future. We used to feel that the company needed us. We gave it to the company and it gave us back." Thus by donating money to those who were having financial difficulties, he responded to their *acham*. This concept reflects this expectation of solidarity, of generosity and mutual assistance between employees and the superior.

In addition to his donor status, employees perceived the CEO as a fair person, in particular because of the absence of religious discrimination. This fairness was more appreciated as the CEO belonged to the Coptic minority.

An Authority Figure Who Is Faithful to the Country

A final feature that we have noted in the person of the former owner, from the employees' point of view, was his commitment to the country. He was described by the employees as a "true Egyptian" and seen as concerned about the country's development, hence the praiseworthy qualifiers *ibn balad* ("son of a country") and *ibn asl* ("son of origin"). The former CEO was perceived as "loyal to his origins" as he invests and lives in his country, unlike those who leave it for reasons of social status.

Discussion and Conclusion

This chapter aims to understand the influence of cultural differences in the context of international post-acquisition integration by analyzing the notion of authority figures. To do this, we have described the good authority figure from the perspective of the French headquarters and the Egyptian subsidiary. This research highlights how the management of post-acquisition integration was affected by a collision between two different and incompatible conceptions of hierarchical relationship. The headquarters granted a great degree of autonomy to its subsidiary according to its subsidiary logic, while the subsidiary was waiting for a new white knight to solve its problems. This autonomy was perceived locally as a form of abandonment by the headquarters, which was a source of frustration and a catalyst of the ensuing crisis. With the involvement of the headquarters and the appointment of an English director, an action initially perceived by the group as transgressive of the local teams, the expectations of local employees were met. Contrary to the perception of headquarters, respect for local teams has been demonstrated by the appointment of a management team from the group, which is a sign of interest and of the importance attached to the subsidiary, according to the latter.

Based on the EPG model (Perlmutter, 1969), the French group adopted a polycentric approach by granting a high degree of autonomy to its subsidiary (e.g., by appointing a local manager considered as capable of effectively managing local teams). However, according to this model, the choice of the headquarters approach depends in particular on the degree of development of the host country. In the more difficult context of developing countries, stronger control by the headquarters may be more appropriate. The ethnocentric approach therefore seems more appropriate for the company studied.

In addition to this subsidiary logic underlying the power relationships in a French context, the autonomy granted by headquarters could be explained by the purpose of the acquisition. As suggested by Slangen (2006), the search for risk reduction related to the Egyptian market and/or an increase in turnover could be possible objectives. In this case, autonomy and the low level of post-acquisition integration would imply less contact with local teams and probably less risk of cultural incidents, thus maximizing the success of the deal. However, a more in-depth reflection and a cultural perspective allowed us to qualify these views because avoiding contact with local teams in itself can lead to cultural incidents. This research shows that a better understanding of the concept of authority figure is crucial for the success of relationships between organizations.

The analysis of the two national cultures' specificities, based on frameworks suggested by qualitative and quantitative approaches, provides additional insight. In connection with the authority figure, the cultural model proposed by Hofstede through the power distance dimension allows an initial comparison. A focus on France and Egypt shows very close scores: 68 and 70, respectively. In fact, these two countries are considered culturally close with a high level of power distance. According to Hofstede's model, power in these two countries would therefore be centralized in the hands of an autocracy. The phase of post-acquisition integration would rationally be easier between two cultures characterized

Autonomy or Abandonment? 71

by a more centralized power in the hands of superiors and a rather similar conception of authority. Paradoxically, we noticed that the degree of autonomy and limited supervision granted by the French group rather reflects a low power distance.

From the headquarters' perspective and according to the second approach, subsidiary management refers to a form of regulation of social relations between superiors and subordinate embedded in the French culture: the principle of moderation (D'Iribarne, 1989, p. 45). As explained by the author, the principle of moderation describes the extent of an authority power depending on whether the situation refers to a normal or a crisis situation. In a common context, the author explains that "it is difficult for the superior to interfere much in the 'business' of those he leads. Indeed, the responsibility of moderation then forbids him from disturbing someone who 'does his work,' in other words, someone who meets their responsibilities." On the contrary, in an uncommon context where the subordinate has difficulty doing his job, "the superior has considerable powers" to help the subordinate to overcome his difficulties. This conception of authority in a French context clearly describes the principle of subsidiarity followed by the acquiring company. On the subsidiary side, the form of social relations between white knights and subordinates is embedded in the local culture. According to Fahmy (2002), the history of Egyptian society shows two fundamental aspects: the wish for a wise savior and the contempt for the ordinary individual. This savior has full power and acts in the collective interest. His wisdom gives him intellectual legitimacy, referring to the country's golden age as the cradle of civilization. To avoid being labeled as ordinary, subordinates are driven by a desire to show up, especially intellectually. In counterpart to the power and the strong authority, subordinates enjoy protection and generosity from their superior. Therefore, understanding these forms of social relations regulation makes it possible to better apprehend the subsidiary's expectations in respect of the headquarters. Based on a Franco-Egyptian case, this research highlights the influence of national culture, through the conception of the authority figure and hierarchical relations, in the context of international post-acquisition integration.

This research findings suggest several avenues for further research. On the one hand, our analysis of the authority figure conception from a cultural perspective does not facilitate taking into account the power issues that exist between headquarters and subsidiary. A strategic analysis focused on the interests of both parties would facilitate extending our study by taking into consideration the power imbalances resulting from the acquisition. On the other hand, we collected our data after the acquisition. A nostalgia for the past may have led to a certain bias in the interviews conducted in the subsidiary. It would thus be relevant to enrich the results relating to the authority figure with future research.

References

Barmeyer, C., Mayrhofer, U. (2002). "Le management interculturel: Facteur de réussite des fusions-acquisitions internationales." *Annales des Mines, Gérer et Comprendre*, 70, pp. 24–33.

Blanchot, F. (2009). "Le management stratégique des fusions acquisitions: motifs, effets, et conditions de réussite." In O. Meier (ed.), *Stratégies de croissance*. Paris: Dunod, pp. 145–160.

Chapman, M. (1996). "Social anthropology, business studies, and cultural issues." *International Studies of Management and Organization*, 26(4), pp. 3–29.

CNUCED. (2016). *Rapport sur l'investissement dans le monde 2016. Nationalité des investisseurs: enjeux et politiques*. Geneva: United Nations.

Datta, D. K. (1991), "Organizational fit and acquisition performance: Effects of post-acquisition integration." *Strategic Management Journal*, 12(4), pp. 2181–2297.

Denison, D. R., Adkins, B., Guidroz, A. M. (2011). "Managing cultural integration in crossborder mergers and acquisitions." In W. H. Mobley, M. Li, and Y. Wang (eds.), *Advances in Global Leadership*, 6. Bingley: Emerald Group, pp. 95–115.

Fahmy, K. (2002). *All the Pasha's Men: Mehmed Ali, His Army and the Making of Modern Egypt*. Cairo: American University in Cairo Press, p. 352.

Hall, E. T. (1976). *Beyond Culture*. New York: Anchor Books.

Hampden-Turner, C., Trompenaars, F. (1993). *The Seven Cultures of Capitalism: Value Systems for Creating Wealth in the United States, Japan, Germany, France, Britain, Sweden, and the Netherlands*. New York: Piatkus.

Harzing, A.-W., Pudelko, M. (2016). "Do we need to distance ourselves from the distance concept? Why home and host country context might matter more than (cultural) distance." *Management International Review*, 56(1), pp. 1–34.

Haspeslagh, P., Jemison, D. (1991). *Managing Acquisitions: Creating Value Through Corporate Renewal*. New York: Free Press.

Hofstede, G. (1980). *Culture's Consequences: Comparing Values, Behaviors, Institutions and Organizations Across Nations*. Thousand Oaks, CA: Sage.

Hofstede, G., Hofstede, G. J., Minkov, M. (2010). *Cultures et organisations*. Paris: Pearson.

House, R. J., Hanges, P. J., Javidan, M., Dorfman, P. W., Gupta V. (2004). *Culture, Leadership, and Organizations: The GLOBE Study of 62 Societies*. Thousand Oaks, CA: Sage.

House, R. J., Javidan, M., Hanges, P., Dorfman, P. (2002). "Understanding cultures and implicit leadership theories across the globe: An introduction to Project GLOBE." *Journal of World Business*, 37(1), pp. 3–10.

Huang, Z., Zhu, H., Brass, D. J. (2016). "Cross-border acquisitions and the asymmetric effect of power distance value difference on long-term post-acquisition performance." *Strategic Management Journal*, 38(4), pp. 972–991.

Iribarne, P. (d'). (1989). *La logique de l'Honneur*. Paris: Seuil.

Iribarne, P. (d'). (2000). "Management et cultures politiques." *Revue française de Gestion*, 128, March–May, pp. 70–75.

Iribarne, P. (d'). (2004). "Face à la complexité des cultures, le management interculturel exige une approche ethnologique." *Management International*, 8(3), pp. 11–19.

Autonomy or Abandonment? 73

Mayrhofer, U., Urban, S. (2011). *Management International. Des pratiques en mutation.* Paris: Pearson.

Miles, M., Huberman, M. (2003). *Analyse des données qualitatives.* De Boeck Université, Brussels, p. 626.

Morschett, D., Schramm-Klein, H., Swoboda, B. (2010). "Decades of research on market entry modes: What do we really know about external antecedents of entry mode choice?" *Journal of International Management,* 16(1), pp. 60–77.

Perlmutter, H. V. (1969). "The tortuous evolution of the multinational corporation." *Columbia Journal of World Business,* 4(1), pp. 9–18.

Samuel, K. E. (2003). "Prévenir les difficultés post-fusion/ acquisition en utilisant la gestion de crise." *Revue Française de Gestion,* 145(4), pp. 41–54.

Schwartz, S. H. (1999). "A theory of cultural values and some implications for work." *Applied Psychology: An International Review,* 48(1), pp. 23–47.

Schwartz, S. H. (2004). "Mapping and interpreting cultural differences around the world." In H. Vinken et al. (eds.), *Comparing Cultures, Dimensions of Culture in a Comparative Perspective.* Leiden: Brill, pp. 43–73.

Shenkar, O. (2001). "Cultural distance revisited: Towards a more rigorous conceptualization and measurement of cultural differences." *Journal of International Business Studies,* 32(3), pp. 519–535.

Shenkar, O. (2012). "Cultural distance revisited: Towards a more rigorous conceptualization and measurement of cultural differences." *Journal of International Business Studies,* 43(1), pp. 1–11.

Slangen, A.H.L. (2006). "National cultural distance and initial foreign acquisition performance: The moderating effect of integration." *Journal of World Business,* 41(2), pp. 161–170.

Trompenaars, F., Hampden-Turner, C. (1998). *Riding the Waves of Culture.* New York: McGraw-Hill.

Villette, M. (2014). "Ethnographie dans l'entreprise." *Annales des Mines, Gérer et comprendre,* 117, pp. 4–9.

Wacheux, F. (2009). *Méthodes qualitatives et recherche en gestion.* Paris: Economica, p. 290.

Wind, Y., Douglas, S., Perlmutter, H. (1973). "Guidelines for developing international marketing strategies." *Journal of Marketing,* 37(2), pp. 14–23.

Yin, R. K. (2003). *Case Study Research: Design and Methods.* Thousand Oaks, CA: Sage, p. 170.

5 Cultural Challenges and Quality Management Practices of a German Multinational in Brazil

Madeleine Bausch, Christoph Barmeyer and Ulrike Mayrhofer

Introduction

Multinational companies (MNCs) often face cultural challenges when implementing organizational and business practices, such as quality management in their foreign subsidiaries (Hadjikhani et al., 2012; Mayrhofer, 2013; Barmeyer and Davoine, 2019). The international transfer of practices can be viewed as a cross-cultural process between individuals in which subjective perception, interpretation and the creation of meaning play an important role (D'Iribarne, 2012). In particular, diverging systems of meanings and misinterpretations may lead to difficulties in communication and implementation. Due to their culture and language, managers from different backgrounds often have diverging assumptions, convictions and interpretations of the content and method of how to implement management practices (Brannen, 2004; Gertsen and Zølner, 2012; Ramirez and Søderberg, 2019); this also applies to quality and quality management (D'Iribarne and Henry, 2007). Culture can be defined as the reference and orientation system of values, interpretations and problem-solving abilities that are inherent in a group or society and which distinguish one group or society from others (Barmeyer and Franklin, 2016). The cultural traits of individuals become most apparent when communicating and cooperating with individuals from different cultures, through language use and behavior in everyday work situations.

German industrial companies are known worldwide for representing high standards of quality, mostly epitomized by the "Made in Germany" label, promising longevity, reliability, robustness, ingenuity and precision (Germany Trade and Invest, 2018; Statista, 2019). It is not only large, well-known multinationals that represent the "Made in Germany" label; above all there are numerous medium-sized family-owned companies that contribute to the hallmark, called "hidden champions" (Simon, 2009). According to Simon, hidden champions are companies that are among the leaders in the world market through following a niche strategy. They are mostly active in the business-to-business sector and are rarely known to the end customer. When locating production facilities in foreign markets, these German companies transfer their quality management practices and standards, and thus their knowledge of how to produce high-quality products, to different production sites across the world, including emerging economies like Brazil. Currently, there are around 1,400 active German companies in Brazil (German-Brazilian Chamber of Commerce, 2019). Many of them started their activities in Brazil in the 1970s because of cheaper labor forces and the hope for an expanding economy in a market with more than 200 million inhabitants (Amal and Tomio, 2015).

While the need to examine German-Brazilian business relationships is evident, it seems surprising that there are hardly any empirical studies on this topic. This research aims to contribute to a better understanding of cultural challenges that can emerge in the implementation of German quality management in Brazil. We will adopt a multi-level perspective to analyze a significant critical incident a German multinational faces in its Brazilian subsidiary. In fact, cultural challenges can be due to political, socioeconomic and technological differences at a societal macro level, or strategic, structural and power-political discrepancies at an organizational meso level. Whenever practices are transferred internationally, managers from different cultural backgrounds interact, and these interactions are therefore also influenced by cultural traits of the individuals at a micro level.

The chapter is divided into six sections. Initially, we will review the existing literature on the transfer of quality management in a cross-cultural context, with a specific focus on quality management in Germany and Brazil. After the presentation of the research methodology, we will analyze our findings concerning a major critical incident in the Brazilian subsidiary of a German multinational using a multi-level perspective. Finally, we will discuss our results and develop some possible solutions for overcoming cultural challenges in German-Brazilian collaboration.

The Cross-Cultural Transfer of Quality Management Practices

For more than two decades, research on international and intercultural management has been devoted to examining and understanding transfer processes across cultures (Kostova, 1999; Brannen, 2004; D'Iribarne and Henry, 2007; Gertsen and Zølner, 2012; Isaac et al., 2019). In general, there seems to be agreement that multinational companies should behave in a culturally sensitive way when transferring practices to foreign production sites in order to be successful.

Although cross-cultural research has so far focused on strategic issues in general (e.g., Kostova, 1999; Brannen, 2004), HRM practices (Schröter and Davoine, 2009), codes of conduct and corporate values (Gertsen and Zølner, 2012) or CSR practices (Gutierrez-Huerter et al., 2020), there is only limited research on the transfer of quality management practices.

76 *Madeleine Bausch et al.*

Most frequently, existing research relates to total quality management (TQM) (D'Iribarne and Henry, 2007; Erçek and Say, 2008), a management fashion of the 1990s.

In one of the few relevant publications, D'Iribarne and Henry (2007) examine the implementation of TQM practices by a French company in its Moroccan subsidiary. The authors show that the company had severe problems in implementing a TQM philosophy but then succeeded in changing the corporate culture, employee motivation and commitment by applying the principles of Islam (including "do not lie," "help others to succeed," "respect for others," "enabling learning"); it then embedded the values of TQM such as *Kaizen* (continuous improvement). The company was thus able to adapt the principles of TQM by connecting it with religious values.

Although international organizations strive to formally align quality management systems worldwide with the help of institutions such as the International Organization for Standardization (ISO), the existing literature reveals that cultures and societies deal differently with conceptions and practices of quality and quality management (Juran and Godfrey, 1999, sec. 36; D'Iribarne and Henry, 2007). In theory, quality is considered universal; in practice, however, quality management is often "imagined" and conceptualized in the specific context of the headquarters before being transferred to the local context of the subsidiaries. Accordingly, the cultural traits of individuals and societal norms influence, mostly unconsciously, the underlying principles of "good" quality (Vecchi and Brennan, 2009).

When German MNCs transfer management practices to Brazil, they are facing not only organizational but also institutional challenges (Geppert and Mayer, 2006) and cultural differences with sometimes difficult transfer processes (Friel and de Villechenon, 2018; Barmeyer and Davoine, 2019). The three levels of analysis are presented in Table 5.1.

Table 5.1 Three levels of analysis and associated characteristics

Level	Associated characteristics
Cultural	Underlying values
	Meaning systems and interpretation processes
	Language and communication styles
	Problem-solving abilities
Institutional	Political stability
	Laws
	Societal norms
	Educational system
	Situation of the labor market
	Trade unions
Organizational	Headquarters-subsidiary relationships
	Internationalization strategy
	History and development
	Corporate values
	Intra-organizational power struggles

First, at a *cultural* level, underlying values influence interpretation processes, behavior and problem-solving mechanisms in intercultural work situations (Barmeyer and Mayrhofer, 2008). Values are defined as "conception[s], explicit or implicit, distinctive of an individual or characteristic of a group, of the desirable which influences the selection from available modes, means and ends of action" (Kluckhohn, 1951: 395). Whereas German culture is primarily characterized by task orientation, direct communication, rationality, long-term thinking and internalized control mechanisms, paired with a relatively high autonomy of the individual (Brannen and Salk, 2000; Thomas et al., 2010), in Brazilian society, values such as personal orientation, emotionality, flexibility, conflict avoidance, collectivism and indirect communication, paternalism and power distance are more pronounced (Azevedo, 2011; Dávila and Elvira, 2012; Bartel-Radic, 2013; Chanlat et al., 2013; de Freitas, 2017).

Second, at an *institutional* level, MNCs have to deal with different institutional frameworks that influence transfer processes primarily through the situations of the labor market, trade unions, educational systems, environmental laws and complex bureaucratic structures as well as shadow economies and corruption (Geppert and Mayer, 2006; Friel and de Villechenon, 2018). Institutions such as the German educational system have developed over centuries and thus shaped the notion of quality and how it is understood. The development of early medieval craft guilds finally led to the emergence of the dual vocational training system, which secures an in-depth "expertise" by engineers and technicians (Juran and Godfrey, 1999; Ewing, 2014). Logical reasoning and analytical thinking coined by (among others) the European Enlightenment movement is a mark of professional and organizational cultures in most of the manufacturing companies. Moreover, inspection services such as TÜV (*Technischer Überwachungsverein*) or *Stiftung Warentest* (a non-profit consumer organization) steadily assess and secure the quality of products and services. Moreover, the social, legal and normative relevance of quality seals such as "Made in Germany" reveal the status of quality in Germany for customers. In contrast, Brazil is a country with a comparatively young history (approximately 200 years) and which still struggles with unstable political and legal institutions. With regard to the educational system, students have traditionally enjoyed a rather generalist education (Havighurst and Moreira, 1969). However, there have been efforts to transfer the German dual vocational system in order to educate specialists as well (iMove Germany, 2016). Whereas for German customers hallmarks of quality seem to be of utmost importance, Brazilian customers tend to valorize products based on their geographic origin. For example, European or North American products are attributed a high quality due to their origin—a term known as *estrangerismo* in Brazil (Bartel-Radic, 2013).

Third, at an *organizational* level, the relationships between parent companies (headquarters) and subsidiaries (Beddi and Mayrhofer,

78 *Madeleine Bausch et al.*

2013) depend on the chosen internationalization strategy (Perlmutter, 1969), organizational history and development (Schein, 2010) and intra-organizational power struggles (Festing and Maletzky, 2011; Dörrenbächer and Geppert, 2017). Using this perspective, the organizational culture, that is, a system of standards, guidelines and corporate values shared by the actors of an organization (Brown, 1998), can play a central role. It corresponds to a collective reference framework that defines behaviors and guides certain decisions and solutions. According to Schein (2010), culture functions at different levels. In MNCs, the organizational culture can be considered as an important mechanism for the coordination of headquarters-subsidiary relationships (Wächter et al., 2003).

Figure 5.1 illustrates the influence of the three levels (cultural, institutional and organizational) on the transfer of quality management practices in the German-Brazilian context.

Methodology: A Single Ethnographic Case Study

In order to investigate intercultural challenges linked to the transfer of quality management practices from a German MNC to its Brazilian subsidiary, we adopted a qualitative, single-case-study design for a German company in Brazil (Piekkari et al., 2009; Marschan-Piekkari and Welch, 2011; Taylor and Søndergaard, 2017). Case studies allow the describing of the phenomenon of interest but also the context in which it occurs (Taylor and Søndergaard, 2017). Thus they provide rich data that allows *understanding* of the motives, interests and points of view of each individual, which is then aggregated to a larger group of individuals (i.e., a company or an organization).

Data Collection and Analysis

The strength of the case study is to combine different data sources in which the *meaning* for the people involved and the stakeholders becomes apparent. The researcher is thus able to get a more holistic view of social phenomena (Geertz, 1973; Caprar, 2011; Primecz et al., 2011). Over six months, the first author conducted 22 semi-structured interviews with quality managers and people responsible for quality and production departments in Germany and Brazil as well as two focus groups within the Brazilian workforce. The interview guide contained questions regarding the transfer process; challenges and success factors in the transfer of quality practices; and collaboration between German and Brazilian colleagues. Moreover, we selected documents such as corporate values, specified quality processes, checklists and assembly instructions, internal email communications and field notes from the ethnographic study.

When doing research in Brazilian organizations, establishing personal relationships with the interviewees and conducting interviews in the

A German Multinational in Brazil 79

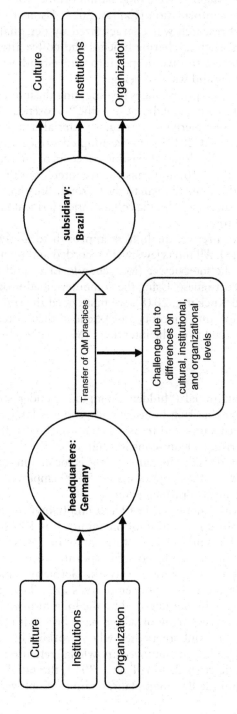

Figure 5.1 A multi-level analysis of quality management transfer in a multinational

80 Madeleine Bausch et al.

interviewee's native language were of great importance for trust-building and served to gather information (Caprar, 2011; Usunier et al., 2019). Therefore, the field research was characterized by personal interaction with the employees, such as sharing lunches and coffee after work; this allowed the researchers to dive deeper into understanding individuals' interests, personalities and ways of being.

As there seem to be no prior studies investigating the intercultural challenges of German-Brazilian collaboration—the "theoretical development of the knowledge base underlying the course material is underdeveloped" (Taylor and Søndergaard, 2017: 32)—we adopted a research design of an inductive nature. We also drew on existing concepts of intercultural interaction (Thomas et al., 2010) and constructive interculturality (Barmeyer and Davoine, 2019), extended them to the German-Brazilian context and looked for cultural specificities in the collaboration (critical incidents) and possible success factors.

We chose an interpretive, qualitative approach to analyze the data (Romani et al., 2018). All interviews were recorded and then transcribed in the language of the interviewee (Marschan-Piekkari and Reis, 2004), either German or Portuguese. Using the computer-aided program MAX-QDA (Rädiker and Kuckartz, 2018), we first coded the transcripts with common codes of existing concepts and extended them afterwards with new codes that emerged from the interviews (Miles et al., 2014).

Case Description

The German multinational ("hidden champion") under study belongs to the mechanical engineering industry and produces large construction machinery (e.g., excavators and transshipment machines). It is part of a larger group comprising 11 divisions in total, of which the studied company represents one division. Its parent plant is located in a small city in southwest Germany and has approximately 9,000 employees worldwide, of whom 500 work at the Brazilian plant.

The enterprise was founded in 1949 as a family-owned company and is now run by the third generation of the family. It is 100% self-funded by the family, which is said to be the "foundation for our success" (home page). The multinational has listed six corporate values (see Box 5.1), which become apparent in several ways in Germany and Brazil. For example, regarding the value "Our employees are a key factor in our success," the company is characterized by the long-term employment of managers and employees, many of whom have been with the company for more than ten years and others their whole working life. It also practices long-term planning and employee knowledge retention. Despite the continuing economic crisis in Brazil since 2014, the family's approach has been to maintain the Brazilian plant, retain its employees and avoid dismissals.

A German Multinational in Brazil 81

Box 5.1 Corporate Values of the German Multinational

"We are independent."
"We are a trustworthy partner."
"We are innovative."
"Our employees are a key factor in our success."
"Highest quality in everything we do."
"We accept responsibility."

Source: Internal documents.

In the 1970s, the German multinational decided to expand its operations to Brazil, where it has a production and sales subsidiary in the federal state of São Paulo. For more than 40 years, the Brazilian plant has been acting in a relatively autonomous way: the workforce is mainly Brazilian (Brazilian managers and workers); only one of the two managing directors is of German origin, and he has more than 10 years' work experience in Brazil. For that reason, the Brazilian plant is structurally called a "sister plant" rather than a classical subsidiary. However, in recent years, due to the strong growth of its activities worldwide, the parent company has been striving to align its foreign production plants in order to secure uniformity and global recognition of the brand. Within the alignment, quality practices are incrementally controlled and readjusted in the Brazilian plant.

A Major Critical Incident: Yellow Is Not Yellow

Due to the holistic case-study approach, we were able to gather many insights into the daily life of German-Brazilian collaboration within the company and the respective focus of the two plants' personnel on the transfer of quality standards and practices. At the beginning of our research, complaints and challenges became apparent, which complicated daily business between the two sites and the successful functioning of the Brazilian subsidiary. These challenges are exemplified by a major critical incident that we will present in more detail.

Presentation of Case Study

The family-owned MNC manufactures parts for construction machines both in Germany and in Brazil. The Brazilian plant imports the parts manufactured in Germany and installs them on site to assemble the entire machine. The corporate design specifies that the machines must be painted with the yellow varnish of the parent company in order to ensure global corporate identity. Due to import barriers and cost issues, the Brazilian subsidiary decided, against the company's internal regulations, to obtain

82 *Madeleine Bausch et al.*

the paint from a local supplier. Initially, this did not pose a problem for the parent company, because the color appeared to be the same (both are yellow). The locally manufactured parts were thus painted in the color of the Brazilian supplier, whereas the parts coming from Germany were painted by the German supplier. The Brazilian workers assembled the parts into a complete machine, which was delivered to the customers.

During a visit to Brazil, the German managers discovered that the yellow tones were slightly different and that the Brazilian machines had two yellow tones: one in the yellow of the Brazilian supplier, the other in the yellow established by the parent company. The German managers raised the issue with the local production manager, but the latter saw no problem with the "two-tone" look: "The machine works! What is the problem?" For the German managers, it was clear: the machines must no longer be delivered varnished like that. The brand and its quality image could suffer serious damage if customers complained. And there was the important company value, "Highest quality in everything we do." In Brazil, however, nobody seemed to take this issue seriously.

Analysis of the Case Study

Our analysis of the critical incident shows that challenges appeared at the cultural, institutional and organizational levels.

First, at a *cultural* level, the case can be explained by differing interpretive patterns: the meaning of quality and its conceptions are thus bound to contexts and differ across cultures (Brannen, 2004; D'Iribarne, 2012; Chevrier and Viegas-Pires, 2013). For the Brazilian managers, a working machine seemed to be enough to fulfill the company's quality requirements, but the German *concept of quality* goes beyond functionality and puts the focus on the outer appearance of the machine as well. This even became apparent in one of the focus groups, when the critical incident was discussed: "the physical aspect is not [so important] because the machines . . . are in the field" (Employee, Production, Brazil). This conception is aligned with contextual and geographic factors, for example, how the machines are used by Brazilian customers:

> A: The Brazilian customer wants to put the machine in a mine. Not in Germany. He uses the machine to move sand from one place to another. But there are other contexts. . . . If it's for a German client, for example, color is very important; the look has to be fine.
>
> B: Here, it goes into a mine. One doesn't even know what color the machine has. There is earth, dust, dirt.
>
> C: For a Brazilian customer, quality means a running machine.
>
> B: Yes, the machine cannot stop.
>
> (Group interview, Quality Management, Brazil)

In Brazil, the functionality and practicability of the machine appear to be of higher relevance than its look or color tone. Moreover, managerial thinking is marked by cost sensitivity in order to place a more affordable product on the market: "[Quality is having] a competitive price, a fair price, . . . because our products are products that live in the competitive world."

(Manager, Production, Brazilian)

This is due to, among others, economic (institutional) factors, that is, the purchasing power and industrial development of the country, which has been in economic crisis since 2014. On average, Brazilian customers spend less money on construction machines than German customers (Field notes). This is due to the fact that in Brazil the company is exposed to competitors from the United States, Korea and Japan, whereas in Germany it is one of the national market leaders. In contrast, German managers emphasize the outer appearance and perfection of the machine:

When we deliver the device, it won't have a scratch or a flaw. That is our claim, that there is a perfect device. And that's what sets us apart from our competitors, when we're there at a trade fair and look at the devices, you see a visual difference.

(Manager, Industrial Engineering, Germany)

In my opinion, . . . the understanding of quality is 120%. That has to be absolutely perfect. Perfect surface. Perfectly laid things. Perfect, simply something perfect.

(Project Manager, Germany)

Each machine that comes out should look the same.

(Employee, Industrial Engineering, Germany)

The German sense of quality thus requires strict conformity to the prototype; a deviation from the standard must not be tolerated, as it is determined in the corporate value concerning quality. Regarding the different color tones, a German manager complains:

There are devices delivered that have two different color tones. . . . there's a lighter one and a darker one, and that's side by side. And there I say: that's not possible at all, you just can't do that!

(Manager, Industrial Engineering, Germany)

Second, these cultural values and interpretations are transferred from members of a society to other members of that society and shaped by

84   *Madeleine Bausch et al.*

socialization and institutions (Barmeyer, 2004; Walther, 2014). One of the important *institutions* that influences the perception and interpretation of the social world is the *educational system*, which varies between the German and Brazilian contexts.

There is compulsory schooling in Germany as a well-developed training system that specifies that technical employees in Germany must have either two or three years of well-founded vocational training or a university or engineering qualification (in German: Dr. and Dipl. Ing.). The vocational training is completed on a dual basis, combining practical and theoretical courses in cooperation with the companies and vocational schools. Most of the trainees specialize in one profession and in a smaller niche domain, so that the alumni acquire an in-depth knowledge in one specific field (Barmeyer and Mayrhofer, 2014). During the apprenticeship years, expert knowledge and attention to detail are meticulously taught and are thus highly valued in Germany (Walther, 2014; Davoine and Deitmer, 2019), contributing to the high quality of German products and the creation of the "Made in Germany" label (Ewing, 2014). Thus, the "love for detail" (in German: *Liebe zum Detail*) is also shaped by the apprenticeship system that most technicians pass through. The German educational system creates "specialists."

Conversely, in Brazil, the educational system is marked, rather, by "general" competences and a broader range of capacities. The private institution SENAI (*Serviço Nacional de Aprendizagem Industrial*, National Service for Industrial Learning; SENAI, 2019) has offered industrial and technical courses as well as qualification programs in collaboration with companies since 1942; however, most students attend colleges or universities to obtain a degree to enter the labor market (Field notes). In a group interview, a Brazilian employee described the situation:

> In Germany, one person is responsible for a product, sometimes for a component. It's all in the details. Yesterday, they told me: the mechanics come from Germany. But the mechanic doesn't do the electrical part. He can't do that. The electrician has to come. The Brazilian is rather generalist. The mechanic also does the electric part. (Employee, Quality Department, Brazilian)

Third, at an *organizational* level, it is interesting to note that, when it comes to quality responsibilities, the different leadership styles between Germany and Brazil become evident. In Germany, the responsibility for quality and security lies more in the hands of every worker (Thomas et al., 2010)—expressed through the German word *Werkerselbstprüfung* (in English: "worker's self-check"). In contrast, in Brazil, it is more in the hands of the managers who are the "safeguards of quality," in the sense of a paternalistic and humanist leadership style (Caldas, 2006; Dávila and Elvira, 2012) which can be traced back to Brazil's colonial heritage

A German Multinational in Brazil   85

(Dávila and Elvira, 2012), and in turn leads to stricter laws protecting the employee:

> It's the boss's responsibility to see that I [as an employee] don't know, not mine. Because the law here in Brazil, it's a bit patriarchal. A law that protects the employee. The employee is the weaker side.
>
> (Directing Manager, Brazil, Brazilian)

> Our employees are also very sensitive when it comes to surfaces and colors. If there is something visually wrong, at the latest when repainting, someone raises his hand and says "something doesn't fit."
>
> (Employee, Industrial Engineering, German)

> The "Werkerselbstprüfung" actually just means that the employee checks the work step he or she is carrying out. There's no one else who says "I'll see if you did it right." . . . So you are responsible for this result.
>
> (Manager, Quality Management, German)

The organizational structure and history (Schein, 2010) are also influencing factors that challenge the collaboration, mainly between the German and Brazilian managers. Due to its high degree of independence from the German plant during the last 40 years, the Brazil plant's managers are used to leading the company "their way"—in line with a polycentric strategy (Perlmutter, 1969)—and they are still striving for independence when it comes to organizational decisions made in Germany. This is also reflected by the two corporate values "We are independent" and "We accept responsibility" (Internal documents). The Brazilian plant continues to act independently (like in the past), but the German company's push toward alignment becomes apparent at the same time.

The increasing interest in introducing and securing German standards thus provokes political disputes (Dörrenbächer and Geppert, 2017) between the German headquarters and the Brazilian subsidiary about decision-making power and influence. Regarding the critical incident, the Brazilian managers insisted on selecting their own color suppliers, as they were used to doing during the previous decades (Internal documents). During the interviews and the field research, a certain "pride" (in Portuguese: *orgulho*) often became apparent among Brazilians. In one of the first interviews, the Brazilian managing director indicated:

> This company here is working. . . . [And with regard to Brazil,] I developed these products, and these products work, there is a market, I sell.

86   Madeleine Bausch et al.

> I don't want to lower my head for [the German company]. . . . Because there are strong managers here, too. There is not much effort to really make an adjustment, because each one has a profitable business unit. So, why should I change?
>
> (Managing Director, Brazil)

The ethnocentric attitude (Thomas and Peterson, 2016) with regard to decision-making and working style is also reported by the European workforce:

> I feel the Brazilians are very proud of what they do and what they represent. I always get to hear that with something like, "yes, we have everything under control. In Europe, you are a bit too over perfectionist. Here, everything is a bit quieter. And we know best how to do it anyway."
>
> (Project Manager, Europe, Germany)

Internal email communication regarding the decision-making on the color supplier demonstrates the ethnocentric attitudes and power struggles within the company. Thus, answers in the response to an email (written in blue) of the German managers are written in red, a color that in Germany in this situation would be used to attract attention and show anger:

> I know in Brazil how [it] works and how much are the taxes and logistics between Brazil and Europe. . . . We also have our own ideas and ways to manage [the Brazilian company].
>
> (Internal documents)

In the words of a German manager who has lived and worked for several years in Brazil: "And one of [the Brazilian managers], who was already in Europe [30 years ago], says that they have no idea at all in Europe."

The pride of "doing it the Brazilian way" also becomes clear through the rejection of expatriation opportunities for the Brazilian workforce. Several times, the German company invited Brazilian employees to learn "the German way" side by side with German technicians. However, some Brazilian managers see no need for assignments: "No, it's not necessary," cites the statement of one of the Brazilian managers.

This type of "pride" in Brazilian society might be the result of a multi-ethnic society in which people are striving for identity affiliation and social belonging. The fact that every person in Brazil has their own racial and ethnic roots makes Brazilian society one of the most hybridized cultures in the world (Sutter et al., 2015; de Freitas, 2017): "Brazil can be seen as an 'archipelago of dissimilar cultural islands, although bathed by the same waves, and crowned by the same stars'" (Bastide, 1980, cited by Sutter et al., 2015: 146).

Table 5.2 summarizes major challenges in both countries according to the three levels analyzed.

A German Multinational in Brazil   87

Table 5.2 A multi-level analysis of major challenges in Germany and Brazil

Level	*Germany*	*Brazil*
Cultural • Meaning of quality • Cultural values	Functionality Appearance of the product Perfection *Liebe zum Detail*; strict rule orientation	Price and competitiveness Functionality and practicability *Orgulho brasileiro*; personal orientation toward the customer
Institutional • Education • Laws	Specialist and detailed "dual" apprenticeship system More equal rights between employer and employee	Generalist (university) education Strong employee protection laws due to colonial heritage
Organizational • Leadership style • Internationalization strategy and history of the company • Decision-making power and micro- political disputes	Participative Striving for alignment and standardization after 40 years Decision-making by the family and German managers	Paternalist/humanist Striving for independence and local adaptation for 40 years Independent decision- making, related to *orgulho brasileiro*

Lessons From the Case Study for German-Brazilian Collaboration

What can companies do to overcome these challenges? Our case study and the existing literature on the topic allow the proposition of several solutions for how to overcome intercultural challenges at the three analyzed levels.

First, at the *cultural* level, we note that the German multinational has developed a culture of negotiation and dialogue between employees and managers across different hierarchical levels. This is achieved by short-term assignments and international meetings as well as the implementation of language courses for employees and managers. Language can be seen as an entrance to culture, and employees from both cultures are thus able to communicate and better understand the behavior of their colleagues from other cultures. Companies could also foster intercultural learning about values, interpretation systems and problem-solving styles of other cultures (Bartel-Radic, 2013). This might be achieved by intercultural awareness training and shared reflection after short-term assignments.

Second, at an *organizational* level, the German company introduced a leadership pair or management dyad (Barmeyer and Davoine, 2019) at the level of managing director: one of the managers is German and responsible for administrative issues (administrative director); the other manager is Brazilian and responsible for technical and production activities (industrial director). The two managing directors are able to facilitate

88 Madeleine Bausch et al.

knowledge transfer and promote mutual understanding. Such management dyads could be introduced for middle- and lower-management positions. The company has also put in place international quality network meetings where quality managers from production sites across the world can discuss common topics. They take place twice a year and serve to build up a personal network for quality managers. During the last few years, the company has benefited considerably from this network, because the establishment of personal contacts is an important component for constructive cooperation and knowledge transfer between the employees. Furthermore, the company can benefit from culturally and technically sensitive boundary spanners, also known as knowledge brokers or multipliers (Barner-Rasmussen et al., 2014; Zølner, 2019). Those individuals who have gained technical know-how and internalized both cultures and languages (German and Brazilian Portuguese) can be important nodes for knowledge flows within the company.

Third, at an *institutional* level, challenges regarding the differences in the educational system might be overcome by the transfer of certain elements of the German dual training system. In this respect, the German company initiated its own vocational training program, *Jovem Talento* (Portuguese for "young talent"). The program is carried out in conjunction with the federal training organization SENAI. In cooperation with a local technical school, the company conducts in-house workshops and training courses in which young people learn and deepen their technical skills and abilities both practically and theoretically. The transfer makes the German company a mediator of the system, but also an initiator of higher quality education in Brazil.

Conclusion

In this chapter, we have examined some major challenges faced by a German multinational company when transferring quality management practices from a German to a Brazilian plant. Our qualitative, ethnographic case study of a German "hidden champion" reveals how difficulties arise due to cultural and institutional differences as well as organizational micropolitical and power struggles. We exemplified these challenges with one critical incident regarding the painting of construction machines the company manufactures partly in Germany and assembles in Brazil.

The analysis of the case indicates significant differences with regard to cultural values; interpretation systems and the meaning of quality; and educational systems and legal systems regarding the protection of employees. It also shows that cultural, institutional and organizational characteristics are interwoven and influence each other. For example, in Germany, a specialist educational system conditions the cultural value of "love for detail," and at the same time favors autonomous decision-making and participative leadership. Conversely, in Brazil, strong employee protection

A German Multinational in Brazil 89

laws springing from the colonial heritage reinforce the paternalist leadership style. However, at the same time, the interpretation of *orgulho brasileiro* is reflected in a striving for independence from the German headquarters by the Brazilian managers—a quite contradictory characteristic to the paternalistic leadership style. This type of ambiguity in the Brazilian culture has also been reported by other authors (Martins, 2002; Caldas, 2006; Bueno, 2010; Sutter et al., 2015). For example, Martins (2002: 67) emphasizes that Brazil bundles multiple ethnicities and religions, and thus "a set of identity meanings that are similar and conflicting at the same time." As indicated by Caldas and Wood (1999), cited by Bueno (2010: 30): "almost nothing is what it seems to be, and what it is what it seems to be, it could be something else" (authors' translation).

References

Amal, M., Tomio, B. T. (2015). "Institutional distance and Brazilian outward foreign direct investment." *M@n@gement*, 18(1), pp. 78–101. https://doi.org/10.3917/mana.181.0078.

Azevedo, G. (2011). "Intercultural integration in Sino-Brazilian joint ventures." In H. Primecz, L. Romani, and S. Sackmann (eds.), *Cross-cultural management in practice: Culture and negotiated meanings*. Cheltenham: Edward Elgar, pp. 112–124.

Barmeyer, C. (2004). "Learning styles and their impact on cross-cultural training: An international comparison in France, Germany and Quebec." *International Journal of Intercultural Relations*, 28(6), pp. 577–594. https://doi.org/10.1016/j.ijintrel.2005.01.011.

Barmeyer, C., Davoine, E. (2019). "Facilitating intercultural negotiated practices in joint ventures: The case of a French-German railway organization." *International Business Review*, 28(1), pp. 1–11. https://doi.org/10.1016/j.ibusrev.2018.06.001.

Barmeyer, C., Franklin, P. (2016). *Intercultural management: A case-based approach to achieving complementarity and synergy*. London: Palgrave.

Barmeyer, C., Mayrhofer, U. (2008). "The contribution of intercultural management to the success of international mergers and acquisitions: An analysis of the EADS group." *International Business Review*, 17(1), pp. 28–38. https://doi.org/10.1016/j.ibusrev.2007.12.001.

Barmeyer, C., Mayrhofer, U. (2014). "How has the French cultural and institutional context shaped the organization of the Airbus Group?" *International Journal of Organizational Analysis*, 22(4), pp. 440–462. https://hal-univ-lyon3.archives-ouvertes.fr/hal-01071390.

Barner-Rasmussen, W., Ehrnrooth, M., Koveshnikov, A., Mäkelä, K. (2014). "Cultural and language skills as resources for boundary spanning within the MNC." *Journal of International Business Studies*, 45(7), pp. 886–905. https://doi.org/10.1057/jibs.2014.7.

Bartel-Radic, A. (2013). "'Estrangeirismo' and flexibility: Intercultural learning in Brazilian MNCs." *Management international/International Management/Gestiòn Internacional*, 17(4), pp. 239–253. https://doi.org/10.7202/1020680ar.

90 Madeleine Bausch et al.

Beddi, H., Mayrhofer, U. (2013). "Headquarters-subsidiaries relationships of French multinationals in emerging markets." *Multinational Business Review*, 21(2), pp. 174–194. https://doi.org/10.1108/MBR-12-2012-1041.

Brannen, M. Y. (2004). "When Mickey loses face: Recontextualization, semantic fit, and the semiotics of foreignness." *Academy of Management Review*, 29(4), pp. 593–616. https://doi.org/10.5465/amr.2004.14497613.

Brannen, M. Y., Salk, J. E. (2000). "Partnering across borders: Negotiating organizational culture in a German-Japanese joint venture." *Human Relations*, 53(4), pp. 451–487. https://doi.org/10.1177%2F0018726700534001.

Brown, A. (1998). *Organisational culture*. Harlow: Prentice Hall.

Bueno, J. M. (2010). *Brasileiros e estrangeiros na construção de um cotidiano organizacional intercultural*. Dissertation, Fundação Getulio Vargas, São Paulo. https://bibliotecadigital.fgv.br/dspace/bitstream/handle/10438/4459/71060100679.pdf.

Caldas, M., Wood, T., Jr. (1999). *Transformação e realidade organizacional: uma perspectiva brasileira*. São Paulo: Editora Atlas.

Caldas, M. P. (2006). "Conceptualizing Brazilian multiple and fluid cultural profiles. Management research." *Journal of the Iberoamerican Academy of Management*, 4(3), pp. 169–180. https://doi.org/10.2753/JMR1536-5433040303.

Caprar, D. (2011). "Foreign locals: A cautionary tale on the culture of MNC local employees." *Journal of International Business Studies*, 42(5), pp. 608–628. https://doi.org/10.1057/jibs.2011.9.

Chanlat, J. F., Davel, E., Dupuis, J. P. (eds.). (2013). *Cross-cultural management: Culture and management across the world*. Oxford: Routledge. https://doi.org/10.4324/9780203066805.

Chevrier, S., Viegas-Pires, M. (2013). "Delegating effectively across cultures." *Journal of World Business*, 48(3), pp. 431–439. https://doi.org/10.1016/j.jwb.2012.07.026.

Dávila, A., Elvira, M. M. (2012). "Humanistic leadership: Lessons from Latin America." *Journal of World Business*, 47(4), pp. 548–554 https://doi.org/10.1016/j.jwb.2012.01.008.

Davoine, E., Deitmer, L. (2019). "German dual training through apprenticeships: An exportable model?" In J. L. Cerdin and J. M. Peretti (eds.), *Learning and its success*. London: ISTE.

De Freitas, M. E. (2017). "Managing diversity in Brazil." In J. F. Chanlat and M. Özbilgin (eds.), *Management and Diversity*, 3, pp. 113–157, https://doi.org/10.7202/1015807ar.

D'Iribarne, P. (2012). *Managing corporate values in diverse national cultures: The challenge of differences*. London: Routledge. https://doi.org/10.4324/9780203128114.

D'Iribarne, P., Henry, A. (2007). *Successful companies in the developing world: Managing in synergy with cultures*. Paris: Agence Française de Développement (AFD), Research Department.

Dörrenbächer, C., Geppert, M. (eds.). (2017). *Multinational corporations and organization theory: Post millennium perspectives*. Bingley: Emerald Group. https://doi.org/10.1016/j.jwb.2012.01.008.

Erçek, M., Say, A. (2008). "Discursive ambiguity, professional networks, and peripheral contexts: The translation of total quality management in Turkey, 1991–2002." *International Studies of Management & Organization*, 38(4), pp. 78–99. https://doi.org/10.2753/IMO0020-8825380404.

A German Multinational in Brazil 91

Ewing, J. (2014). *Germany's economic renaissance: Lessons for the United States.* New York: Palgrave. https://doi.org/10.1057/9781137340542.

Festing, M., Maletzky, M. (2011). "Cross-cultural leadership adjustment—A multi-level framework based on the theory of structuration." *Human Resource Management Review*, 21(3), pp. 186–200. https://doi.org/10.1016/j.hrmr.2011.02.005.

Friel, D., De Villechenon, F. P. (2018). "Adapting a lean production program to national institutions in Latin America: Danone in Argentina and Brazil." *Journal of International Management*, 24(3), pp. 284–299. https://doi.org/10.1016/j.intman.2018.03.001.

Geertz, C. (1973). *The interpretation of cultures.* New York: Basic Books.

Geppert, M., Mayer, M. (eds.). (2006). *Global, national, and local practices in multinational companies.* Houndmills: Palgrave Macmillan.

German-Brazilian Chamber of Commerce. (2019). www.ahkbrasilien.com.br/de/, accessed October 16, 2019.

Germany Trade and Invest. (2018). *Made in Germany. Das Erfolgslabel auf dem Prüfstand.* www.gtai.de/GTAI/Navigation/DE/Trade/Maerkte/Future/made-in-germany.html, accessed October 16, 2019.

Gertsen, M. C., Zølner, M. (2012). "Recontextualization of the corporate values of a Danish MNC in a subsidiary in Bangalore." *Group & Organization Management*, 37(1), pp. 101–132. https://doi.org/10.1177%2F1059601111432747.

Gutierrez-Huerter, O., Moon, J., Gold, S., Chapple, W. (2020). "Micro-processes of translation in the transfer of practices from MNE headquarters to foreign subsidiaries: The role of subsidiary translators." *Journal of International Business Studies*, 51, pp. 389–413. https://doi.org/10.1057/s41267-019-00234-8.

Hadjikhani, A., Elg, U., Ghauri, P. (eds.). (2012). *Business, society and politics: Multinationals in emerging markets.* Bingley: Emerald Group. https://doi.org/10.1108/S1876-066X(2012)0000028008.

Havighurst, R. J., Moreira, J. R. (1969). *Society and education in Brazil.* Pittsburgh: University of Pittsburgh Press.

iMove Germany. (2016). *Duale Ausbildung auf dem Vormarsch in Brasilien*, July 11. www.imove-germany.de/cps/rde/xchg/imove_projekt_de/hs.xsl/alle_news.htm?content-url=/cps/rde/xchg/imove_projekt_de/hs.xsl/27604.htm, accessed October 16, 2019.

Isaac, V. R., Borini, F. M., Raziq, M. M., Benito, G.R.G. (2019). "From local to global innovation: The role of subsidiaries' external relational embeddedness in an emerging market." *International Business Review*, 28(4), pp. 638–646. https://doi.org/10.1016/j.ibusrev.2018.12.009.

Juran, J., Godfrey, A. B. (1999). *Quality handbook.* New York: McGraw-Hill.

Kluckhohn, C. K. (1951). "Values and value orientations in the theory of action." In T. Parsons and E. A. Shils (eds.), *Toward a general theory of action.* Cambridge, MA: Harvard University Press, pp. 388–433. http://doi.org/10.4159/harvard.9780674863507.

Kostova, T. (1999). "Transnational transfer of strategic organizational practices: A contextual perspective." *Academy of Management Review*, 24(2), pp. 308–324. https://doi.org/10.5465/amr.1999.1893938.

Marschan-Piekkari, R., Reis, C. (2004). "Language and languages in cross-cultural interviewing." In R. Marschan-Piekkari and C. Welch (eds.), *Handbook of qualitative research methods for international business.* Cheltenham: Edward Elgar, pp. 224–244.

92 Madeleine Bausch et al.

Marschan-Piekkari, R., Welch, C. (2011). *Rethinking the case study in international business and management research*. Cheltenham: Edward Elgar.

Martins, P. H. (2002). "Cultura autoritária e aventura da brasilidade." In J. A. Burity (ed.), *Cultura e Identidade: Perspectivas interdisciplinares*. Rio de Janeiro: DP&A.

Mayrhofer, U. (2013). *Management of multinational companies: A French perspective*. Basingstoke: Palgrave Macmillan.

Miles, M. B., Huberman, A. M., Saldana, J. (2014). *Qualitative data analysis*. London: SAGE. https://doi.org/10.1080/10572252.2015.975966.

Perlmutter, H. W. (1969). "The tortuous evolution of the multinational company." *Columbia Journal of World Business*, 1, pp. 9–18.

Piekkari, R., Welch, C., Paavilainen, E. (2009). "The case study as disciplinary convention: Evidence from international business journals." *Organizational Research Methods*, 12(3), pp. 567–589. https://doi.org/10.1177%2F1094428108319905.

Primecz, H., Romani, L., S. Sackmann (2011). *Cross-cultural management in practice: Culture and negotiated meanings*. Cheltenham: Edward Elgar.

Rädiker, S., Kuckartz, U. (2018). *Analyse qualitativer Daten mit MAXQDA: Text, audio und video*. Wiesbaden: Springer. https://doi.org/10.1007/978-3-658-22095-2.

Ramirez, J., Søderberg, A. M. (2019). "Recontextualizing Scandinavian practices in a Latin American regional office. Management research." *Journal of the Iberoamerican Academy of Management*, forthcoming. https://doi.org/10.1108/MRJIAM-12-2018-0895.

Romani, L., Barmeyer, C., Primecz, H., Pilhofer, K. (2018). "Cross-cultural management studies: State of the field in the four research paradigms." *International Studies of Management & Organization*, 48(3), pp. 247–263. https://doi.org/1 0.1080/00208825.2018.1480918.

Schein, E. H. (2010). *Organizational culture and leadership*. San Francisco: John Wiley & Sons.

Schröter, O., Davoine, E. (2009). "The cross-national transfer of HRM practices in multinational companies towards their Swiss subsidiaries." *Dossier de la Revue Economique et Sociale en anglais*, 107(1), pp. 1–24.

SENAI (Serviço Nacional de Aprendizagem Industrial). (2019). www.portaldaindustria.com.br/senai/, accessed October 16, 2019.

Simon, H. (2009). *Hidden champions of the twenty-first century: The success strategies of unknown world market leaders*. Berlin: Springer Science & Business Media. https://doi.org/10.1007/978-0-387-98147-5.

Statista (2019). *Made-in-country-index*, July 23. https://de.statista.com/statistik/daten/studie/676530/umfrage/made-in-country-index-gesamtranking-2017/, accessed October 16, 2019.

Sutter, M. B., Mac Lennan, M.L.F., Tiscoski, G. P., Polo, E. F. (2015). "Brazilianness: A look at the multiple faces of the Brazilian national identity." *Future Studies Research Journal: Trends and Strategy*, 7(1), pp. 130–156. https://doi.org/10.24023/FutureJournal/2175-5825/2015.v7i1.191.

Taylor, M. L., Søndergaard, M. (2017). *Unraveling the mysteries of case study research: A guide for business and management students*. Cheltenham: Edward Elgar.

Thomas, A., Kinast, E. U., Schroll-Machl, S. (2010). *Handbook of intercultural communication and cooperation*. Göttingen: Vandenhoeck & Ruprecht. https://doi.org/10.13109/9783666403279.

Thomas, D. C., Peterson, M. F. (2016). *Cross-cultural management: Essential concepts.* Los Angeles: SAGE.

Usunier, J. C., Van Herk, H., Lee, J. A. (2019). *International and cross-cultural business research.* London: SAGE.

Vecchi, A., Brennan, L. (2009). "Quality management: A cross-cultural perspective." *Cross Cultural Management: An International Journal,* 16(2), pp. 149–164. https://doi.org/10.1108/13527600910953900.

Wächter, H., Peters, R., Tempel, A., Müller-Carmen, M. (2003). *The "country-of-origin effect" in the cross national management of human resources: Results and case study evidence of research on American multinational companies in Germany.* Munich: Rainer Hampp Verlag.

Walther, M. (2014). *Repatriation to France and Germany: A comparative study based on Bourdieu's theory of practice.* Wiesbaden: Springer Gabler. https://doi.org/10.1007/978-3-658-05700-8.

Zølner, M. (2019). "Local intermediaries and their organisational identification in a French subsidiary." *European Journal of International Management,* 13(1), pp. 88–110, https://doi.org/10.1504/EJIM.2019.096504.

Part II

Ethical and Social Responsibility Issues in International Management

Part I of the book analyzed the cultural and societal challenges of international management through strategic decision-making and implementation. Part II deals with issues of ethics and societal responsibility in international management.

In Chapter 6, Suzanne M. Apitsa considers CSR actions as a means for multinationals to find a balance between global coherence and local adaptability. Africa is marked by a certain number of problems that are key CSR issues: poverty, diseases and pandemics (HIV, Ebola, etc.), corruption, hunger, malnutrition, climate change, and so forth. What are the CSR action mechanisms at work in the HRM of international companies in Africa, particularly in Cameroon?

In Chapter 7, Hamza Asshidi explores how ethical tools are designed and implemented in a context of cultural diversity within multinational companies. So far, the literature has focused on comparing local variants of internationally distributed ethical tools, adapted to the targeted contexts. The process of developing and implementing these tools in different cultural contexts has itself hardly been considered. It is this process that this chapter intends to study. It is built on the basis of the study of seven exploratory cases of multinational enterprises—four from France and one each from Switzerland, the United States and Japan.

In Chapter 8, Gildas Lusteau and Isabelle Barth describe and interpret the challenges and evolution of corporate social responsibility (CSR) in China. The chapter highlights how organizational social responsibility—a concept of western origin—can be rooted in Chinese and Confucian culture and even in the ideological perspectives developed by successive leaders of communist China. The authors also study the break with the "post-'80s" generation, resulting from the one-child policy endorsed by Deng Xiaoping in 1978.

In Chapter 9, Laure Dikmen studies the interpenetration of the religious order and the economic order through 119 questionnaires administered to members of the Turkish employers' association, the MÜSIAD. As the

96 Ethical and Social Responsibility Issues

Muslim population is projected to increase from 23.4% of the world's population in 2010 (1.6 billion) to 26.4% in 2030 (2.2 billion), the considerable weight of Islam in the world leads to a profound reflection on the ideological, sociological, economic, strategic and political issues that this religion carries today.

6 CSR Action Mechanisms of International Companies

An Analysis in the Light of African Realities

Suzanne M. Apitsa

Introduction

This chapter focuses on the CSR action mechanisms deployed by international companies in Africa. Africa is marked by a number of problems that are expressed as CSR issues: poverty, diseases and pandemics (HIV, Ebola, etc.), corruption, hunger, malnutrition, climate change and so on. The general question posed in our research is to understand "how" African realities drive CSR mechanisms in the international human resources management (HRMi) of international companies located there. To respond to this question, we study the HRMi policies of two international companies established in Cameroon (a multinational and an international SME). HRMi requires putting in place a set of tools to coordinate and control the activities of subsidiaries. These tools must contribute to the development of skills and motivation necessary for the international competitiveness of the company (Bartlett and Ghoshal, 2002; Jaussaud and Schaaper, 2006; Sparrow et al., 2017). Few existing studies analyze the CSR action mechanisms deployed by companies in the context of the management of their activities abroad, particularly in Africa (Boiral, 2008; Golli and Yahiaoui, 2009; Koleva and Gherib, 2012; Harison and Obrecht, 2013; Levermore, 2014; Dartey-Baah et al., 2015; Adanhounme, 2015; Vig, 2016; Kamdem, 2016). In the field of international management, most of the work focuses on the construction of CSR strategies by multinationals (Bondy and Starkey, 2014; Pestre, 2011, 2014).

Internationalized companies must develop relevant practices to cope with local host country contingencies on the one hand, and on the other hand they must respect the harmony and consistency of their policies with headquarters practices (Kostova and Roth, 2002). CSR brings an additional dimension to this tension (Husted and Allen, 2006). CSR, on the one hand, is part of the mandatory global mechanisms defined by international institutions for all organizations, regardless of their size and nationality (The Global Compact and ILO, 2010; European Commission, 2011). On the other hand, existing disparities between countries make it necessary to take into account contextual contingencies in the application of international CSR principles (Apitsa, 2019).

98 *Suzanne M. Apitsa*

Thus two research questions emerge from this dilemma: First, what are the CSR action mechanisms at work in the HRMi of international companies in Africa? The World Business Council for Sustainable Development (Holme and Watts, 2000) defines corporate social responsibility as a company's ongoing commitment to ethical behavior and to contribute to economic development, while improving the quality of life of its employees and their families, as well as that of the local community and society at large. This orientation is part of the ISO 26000 international standard where the CSR guidelines for all organizations are provided. These must ensure in respect of their employees full and secure employment, health, well-being and safety at work, work-life balance, equality of opportunity, equity, promotion of diversity, respect for people and social solidarity . . . (ISO 26000, 2010). In Africa, societal problems are particularly strong, and issues related to the health, safety, well-being at work of employees and so forth vary to different degrees according to the countries concerned, and the management methods and tools of companies, whether national or international. If CSR is an additional issue at the center of strategic tensions of internationalization of companies, then the second research question is, can CSR action mechanisms be able to regulate the balance between the search for global coherence and the taking into account of local specificities in the HRMi activity? The peculiarities of national contexts invite multinationals not to ignore the abundance of values that collide outside of original contexts (Holme and Watts, 2000). For example, in Africa, the competitive environment imposes constraints that companies must not be deaf to, such as cultural values (Apitsa, 2013).

In the first part of this chapter, we present the challenges of CSR in Africa as well as its specificities on the international scene. The analysis of the different academic works in the field allows us to propose a reading grid that we use. In the second part, we outline our methodological approach and our field of investigation: two cases of international companies (a multinational and an international SME) located in Cameroon, "Africa in miniature." Finally, the third part highlights the results from these two cases. They show that CSR expresses itself in the practice of HRMi not as a management tool but as a banal and philanthropic mechanism in the daily management of human resources. Finally, a discussion of our findings is presented, and the conclusion section highlights their managerial implications.

Literature Review

Africa is now an increasingly important location in global economic development. It is therefore appropriate to look at the conceptual and analytical framework of HRMi in its African context.

CSR in Africa, a Concept at the Heart of the Regulation of Economic and Social Action

In Africa, CSR is an emerging concept closely linked to the concepts of good governance and ethics. Without being clearly named as such, the term resonates with the structural reforms (structural adjustment programs (SAP)) imposed by financial institutions (World Bank, IMF). These "Washington Consensus"[1] reforms are aimed at integrating Africa into the global economy and promoting African private enterprise. Many studies, which refer to the SAP, emphasize that it has denigrated the role of the state in social and economic organization and has not considered the peculiarities of African countries (Williamson, 1990; Dia, 1996). Indeed, African states, faced with "mismanagement" by their leaders, have been forced, as part of these reforms, to withdraw from many of their responsibilities, to relegate them to private companies and regain some legitimacy.

Undoubtedly, these reforms require more responsibilities from leaders, and therefore the application of the rules of good governance and ethics. One of the consequences of the reforms is the liberalization of the economy, which has allowed the inflow of foreign capital through a process of privatization of sectors of activity previously owned by public enterprises. This phenomenon has encouraged most business through the acquisition of enterprises and increased the number of FDI (foreign direct investment) inputs. Consequently, in order to prevent multinationals from acting opportunistically and favoring the economy over society, it was necessary to regulate economic action by tightening the legislative and regulatory measures in the countries and deregulating the markets. At the same time, people who witnessed the weakening of the power of African national states discovered the disparities between rich countries (North) and poor countries (South), disparities reinforced by globalization as emphasized by the economist and Nobel laureate, Joseph Stiglitz (2014). Petitioned by international institutions, non-governmental organizations (NGOs) and movements fighting inequalities, multinationals have been called to respect the principles of development to meet the needs of the present without compromising the ability of future generations to meet their own needs (Brundtland Report, 1987). The underlying idea is that these multinationals must act on the CSR issues of the countries where they are present.

However, in this decade, we have seen the emancipation of African civil society, unaccustomed to making demands and engaging in strikes, revealing an awareness that calls for the promotion of corporate responsibility. We can note the demonstrations against the cost of living in some African countries in the decade of the 2000s. The question of the respecting the principles of ethics and good governance has thus arisen without the term CSR being really used in Africa.

100   *Suzanne M. Apitsa*

African countries are facing the challenges of economic growth, poverty reduction, the fight against hunger and pandemics (HIV, Ebola), security, crop failure and climate change. In a context of competitive intensity and uncertainties related to investment barriers, integrating CSR mechanisms into its HRMi may be a distinctive advantage (Porter and Kramer, 2006). Does the challenge of such an approach, in the light of African realities, require to deny their peculiarities when existing social and societal problems are strong? The underlying issue concerns the universal scope of CSR principles and standards in addressing country disparities. This challenge rests, on the one hand, on the subtle global/local/transnational debate of the international strategies of firms abroad, and on the other hand, on the ambiguity maintained by the global principles of CSR, at the same time mandatory, voluntary and utilitarian. This brings us to the specificities of international CSR. What is it concretely?

The Specificities of CSR at the International Level

In a perspective of internationalization of companies, the existing literature states that the global corporate culture requires particular CSR practices according to each cultural location (Deresky, 2008; Mayrhofer, 2011). These authors defend cultural relativism, an issue debated in international management research, and concerns the dilemma of standardization *versus* adaptation of management practices and tools of companies abroad. International CSR is currently going through this debate. Studies analyzing the strategic process of CSR training of multinationals highlight, in each case study, the global *versus* local cleavage of international CSR (Arthaud-Day, 2005; Husted and Allen, 2006; Barin Cruz et al., 2008). The authors explain that multinationals operate in different geographical areas, and therefore CSR is subject to the same types of strategic tensions abroad. In Africa, as part of the fight against AIDS, Pestre (2011) studies the process of building the Lafarge Group's CSR strategy. The results, which support the work of Logsdon and Wood (2002) and Arthaud-Day (2005), show the existence of a transnational (hybrid) CSR strategy implemented by Lafarge. Transnational CSR is a strategic alternative that allows the multinational to develop combined strategic capabilities in terms of global integration (global CSR strategy: normative principles and standards developed by international institutions and signed by most countries) and local adaptation (local CSR: taking into account the specificities of the countries). In other works, Pestre (2014) deepens the analysis of the process of building the CSR strategy in five French multinationals through the analysis of the relationship between headquarters and subsidiaries. It describes three factors that condition the strategic orientation of the international CSR of the firms studied: institutional, strategic and specific. For the author, these factors make it possible to determine the strategic logic of CSR (global, local or transnational) of multinationals. Whatever the CSR strategy identified, CSR action mechanisms are not studied.

CSR Action Mechanisms   101

In Africa, the review of the literature in international management shows that African cultural particularities require adapting the tools and modes of management of the multinational firms to the setting context (D'Iribarne, 2003; Apitsa, 2013). In terms of CSR, this is an adapted approach to CSR (Prahalad, 2005, Lado, 2016). For these authors, the local CSR approach is necessary because the CSR issues are not the same in all countries. The findings made by these authors affirm that in Africa, even if the standard of living, human suffering, unemployment, HIV, Ebola and so forth are essential issues for CSR, the degree of priority differs because the needs of each country are different (Reed, 2002).

To promote CSR, many principles and standards have been implemented by international institutions to guide companies in their approach: the International Organization for Standardization ISO 9001 (quality), 14001 (environment), 26000 (social) and the Occupational Health and Safety Assessment Series (OHASAS) 18001 (occupational health and safety). It is for companies to combine their economic approach with the implementation of concrete action mechanisms that prove their commitment to CSR (Boiral, 2008). In Africa, does the challenge of such an approach, in the light of African realities, require consideration of their particularities?

We now present the conceptual framework deployed to identify operational descriptors to the questions posed by the research.

The Conceptual Framework of CSR

The conceptual framework of CSR is based on the concept of stakeholders. This reference framework of CSR was built within three theoretical approaches, structured around business ethics, social issue management and business and society. Proponents of these three approaches agree that firms would be able to take charge of the common good. They propose three levels of approaches that underpin the principles of corporate responsibility: the principles of societal legitimacy (institutional level), public responsibility (organizational level) and managerial (individual level). The School of Business Ethics (Goodpaster and Matthews, 1983) supports an institutional approach that integrates the moral and even ethical dimension. For this school, the company is subject to the same rules as humans, which supposes that the behavior of the company is in line with the norms and values of society. This approach allows the adoption of CSR only through ethical or moral considerations. It ignores the capitalist environment that encompasses the company and influences its purpose. However, within companies, ethical behavior is limited by organizational constraints. The current social issue management approach (Freeman, 1984) refines the classic economic thesis and integrates the concept of stakeholders.[2] It delineates the dimensions of corporate responsibility (economic, ethical, legal and discretionary). This trend advocates a

102 *Suzanne M. Apitsa*

pragmatic view of CSR and considers the company as a social and political actor (Freeman, 1984). The School of Business and Society (Wood, 1991) is part of a contractual approach to CSR. Wood (1991) builds on the work of Carroll (1979) to demonstrate the interdependent relationship between business and society. The author considers the company as a social institution that must serve society to be legitimate. To define his approach, he is interested in the CSR policies and programs as well as their observable results (social impacts of the company's behavior, programs used by the firm to face its social responsibility and improve its responsiveness to the expectations of external actors and policies implemented by the company to manage societal issues and the interests of stakeholders). Wood's (1991) approach admits a positive relationship between social responsibility and corporate performance and advocates a proactive attitude. In the framework of the study of the CSR strategies of the foreign multinational, authors have established so-called graded approaches of CSR strategies that highlight the practices of the companies in the matter. In this vein, Martinet and Payaud (2008) have identified four types of CSR strategy deployed by the multinational companies: cosmetic, annex or peripheral, integrated and bottom of the pyramid (BoP). This last characteristic was developed by Prahalad (2005). It concerns poor countries and allows the company to deploy CSR actions essential to redraw the economic fabric and make it reliable. In agreement with Pereira Pündrich and Mercuri (2011), the graduated approach of Martinet and Payaud (2008) is interesting for understanding CSR in MNCs but depends on the company's capabilities, objectives and needs.

To understand the approach of social responsibility of multinationals through mechanisms of action, Carroll (1991) has proposed four possible dimensions of CSR, which he describes as pyramids:

- The philanthropic responsibility that is generally expected by the stakeholders. It consists of giving them financial and humanitarian contributions. The company is perceived in this case as a good citizen. Carroll emphasizes the importance of this component in the societal approach without making it a dominant criterion.
- The ethical responsibility that allows companies to respond, in full transparency, to the expectations of society. Uncodified laws, rules of behavior and implicit values prevail for companies and stakeholders.
- The legal responsibility ensures the stakeholders that the companies carry out their activities and obtain profits by respecting the written law.
- Economic responsibility reinforces the traditional idea that companies have an obligation to produce the goods and services needed by consumers to meet their needs while maximizing their own profits.

This last "economic" responsibility represents for Carroll (1999) the primordial precondition for the realization of the three other responsibilities (philanthropic, ethical, legal). According to the author, companies, if economically and legally stable, can develop philanthropic and ethical initiatives. This model has received some criticism (Pasquero, 2005), but despite this, it is relevant to meet the expectations of this research.

Methodology

Our field of study is Cameroon. This country is located in Central Africa and is classified among the poor countries. Called "Africa in miniature," it covers a diversity of cultures and ethnicities. Its economic situation is improving, with growth reaching 3.8% in 2018 and accelerating to 4.4% in 2019. These growth figures do not enable it to escape its ranking in the list of poor countries. The country has an extremely young population, half of which is under 20 years old. This constitutes a heavy burden for an essentially agricultural economy but also a potential force for development. The employment situation in Cameroon is difficult to assess because of the weight of the informal sector. The illiteracy rate is still high despite the ever-increasing literacy rate (77% for men and 60% for women). At the regional level, the country is marked by humanitarian and security crises on the northern borders with Nigeria and on the east with the Central African Republic. This causes displacement of refugees fleeing inland or to neighboring countries. In the interior of the country, there is the political crisis in the anglophone region. In addition to these crises, there are diseases and pandemics (prevalence of HIV/AIDS) and problems related to climate, water, deforestation, biodiversity and so forth.

Sample

Our study is in respect of two cases of French international companies (a multinational and an international SME). They are active in the insurance and distribution sectors, respectively.

The multinational insurance company is a major player at the global and local levels. It is present in more than 62 countries including eight in Africa. It offers its services to individuals and businesses. In Africa, it is a specialist in understanding and managing risk for its clients. The company is positioned as a player in CSR and diversity, and has signed the Diversity Charter. It is promoted as a responsible and socially responsible company with one objective: to meet the demands and opportunities of its environment (secondary sources).

The international SME works in the electrical equipment distribution sector (BT-MT-HT, lamps, inverters, cables, generators, etc.). It is a leader in its sector of activity. Its process of internationalization is gradual: the

104 *Suzanne M. Apitsa*

parent company initiated its international commitment through exporting, then through the creation of subsidiaries in several African countries.

It seemed appropriate to invest empirically in these two cases of international companies because they are naturally, by their business, motivated by CSR considerations. In addition, whether large or small, societal phenomena require the contribution of any organization (Brundtland Report, 1987). However, the financial vulnerability of SMEs raises questions about their ability to commit to social and societal causes. Penetrating this type of company in Africa allows us to study in depth a subject that has been only marginally researched in the field of the international management and beyond.

Methodological Approach

Our methodological approach adopts a posture of interpretative meaning-practice (Welch et al., 2011). This case-based stance (Yin, 2014) refers, according to Milliot and Freeman (2015), to an idiographic project associated with an exploratory research objective. The abductive inference logic uses qualitative data based on interviews, observations, secondary data (Internet, newspapers and magazines) and internal documents. As a result of the use of the documentary sources, we requested face-to-face interviews, which were later supplemented by telephone interviews. The interviews were conducted using an interview guide built around eight themes: managerial policy/governance, CSR, economy, social, ethics, legislation, diversity and social expectations. This structure was developed from Carroll's (1991) reading grid and supplemented by that of the HRMi and international CSR. The immersion in the reality of the employees' lives made it possible to collect the necessary data that can't be completely obtained during face-to-face interviews. Thirty interviews (23 face-to-face and 7 by telephone) were collected from field actors with different profiles (expatriates, senior and middle managers, subordinates). Our research protocol is based on content analysis (Glazer and Strauss, 1967). Table 6.1 presents a summary of the elements of the field of study.

Results and Discussion

In the management of the companies studied, the empirical data shows, to varying degrees and convergence, that CSR action mechanisms operate and reflect both a managerial willingness and a response to the pressures of international institutions, employees and civil society. They also bring to light the expectations expressed by employees, questioning the commitment and the management methods and tools of these companies. Within the strategic tensions of the HRMi, can regulation be possible thanks to the CSR action mechanisms identified?

Table 6.1 Sample description

Characteristics	Multinational	International SMEs
Nationality of firms	French	French
Year of implantation	1980	1980
Activity area	Insurance	Distribution of electrical equipment
Nationality of managers in key positions of subsidiaries	Cameroonian	Cameroonian
Number of expatriates posted to subsidiaries	1	0
Number of employees	90	30
Number of interviews	13 face-to-face 4 by phone Total number of interviews: 30	10 face-to-face 3 by phone
Status of informants	Administrator (expatriate) General manager Directors of departments Subordinates	French boss General manager Intermediate manager Secretaries Subordinates
CSR	Governance Ethics Diversity Fight against AIDS (HIV) Fight against malnutrition (actions dedicated to nutrition) Working conditions Protection of customers' personal data	Governance Ethics Diversity Health actions dedicated to employees Solidarity actions dedicated to schools and churches (civil society) Working conditions Quality
Duration of interviews	1–2 hours	
Analysis design	Content analysis	
Theme interview grid	Managerial policy/governance—CSR—economy—social—ethics—legislation—diversity—social expectations	

CSR, Managerial Will and Pressure of Institutions: Global Integration

The results show that CSR mechanisms such as governance, ethical principles and the ISO 9001 standard are used in the day-to-day management of each subsidiary. These mechanisms find meaning in African realities.

106 *Suzanne M. Apitsa*

Governance, Ethical Principles and ISO 9001 Standard

In the multinational insurance company, the governance mechanism is an internal control tool designed to prevent and control the risks associated with insurance services provision.

> In 2008, a process was launched to harmonize corporate governance standards within the Group: harmonization of the rules relating to the size and composition of management bodies, the criteria for independence of directors, the role of Committees and Directors Compensation Policy. These standards require, in particular, that an audit committee and a "multinational" compensation committee be set up on the boards of directors of the Group's main subsidiaries.
>
> (Multinational)

This verbatim statement highlights the importance of good corporate governance and respect for the ethical principles set out in the international CSR framework (The Global Pact/ILT, 2010). This translates into a degree of transparency and respect for the rules governing the remuneration of the subsidiaries' hierarchy. This ethics principle is used here to respond to the institutional pressures exerted by the political authorities on stock options (bonus envelope, conflicts of interest). It also assumes that the rules for preserving the personal data of customers are applied. The latter is a commitment to the core business of the multinational.

> The management of personal and sensitive data of our customers confers a new responsibility, that of protecting their data because we are convinced that it is an expectation of the society as a whole but also, we have for ambition to build a lasting relationship of trust with our customers.
>
> (Multinational)

This empirical data points to the ISO 9001 standard as the required quality standard of the service to be delivered to the customer.

We deduce an ethical responsibility to satisfy the rules of behavior and expectations of stakeholders. The application of these rules results in a legal liability (Carroll, 1991).

In the case of the SME, results from secondary data reveal that it is managed locally through reporting. The latter contributes in a homogeneous and coherent way to the dissemination of information and results of the group. Here, management is designed in a standardized way.

The data from the interviews show that the SME has a very technical culture based on the notion of quality, which is reflected among other things by the following responses:

> Technique is our greatest strength.
>
> (International SME)

> Our strength is quality. We operate in the field of electricity. Electricity requires safety standards. Avoid selling poor quality cables. We are a French subsidiary and we are forced to European standards.
>
> (International SME)

> Customer satisfaction is our priority.
>
> (International SME)

ISO 9001 (quality) is at the heart of the SME's orientation. It is a standard certification mechanism established at the international level. The quality and technical prowess of the product enables the SME to meet the customer's requirements, to ascertain the level of customer satisfaction and to measure its performance. CSR is a legal, ethical and economic responsibility (Carroll, 1991).

Governance, ethical principles and the ISO 9001 standard are in fact standard mechanisms of CSR action, deployed to varying degrees in the practices of both companies. They correspond to the logic of global integration. They are part of the logic of economic, legal and ethical legitimacy in the sense of Carroll (1991). At the heart of African cultural realities, ethics reflects a certain legitimacy that values the behavior of an individual in the community (Apitsa, 2018). As for the notion of quality, it is expressed in the economic realities of individuals marked by poverty. As a result, they have little regard for the quality of a product and rather focus on its price (Anglès and Apitsa, 2017).

Career Management: Diversity Charter and ISO 26000 Standard

Our immersion in the multinational allowed us to observe that local executives now held key positions of responsibility in the subsidiary. The deputy director general, a local executive, has been promoted to the post of director general of the Cameroon subsidiary. All other executive positions were allocated to local executives.

> The challenge is to become a "favourite company" by placing the men and women of the group at the center of the preparation and achievement by 2012 of this ambition. It shows the extraordinary richness of our collaborators. Their diversity is a key element of the group's resource strategy.
>
> (Documentary sources, Multinational)

The multinational is a signatory of the diversity charter. This reinforces one of the international principles of CSR, which is the promotion of diversity (ISO 26000). The employees themselves did not believe it, as evidenced by these verbatim reports.

108 *Suzanne M. Apitsa*

So, they advocate cultural diversity without associating us. In reality, if they do not question us, if they do not associate with us, if we do not take part in forums for exchange together, how will they know what we can bring them? We want to participate. The Multinational says, "Think global and act local," but how do you integrate that local thinking into the group's thinking? How to take into account our Africanity in what is done so that we too can recognize our contributions in the decisions that are made? In fact, there are still social issues that we discuss here, and we still need to know how others have solved it.

(Multinational)

I think the big authorities in France know that there are positions that can't be moved at the moment.

(Multinational)

The Diversity Charter is a response to institutional, strategic and managerial pressures that reveals a shift in HRMi. Reinforcing this analysis, in the case of the SME, the data reveal that it has not signed a diversity charter but is in the process of promoting local executives to key positions.

In 2005, we signed up to promote African managers.

(International SME)

Entrusting key management positions to local executives reflects headquarters' confidence in the words of local leaders:

Our relationship with the French headquarters is very much based on trust.

(International SME)

One can question the motives behind this career management policy in Cameroon. Is the ethical behavior of the headquarters questioned through the accountability of local executives in key positions? Notwithstanding, the ethical responsibility (Carroll, 1991) related to the management of careers of local executives is actuated as a demonstration of the trust of the head office toward the local resources and in line with economic development. The presence of multinationals in a country raises strong expectations in economic terms. At the heart of African economic realities, they play a proactive role for employment. In reference to the ISO 26000 standard, the CSR standard certification mechanism, the empowerment of a local executive is part of a logic of legitimacy of managerial ethics (Carroll, 1991), which, in the African cultural realities, values the social status of the executive within his community.

CSR, Managerial Will, Social Pressure and Societal/Local Reactivity

At the heart of social and societal realities in Africa, to different degrees in the two case studies, the results reveal a set of voluntary and utilitarian actions dedicated to employees and civil society.

Employee Health Actions

Empirical data indicates that managers support the health of employees in HRMi.

> We have an AIDS plan that has been in place for 3 years with free and voluntary screening. And astonishingly, no one has failed, without having to press. Everyone went there. We have 1% of personnel with AIDS in our workforce.
>
> (Multinational)

> Every year we have one, two or three HIV conferences for employees. Last year, the children of collaborators were associated. And now we associate the spouses.
>
> (Multinational)

> I have health insurance. When I'm sick, I can go and look after myself. There are too many diseases in Africa and if we do not have the money, we die. Society supports us in this case. If I was in another company, I would not even have that.
>
> (International SME)

Health is a CSR mechanism operated in projects to fight against pandemics (HIV/AIDS) and diseases, and against malnutrition (actions dedicated to nutrition). The latter is carried out at nutritional conferences given by specialists on site and during working hours.

> We have noticed that here obesity and diabetes are devastating for both men and women.
>
> (Multinational)

> People are eating poorly. They continue to feed themselves as their parents fed when parents did hard work either in agriculture or otherwise. Now when you're sitting all day in the office if you feed that way, you'll have a problem after a few years, that's obvious. We went to get two ladies, nutritionist doctors from the general hospital who come to give us conferences and inform us about how to feed ourselves, how we have to change our ways of feeding ourselves to avoid finding ourselves after with hip problems, knees or excess weight that lead to diabetes, high blood pressure, etc.
>
> (Multinational)

110   *Suzanne M. Apitsa*

We can perceive through this verbatim report the link between culture and poverty in Africa. "If people eat badly," it's because they have neither the culture of balanced eating nor the financial means.

Degenerative diseases and pandemics are part of social reality in Africa. Philanthropic responsibility (Carroll, 1991) is here at work through the humanitarian and financial actions of the multinationals. It is a proactive behavior that ensures the well-being of everyone in the country (civil society and government). The CSR mechanism is voluntarist and utilitarian.

Solidarity Actions Dedicated to Employees

The results show a certain peculiarity in the case of the SME. In employee management, they reveal that local managers have implemented practices that they themselves describe as "solidaristic and humane management": the provision of micro-credit and throwing parties for employees/partners.

> We have a micro-credit loan facility. To help employees meet their children's back-to-school expenses, we are granting a zero-interest loan. The amount to be reimbursed (payroll deduction) is capped at a percentage of net salary.
>
> (International SME)

> We are organizing a party for May 1st where each employee comes as a couple. We are also organizing a Christmas tree in December. This is a normal gesture to allow our employees to offer a toy, a Christmas present to their children. Here very few companies of our size do it. It's rare.
>
> (International SME)

Solidarity is a CSR mechanism that reflects the voluntary and philanthropic commitment of the international SME. It is deployed to motivate employees and meet economic goals (Carroll, 1991). The voluntary integration of targeted solidarity actions enables employees to flourish, to be motivated and to contribute more to the competitiveness objectives of their company. The parties for employees with their partners reinforce this objective. It is a socially responsible practice of leaders that takes shape in the local culture (sociability of African communities).

Solidarity and Mutual Aid Actions Dedicated to Civil Society

Our direct immersion in the SME allowed us to note from the outset that it participated in projects aimed at civil society. During our presence in the field, we observed how the international SME offered free light bulbs and power cables to school and church leaders:

> We support these schools and also the churches that ask us for help with their electrical equipment, we provide them with cables and bulbs.
> (International SME)

This solidarity and humanitarian action reflect philanthropic and ethical responsibilities (Carroll, 1991). It is an example of anchoring local potential and development leverage. Cameroon is a poor country. School infrastructure is very modest.

CSR, a Response to New Social Pressures: Employee Expectations

Well-Being at Work and the OHSAS 18001 Standard

In the case of the multinational, the data collected show that employees aspire to have the best working conditions for their well-being at work.

> The only thing that sometimes, I would not say is problematic but annoying to people, is the importance of reporting to the group. We are asking for more and more things, but we are also asking for more and more things in an increasingly shortened time.
> (Multinational)
> If an employee is asked to handle 10 claims files per day; if he has not done so, he can explain why. If he did, he can also explain why.
> (Multinational)

Employees are under double pressure: one linked to the reduction of deadlines for completion of tasks (admitted by new social tools, reporting) and the other related to the productivity constraint. The CSR action mechanism is here called to be activated to address productivity pressures.

Employability, Occupational Health and ISO 26000 and OHASAS 18001 Standards

In the case of SMEs, we observed during our presence in the field that the SME used a lot of technical assistance from France.

> We need training on the products we sell. The customer must have all the technical information even on the ecological details. Before we neglected all that but today it is no longer possible even for our health and for customer satisfaction.
> (International SME)

112 *Suzanne M. Apitsa*

This verbatim report highlights the training needs of employees and the concern to preserve their health at work. It calls for legal responsibility (Carroll, 1991), which requires the SME to operate two CSR action mechanisms of employee training and safeguarding their health at work.

Discussion

The existing literature, which we have explored, has provided guidelines for our research. The conceptual framework of CSR adopted and developed by Carroll (1991) has identified, to varying degrees, the nature of the CSR of the companies studied. This operational framework unveiled the mechanisms of CSR action at work in the HRMi of the two companies that are subjects of this study: governance, ethics, quality, diversity charter, health actions (fight against HIV/AIDS, fight against malnutrition) solidarity actions dedicated to employees (micro-credit, throwing of parties) and civil society actions (donations of infrastructure to schools and churches). These CSR action mechanisms are set out in the international standards and certification standards (Global Compact, ISO 9001, ISO 26000 and OHASAS 18001) that the companies studied operate on a voluntary, utilitarian and mandatory basis.

Our results highlight the specificities of each company in terms of CSR. In a convergent way, the mechanisms of CSR action at work in the SME appear in the practices of its HRMi without being so named. The results show that both companies are concerned about problems of economic development, health, nutrition, solidarity and mutual aid, and the fight against poverty. These realities presuppose strong expectations from both internal (employees) and external stakeholders (NGOs, civil society, government) (The Global Compact/ILO, 2010; EC, 2011). Our results show that the companies studied are neither deaf nor impervious to these problems because they directly and indirectly affect the lives of their local subsidiaries. Their commitment is consistent with the logic of responsibility that is both philanthropic, ethical, legal and economic (Caroll, 1991). The mobilization by these companies of CSR action mechanisms can be understood as strong signals addressed to stakeholders. These social initiatives, derived from a utilitarian and opportunistic view of CSR (bottom of pyramid), can bring significant benefits to multinationals (Porter and Kramer, 2006; Prahalad, 2005). The assumption shared in the literature, although not empirically proven, is that CSR actions can have social and economic benefits. Our results reveal that within the firms studied, social expectations are new. They are relayed by the work values of a heterogeneous population and are characterized by a desire for well-being at work, employability and health at work. These results are in line with the literature on HRM and show that in terms of working conditions, short-term constraints, the obsession with results (case of the multinationals) and the need for training to develop its performance (case of SMEs) combine and reveal the pressure that still exists among managers and employees (Freudenberger, 1974; Bennett and Robinson, 2000). Another reading in relation to these results is the parallel comparison that can be made with the economic and cultural context and the technological advances in Africa. The expression of the new expectations of the employees is part of the movement of the emancipation of civil society not accustomed to making claims, and the phenomenon of development (opening to the world by television, tools of communication, globalization) which participates in changes in mentalities and freedom of expression in some cases. Our results in the two case studies illustrate the existence of pressures that are institutional (CSR principles in terms of working conditions, OHASAS standards), legal (labor code, employment contract), economic (productivity search) and local (employees, culture, new communication tools).

Our results show that the CSR action mechanisms uncovered by this research can contribute to a regulation located between global integration and local reactivity. Global integration is expressed through the standard principles and international certification standards of CSR. Local responsiveness is clearly demonstrated in targeted action mechanisms dedicated to employees, their families and civil society. These mechanisms give the stakeholders positive signals of ethical awareness of the management practices of the companies studied.

Conclusion and Managerial Proposals

This research, at the heart of African social and societal realities, makes it possible to conclude that CSR in Africa is a real challenge because it is at the center of managerial, social and cultural innovation. To meet the challenge without compromising competitiveness goals at the local level, we urge international companies to strengthen their proactive and utilitarian approach in the different areas of CSR.

The implementation of the CSR mechanism can be seen as a means of recognizing the human dimension in business management tools on the one hand, and as a mechanism for integrating values of solidarity and mutual aid in the management of firms—an anchor value at the heart of the social and cultural reality of African communities. Moreover, at the economic level, the employment of local employees by international companies reinforces their status and social rank among their communities and ultimately is a source of well-being for these communities.

Africa is marked by conflicts of all kinds, by various health crises, by terrorism, by political instability and so forth. In the particular case of Cameroon, the level of poverty is high, and people are struggle to pay health costs. The results of our study show initiatives by the multinational in respect of nutrition. To fight against poverty, NGOs and the international community encourage people toward solidarity in order to help poor countries or at-risk people. These institutions should go

114 *Suzanne M. Apitsa*

beyond solidarity mechanisms by creating or introducing educational tools on nutrition to reduce or even prevent degenerative diseases in these poor countries. The media (as is the case in developed countries) should also take charge of this responsibility. Companies in their commitment must support this change by investing more in advertising campaigns; they are also invited to go further by supporting employees in their local associations (tontines), which can serve as an efficient and close vector for the implementation of these actions. This will enhance their image as good citizens and humanists with civil society and other stakeholders.

This research no doubt has its limitations but, by this Cameroonian experience, it shows that CSR resonates in Africa through the realities facing African societies that challenge any individual or group actor and ask for their contribution.

Notes

1. The Washington Consensus is a program that emphasizes macroeconomic discipline, including fiscal discipline, market economy and openness to the world, and foreign direct investment in business.
2. A stakeholder is "any group or individual who can or is affected by the achievement of the goals of an organization. In the broad sense, the term includes suppliers, customers, shareholders, employees, communities, political groups; political authorities (national and territorial); the media, etc." (Freeman, 1984).

References

Adanhounme, A. B. (2015). "La gestion des ressources humaines et le problème de l'encastrement de l'entreprise en Afrique: l'exemple d'une mine au Ghana." *Revue Recherches en Sciences de Gestion*, 106, pp. 91–111.

Anglès, V., Apitsa, S. M. (2017). *CODIREL Cameroun: quelle stratégie pour la durabilité d'un modèle français de distribution au Cameroun?* Paris: Centrale des Cas et Médias Pédagogiques (CCMP), KEDGE-MI-004, December 30.

Apitsa, S. (2018). "Vers une responsabilisation totale des cadres locaux aux postes clés dans les multinationales en Afrique: rupture et innovation ou réduction des coûts liés à l'expatriation ?", 27 pages, 8ème Conférence Atlas Afmi, Continuité et ruptures en management international Atlas 10 ans déjà!», Paris.

Apitsa, S. M. (2013). "L'hybridation des pratiques de GRH à l'international par le truchement de l'ethnicité en Afrique." *Gérer et Comprendre*, 113, pp. 51–61.

Apitsa, S. M. (2019). "La responsabilité Sociale des Entreprises (RSE) des acteurs portuaires en Afrique: une grille de lecture en termes de défi environnemental." In M. Tchindjang, B. Steck, and A. Bopda (Eds.), *Construire la ville portuaire de demain en Afrique Atlantique*. Caen: EMS, pp. 415–438.

Arthaud-Day, M. L. (2005). "Transnational corporate social responsibility: A tridimensional approach to international CSR research." *Business Ethics Quarterly*, 15(1), pp. 1–22.

Barin Cruz, L., Pedrozo, A., Chebbi, H. (2008). "Le processus de formation d'une stratégie intégrée de développement durable entre siège et filiales: cas de deux

CSR Action Mechanisms 115

groupes français de la grande distribution." *Management International*, 12(2), pp. 81–96.

Bartlett, C. A., Ghoshal, S. (2002). "Building a competitive advantage through people." *Sloan Management Review*, Winter, pp. 34–41.

Bennett, R. J., Robinson, S. L. (2000). "Development of measure of workplace deviance." *Journal of Applied Psychology*, 85, pp. 349–360.

Boiral, O. (2008). "Les pays du sud à l'épreuve des normes ISO: vers un sous-développement durable?" *Management International*, 12(2), pp. 49–63.

Bondy, K., Starkey, K. (2014). "The dilemmas of internationalization: Corporate social responsibility in the multinational corporation." *British Journal of Management*, 25(1), pp. 4–22.

Brundtland, G. H. (ed.). (1987). *Our Common Future: Report of the World Commission on Environment and Development*. Oxford: Oxford University Press.

Carroll, A. B. (1979). "A three-dimensional conceptual model of corporate performance." *Academy of Management Review*, 4(4), pp. 497–505.

Carroll, A. B. (1991). "The pyramid of corporate social responsibility: Toward the moral management of organizational stakeholders." *Business Horizons*, 34(4), pp. 39–48.

Carroll, A. B. (1999). "Corporate social responsibility: Evolution of a definitional construct." *Business and Society*, 38(3), pp. 268–295.

Commission Européenne. (2011). *Responsabilité sociale des entreprises: Une nouvelle stratégie de l'UE pour la période 2011–2014*. https://eur-lex.europa.eu/LexUriServ/LexUriServ.do?uri=COM:2011:0681:FIN:FR:PDF.

Dartey-Baah, K., Amponsah-Tawiah, K., Agbeibor, V. (2015). "Corporate social responsibility in Ghana's national development." *Africa Today*, 62(2), pp. 71–92.

Deresky, H. (2008). *International Management: Managing Across Borders and Cultures*. Bombay: Pearson International.

Dia, M. (1996). *Africa's Management in the 1990s and Beyond: Reconciling Indigenous and Transplanted Institutions*. Washington, DC: World Bank.

D'Iribarne, P. (2003). *Le tiers-monde qui réussit: nouveaux modèles*. O. Jacob, Paris.

Freeman, R. E. (1984). *Strategic Management: A Stakeholders Approach*. Boston: Pitman.

Freudenberger, H. J. (1974). "Staff burn-out." *Journal of Social Issues*, 30(1), pp. 159–165.

Glazer, B., Strauss, A. (1967). *The Discovery of Grounded Theory: Strategies for Qualitative Research*. Chicago: Aldine.

Global Compact and ILT. (2010). *Les principes du travail du Pacte Mondial des Nations Unies: Guide pour les entreprises*. Genève, 53 pp.

Golli, A., Yahiaoui, D. (2009). "Responsabilité sociale des entreprises: analyse du modèle de Carroll (1991) et application au cas tunisien." *Management & Avenir*, 3(23), pp. 139–152.

Goodpaster, K., Matthews, J. B. (1983). "Can a corporation have a conscience?" In T. L. Beauchamp and N. E. Bowie (eds.), *Ethical Theory and Business*. Englewood Cliffs, NJ: Prentice-Hall, pp. 81–83.

Harison, V., Obrecht, J.-J. (2013). "Essai d'évaluation de la RSE dans les industries extractives: le cas du projet Ambatovy à Madagascar." In V. Carbone, S. Nivoix, and J.-P. Lemaire (eds.), *Nouveaux défis du management international*. Paris: Gualino Lextenso, pp. 244–263.

116   Suzanne M. Apitsa

Holme, R., Watts, P. (2000). *Corporate Social Responsibility: Making Good Business Sense*. Geneva: World Business Council for Sustainable Development, January.

Husted, B. W., Allen, D. B. (2006). "Corporate social responsibility in the multinational enterprise: Strategic and institutional approach." *Journal of International Business Studies*, 37, pp. 838–849.

International Organization for Standardization 26000. (2010). *Lignes directrices relatives à la responsabilité sociétale, traduction française de la version ISO 26000 de novembre* ["Participating in the Future International Standard ISO 26000 on Social Responsibility," ISO Central Secretariat: Geneva, 2006]. Paris: AFNOR, 145 pp.

Jaussaud, J., Schaaper, J. (2006). "Control mechanisms of the subsidiary by multinational firms: A multinational perspective." *Journal of International Management*, 12, pp. 23–45.

Kamdem, E. (2016). *Innovation entrepreneuriale et développement durable en Afrique: Défis et opportunités*. Paris: L'Harmattan.

Koleva, P., Gherib, J. (2012). "La responsabilité sociale des entreprises en Tunisie: une lecture institutionnaliste." *Revue Tiers Monde*, 212(4), pp. 83–99.

Kostova, T., Roth, K. (2002). "Adoption of an organizational practices by subsidiaries of multinationals corporation: Institutional and relational effects." *Academy of Management Journal*, 45, pp. 215–233.

Lado, H. (2016). "Les responsabilités sociétales obligatoires et volontaires des entreprises." *Revue française de Gestion*, 260, pp. 143–157.

Levermore, R. (2014). "Organizational geographies and corporate responsibility: A case study of Japanese multinational corporations operating in South Africa and Tanzania." *Journal of Corporate Citizenship*, 56, pp. 67–82.

Logsdon, J. M., Wood, D. J. (2002). "Business citizenship from domestic to global level of analysis." *Business Ethics Quarterly*, 12(2), pp. 155–187.

Martinet, A. C., Payaud, M. A. (2008). "Formes de RSE et entreprises sociales: une hybridation des stratégies." *Revue française de gestion*, 26(1), pp. 199–214.

Mayrhofer, U. (2011). "La gestion des relations siège-filiales. Un enjeu stratégique pour les multinationales." *Revue Française de Gestion*, 212(3), pp. 65–75.

Milliot, E., Freeman, S. (2015). *Case Study Research in Social Sciences: A Paradigmatic Alignment Framework*. 41th Annual Conference of the European International Business Academy (EIBA), Rio de Janeiro, Brazil, December 1–3, 24 pp.

Pasquero, J. (2005). "La responsabilité sociale de l'entreprise comme objet des sciences de gestion: le concept et sa portée." In M.F.B. Turcotte and A. Salmon (eds.), *Responsabilité sociale et environnementale de l'entreprise*. Québec: Presse de l'Université du Québec, pp. 112–143.

Pereira Pündrich, A., Mercuri, S. (2011). "La mise en oeuvre de la responsabilité sociale au sein des firmes multinationales: une analyse de Google en France et au Brésil." In U. Mayrhofer (ed.), *Le management des firmes multinationales*. Paris: Vuibert, pp. 243–258.

Pestre, F. (2011). "Construire une stratégie de responsabilité sociale de la firme multinationale: le cas du groupe Lafarge." *Revue française de gestion*, 212, pp. 109–125.

Pestre, F. (2014). "Les stratégies de RSE locale, globale et transnationale dans l'entreprise multinationale." *Management International*, 18, pp. 21–41.

Porter, M., Kramer, M. (2006). "Strategy and society: 'The link between competitive advantage and corporate social responsibility.'" *Harvard Business Review*, 84(12), pp. 78–92.

Prahalad, C. K. (2005). *The Fortune at the Bottom of the Pyramid.* Upper Saddle River, NJ: Wharton School.

Reed, D. (2002). "Employing normative stakeholder theory in developing countries: Critical theory perspective." *Business and Society*, 41(2), pp. 166–207.

Sparrow, P., Brewster, C., Chung, C. (2017). *Globalizing Human Resource Management.* London: Routledge.

Stiglitz, J. E. (2014). *Le prix de l'inégalité, édition traduite de "The Price of Inequality."* Arles: Babel.

Vig, S. (2016). "Corporate social responsibility in sub-Saharan Africa: Sustainable development in its embryonic form." *African Journal of Economic and Management Studies*, 7(3), pp. 434–437.

Welch, C., Piekkari, R., Plakoyiannaki, E., Paavilainen-Mäntymäki, E. (2011). "Theorizing from case studies: Towards a pluralist future for international business research." *Journal of International Business Studies*, 42(5), pp. 740–762.

Williamson, J. (1990). "What should the World Bank think about the Washington consensus?" *World Bank Research Observer*, 15(2), pp. 251–264.

Wood, D. (1991). "Corporate social performance revisited." *Academy of Management Review*, 16, pp. 691–718.

Yin, R. K. (2014). *Case Study Research: Design and Methods* (5th ed.). Los Angeles: Sage.

7 The Ethical Tools of Multinationals

A Proof of Cultural Diversity

Hamza Asshidi

Introduction

Business ethics has been a significant area of study since the 1970s (Allhoff, 2011), particularly from an international perspective; however, it takes relatively little account of the intercultural dimension. This research takes national contexts as given and compares them to assess their differences and similarities. Other studies have examined whether western value systems can be transposed to non-western contexts, such as the ethical virtues of MacIntyre from the United Kingdom to Sri Lanka (Fernando and Moore, 2015). Comparative studies on ethical tools have been developed to better adapt and manage intercultural relations in business and to solve ethical dilemmas (Moon and Williams, 2000). Here, the definition of an ethical tool, namely "ethical formalization," responds to "a double challenge: it allows the company to react to the pressures of its environment and constitutes a means of internal regulation" (Mercier, 2002). Within the framework of this chapter, these may include not only ethical charters but also corporate values, ethical training or corporate seminars. Some consider that ethical charters are a decoy (Holtzhausen, 2015), but overall, they are rather seen as tools that can, depending on their use and form, take on an insurance and risk prevention function, particularly legal ones (Adelstein and Clegg, 2016).

The existing research has focused mainly on the result but too little on the process of adapting tools to suit different cultures. In other words, there has been a strong focus so far on comparing different ethical tools existing internationally rather than on developing and implementing these tools in different cultural contexts. This is where the gap in the current literature lies. Ethical tools are not necessarily understood in the same way in a cultural context other than that of the native culture of a multinational company, where mores, traditions, conceptions of work, and interpersonal relations are sometimes very different (Buller and McEvoy, 1999). The way in which ethical tools are designed and then transposed in different countries from a cultural point of view, and consequently from an ethical point of view (Thorne and Sanders, 2002), remains insufficiently known.

The Ethical Tools of Multinationals   119

And yet, it is an essential element in improving the integration of the corporate cultures of multinationals into a global environment.

Buller and McEvoy (1999) show the need for multinationals to take into account the cultural and ethical differences that may exist between the different countries in which they operate. By analyzing the case of subsidiaries of large companies in Morocco and Mexico, D'Iribarne (2002) shows how universal, global ethical tools can be adapted locally to suit both employees and managers. From a similar perspective, it has been shown that subsidiaries of the same company may differently interpret the same ethical values promoted by the parent company (Barmeyer and Davoine, 2013). In addition, the difficulties that companies may encounter in implementing a code of ethics in a foreign subsidiary have also been highlighted (Helin and Sandström, 2008). In line with these studies, we propose the exploration regarding how ethical tools "travel" internationally within the same multinational company. Our central question can therefore be formulated as follows: how are ethical tools designed and implemented in a context of cultural diversity within multinational companies?

In order to answer this question, we will first present a literature review that shows the lack of research on this issue. We will then detail the methodology of this chapter based on seven exploratory cases of multinational companies and provide the results of the case studies. The chapter closes with a discussion on the results of the study, and the conclusion section provides some suggested areas for further research.

The Literature on Business Ethics: An Intercultural Perspective Still Insufficiently Studied

Business ethics is an area that is becoming increasingly important in the literature, but it has not been sufficiently studied in terms of cultural diversity.

Business Ethics and International Affairs: An Area of Growing Importance

Some trace the origin of ethics in business back to antiquity to the Greek philosopher Aristotle to show that it has evolved through time taking on different forms, and that it has developed through multiple themes such as sustainable development, ethical management, corruption, diversity and gender (Luetge, 2015). Business ethics is a sub-domain of ethics that aims to provide companies with an effective operating framework to guide managers in their daily work (Kolk and Van Tulder, 2004; Kaptein and Wempe, 2002), and thus provides an effective ethical framework. The modern origin of this research in business ethics can be dated back to the 1970s (Mele, 2015). More specifically, it dates back to the debate on corporate social responsibility (CSR) between Milton Friedman (1970), who believed that companies have no obligations in this area, and Robert E. Freeman (1984, 1994), who saw it as a duty to employees, consumers and the environment in particular (Allhoff and Vaidya, 2008a). CSR is a protean and rich concept that can take on and cover many different realities (Martinet and Payaud, 2007, 2013; Pesqueux, 2009). We will focus on its ethical aspect.

Over the decades, business ethics has become increasingly important in management science research. International trade and ethics are now more often studied together (Doh et al., 2010), which is a result of the decline in the power of nation states, the emergence of NGOs, the proliferation of self-regulatory bodies or the essential changes affecting multinationals themselves in terms of responsibilities, roles and structures (Doh et al., 2010).

One of the main reasons for the growing interest in ethics review tools is to be found in the United States. The Sarbanes-Oxley Act (SOX) of 2002 requires US and foreign companies (if listed on a stock exchange in the United States) to adopt significant internal control tools, particularly to limit the risk of financial fraud (Callaghan et al., 2012). The law also requires companies to declare the adoption of a code of ethics that encourages compliance with US law (Canary and Jennings, 2008); this code must be imposed on corporate finance managers. Companies must justify, if necessary, the absence of such a code. De facto, foreign subsidiaries of American companies have had to comply with this law, as have European companies listed in the United States, which has accelerated the dissemination of codes and ethical charters (Barmeyer and Davoine, 2007). This movement has been accompanied by the creation of positions such as company lawyer or "compliance officer" within many companies. These personnel are invested with organizing the implementation of ethics assessment tools, and to promote them, in order to prevent any legal or reputational risk to companies. In some cases, particularly in Europe, this task falls on human resources management departments, following a less than legal management approach. Thus, beyond the legal dimension, human resources management is becoming increasingly important in this field, explicitly linking international affairs and ethics.

Ethical Charters and Cultural Differences Between Countries

The notion of "culture" refers to the socialization within a group. It is often reduced to ethnic or national origins (Kirchmeyer and Cohen, 1992; Watson et al., 1993), referring to the nation in which a person has spent the longest and most formative part of their life (Hambrick et al., 1998). Nevertheless, culture can also refer to the socialization that takes place within all types of social groups (regional, religious, professional, social class, etc.), provided that its members collectively share some norms, values and traditions that differ from those of other groups (Cox, 1993). Thus, culture can be seen as a model of deeply rooted values and assumptions about social functioning

The Ethical Tools of Multinationals 121

that are shared by a group of interacting individuals (Geertz, 1973; Adler, 2002; Maznevski et al., 2006). These cultural values impact the perception, processing and interpretation of information and shape individual behaviors (Hambrick et al., 1998).

Some believe that universal and global ethical charters are fundamentally fake or a sham (Holtzhausen, 2015). Presented as objective and rational, charters are in fact a tool of power. Holtzhausen affirms that it should be preferred as an individual and contextualized morality in organizations, the only guarantee of ethics in the corporate environment. Several studies have sought to understand the very nature of ethical charters, their development and implementation processes. Thus, by studying the ethical charters of 50 large multinational companies in the field of child labor, Kolk and Van Tulder show that universalism does not prevail (2004).

Different key factors impact business ethics standards and attitudes in an intercultural context. National culture, in particular, serves as a social foundation that generates and shapes the interactions of institutional, organizational and personal factors. These three factors combined influence the perception of ethical standards in business in a unique way, considered unique to each culture (Stajkovic and Luthans, 1997). Therefore, the national cultural context is key to understanding business ethics and must be taken into consideration by multinationals. Research has shown how relevant the existence of a moral community within the company is to the definition of good and evil, based notably on the national culture shared by employees (D'Iribarne, 2003b).

The Ethical Standards of Multinationals Confronted With Globalization, a Poorly Addressed Subject

The need for multinationals to match their corporate ethics with the globalization of their activities has also been demonstrated by Talaulicar (2009), who highlights how the diversity of cultural and legal environments can create complications in the implementation of corporate ethics. The development and implementation of global ethical charters, which should be respected by all employees of a multinational company, is justified by legitimate arguments. However, difficulties may arise. This was the case for legal disputes involving Walmart and Honeywell when the latter implemented its ethical codes in its German subsidiaries (Talaulicar, 2009). Besides this chapter, only a few other works have really addressed this issue. D'Iribarne (2002) carries out a study fairly close to our study but focusing on two subsidiaries, owned by different companies and located in Mexico and Morocco, to illustrate the relevance of adapting multinationals' global ethical tools to foreign subsidiaries in order to give them meaning and enable employees from very different backgrounds to appropriate these tools. Similarly, D'Iribarne (2009) analyzes Lafarge's ethics charter to understand how this multinational company has deployed it in all its subsidiaries. Barmeyer

122 *Hamza Asshidi*

and Davoine (2013) analyzed how different subsidiaries of a multinational group can appropriate and interpret the values transmitted by their parent company. Thus, some ethical elements have been recontextualized by employees of a foreign subsidiary and have been understood differently from the meaning given to them in their initial cultural context (Barmeyer and Davoine, 2013). Then, Helin and Sandström (2008) highlighted the difficulties that a US company may encounter in implementing a code of ethics in a foreign subsidiary, in this case in Sweden; this empirical study sheds light on the national culture and a certain resistance by Swedish employees toward the parent company. They conclude that more emphasis should be placed on the process of implementing ethical charters than on their content. It is precisely this question of the process of implementing ethical tools that we focus on, in order to better understand how employees of a group's foreign subsidiaries can effectively and sustainably integrate these tools, despite given cultural differences.

Methodology and Results

Methodology: A Multi-case Exploratory Study

This chapter uses an inductive research design based on seven exploratory case studies of multinational companies.

This chapter aims to understand how multinationals develop and implement their ethical tools in a context of cultural diversity. It sheds light on the "journey" of these ethical tools and on their confrontation with the national cultures of the countries where they are established. We seek to

Table 7.1 Presentation of the multinationals interviewed

	Country of origin	Activities	International locations
A	United States	Semiconductor industry	Dozens of sites in 17 countries
B	France	Automotive industry	21 countries of operation
C	France	Engineering, consulting and project management	Dozens of sites in 40 countries
D	France	Plastics and chemistry	6 countries of operation
E	Switzerland	Pharmaceutical industry	140 countries of operation
F	Japan	Design and sale of office equipment	Established on 4 continents
G	France	Digital services	44 countries of operation

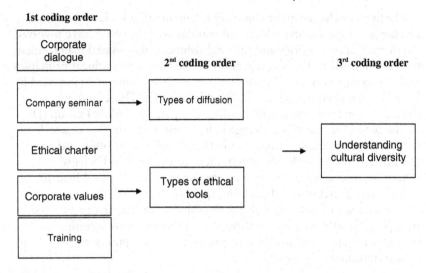

Figure 7.1 Coding scheme (extract)

better understand the opportunities and challenges created by the use of ethical tools by multinationals in culturally different countries.

It is therefore a question of starting in the field to better understand how actors conceive ethics, how they are implemented in an international perspective, and how they are implemented through standards that multinationals design and disseminate. This inductive logic (Bergadaa and Nyeck, 1992; Piekkari and Welch, 2011) has not been used much in our research field. It can contribute to providing a different and enriching insight into the concrete practices of companies and the more or less intuitive methodologies they use.

Depending on the company, we interviewed managers, human resources directors or ethics managers. Some companies have an ethical charter whereas some do not, and their forms vary between the different cases.

The interviews and corporate documentations were analyzed in the light of the international dimension of the companies to show how the subsidiaries were involved in the implementation of ethical tools and how employees in the different countries integrated these standards. Here is an excerpt of the coding undertaken.

Results

Whatever the context in which ethical tools are developed, cultural diversity never seems to be the main source. Two scenarios have been discovered, which can be briefly mentioned.

124 *Hamza Asshidi*

The first is a change in the company's structure that leads to the adoption or change of the company's ethical standards. This could have involved the merger of two entities and the establishment of a general management team, which led to the formalization of the company's ethical principles and values in a very detailed charter, as well as an imperative imposed by international donors such as the World Bank (C). This could also reflect the transition from a financial holding company to a global group (D).

The second scenario is a change in legislation as a driving or accelerating force for the implementation of ethical tools. Most often, although it has not always been clearly stated, there is a change in US legislation or otherwise Japanese legislation with the Japan-Sox (Financial Instruments and Exchange Act, promulgated in Japan in 2006) (F).

The first set of results analyzes the ethical tools that can be used to transpose the ethics of multinationals into their various subsidiaries. The second set focuses on how best to promote the acceptance of these tools by international employees.

General Values for a Relative Inclusion of Cultural Diversity

All the multinationals studied have formulated values that they seek to promote. The idea is to ensure that both employees and managers take ownership of them as best as possible. Two categories of companies can be identified: those that seek to take into account cultural differences in the countries in which they are located and those that do not specifically address this issue.

In the first category, companies seek to formulate and integrate corporate values that take into account cultural differences while trying to overcome them, that is, to implement these values globally to enable employees to work better together. Thus values can be directly linked to the company's vision and mission (A). In this company, these three elements are closely linked and articulated in a dedicated internal document, which is available to the entire group. Synthesized in one page, this document openly echoes the ethical charter. These values that were recently modified mean a change in corporate culture, itself linked to a change in strategy:

> What has changed a lot is not the values part. . . . in fact it is rather the strategic part that is different today. And when you have a change of strategy, in order to have the support of the staff and members of the company, you are obliged to reinforce your vision, your mission and your values. Because that's what the company is all about, that all the employees are all about!
>
> (A)

Similarly, some believe that it is in the "confrontation of different cultures that good practice can be followed and dictated" (C). This interviewee

The Ethical Tools of Multinationals   125

believes that this generates convergences that must be exploited to enable all employees to come together around these values that overlook and go beyond cultural differences. Often, these values are general enough to be adapted to the national cultures in which multinational subsidiaries are located (B), facilitating a form of ownership by employees around the world.

In the second category, companies consider that the values issued by the parent company are equally applicable in all countries where they are located, with no real desire to take cultural diversity into account. The interviews never really linked them to cultural diversity. In these companies, interviewees simply listed and described values but never linked them to cultural diversity (D, E, F). This is particularly true for Japanese companies, where corporate values are deeply rooted in this culture, are characteristic of the country and are very traditional. They are distributed as they stand to all subsidiaries with zeal, even if deviations have been allowed in the French site that was surveyed (F). Thus, during the French translation of the charter, French officials sought to deploy terminology and elements closer to the French reality and culture; the French version of the charter is a little longer and uses more precise wording to allow French employees to better integrate it, and thus compensate for the cultural differences that exist between the two countries (F).

Ethical Training to Transmit Ethical Tools by
Overcoming Cultural Differences

Systematic ethical training for all employees of multinationals contributes to some extent to overcoming cultural differences, as it seeks to spread the same corporate culture to employees from diverse cultural backgrounds. Indeed, it is a question of giving employees tools to enable them to integrate the company's culture, independently of their own national culture.

In some companies, general training is provided for all staff with an annual update (A and C). To ensure that each employee properly integrates the ethical charter, training in a computerized format is provided at the time of recruitment and is redone each year in a shorter format ("refresh") (A). Similarly, training can be provided to all employees, a "code of conduct recycling," to show employees "what is expected of them in terms of ethics and integrity" (E). The training courses can cover major ethical issues of the company (ethical charter, prevention of corruption, competition law) through e-learning modules when they join the group (G).

More targeted training also exists for specific groups of employees. They may, for example, be managers from all the group's subsidiaries who are following a specific training program with a HR department to help them to be in line with the company's values, referred to as an "ethical framework" (200 managers, B). Leadership and co-development training also exist, in line with the group's values, for people at all levels of the

126 Hamza Asshidi

hierarchy and from all the countries where the group operates. The aim is to reach this specific group of employees in all countries, targeting a representative proportion of employees (200 people, around 10%, D). This allows for a rich sharing of experiences and their transfer from the field to the parent company while integrating a maximum of cultural diversity.

The Engagement Survey, a Possible Tool for Taking Cultural Diversity Into Account

Surveys are also conducted among employees to solicit their opinions. In case D, a major engagement survey was implemented among all employees of the company. The aim was to assess employees' adherence to their group from a global point of view, insofar as "the adherence of management is considered essential for the action plans to be as adapted as possible at the local level" (D). This highlights the company's desire to take into consideration the reality of the sites and the countries where they are located, and therefore of the national culture. Indeed, after debriefings and feedback, an action plan was implemented in each site in a specific way in order to accurately reflect the views of the employees concerned. This can therefore make it possible to bring ethical measures into line with the cultural differences specific to each unit (D). The process is the same for all countries.

For Each Country, Its Own Ethical Charter for a Full Recognition of Cultural Diversity in the Service of Employees?

Overall, the ethical charters studied take relatively little account of cultural diversity; they are global, sufficiently general for a margin of interpretation according to cultures, but without any real importance given to the different national cultures. However, in one of the companies (G), the person in charge of the ethics section expresses his regret at the insufficient consideration of cultural differences in the company's ethical systems. Indeed, he speaks of the current ethical charter as a "1.0" charter and would like to move to a "2.0" charter (G). The latter, which could not be achieved due to a lack of resources and "maturity" of the company, should include the different national cultures and leave them a margin for adaptation and interpretation of values. Company G is even considering drafting an Indian code of ethics, because a very large part of its workforce is located in that country. According to this interviewee, personnel do not speak of the company's values in the same way in India as in France, and it is necessary to adapt the systems to the national cultures of the countries where the company is established. For the company this is not just a project; it is a necessity arising from the requirement to match the company's values with those of employees in a very different country. It is about "embedding the value system at the local level, in the Indian reality" (G). One of the examples of

The Ethical Tools of Multinationals   127

value selected by the interviewee is that of honesty, which differs depending on whether you look at it from a French or an Indian perspective. He believes that in India, what is important is "divine honesty," in the sense that it is dictated and promoted by religion, whereas in France, it is rather the individual who is at the center of ethical reasoning. An ethical charter for India would, in his view, allow a better match between the company's culture and India's national culture. It is a project in progress.

Putting Global Principles Into Practice:
A Full Integration of Cultural Diversity

Without going so far as to draw up an ethical charter for each country, companies can try to put their ethical principles into practice to ensure that they are better accepted and applied. Only one company has taken the initiative to do this (E). In France, and nowhere else in this group, a work of "putting values into practice" has been carried out to enable a "common management culture" (E). This "translation of values into concrete actions to have an impact on the management culture" (E) is all the more important as the group does not come from France but from Switzerland. Values are "each time translated into [behavioral] frameworks that are sufficiently standardized and precise" (E). It is to allow for a real integration of values by employees and managers, to avoid "subjective biases" (E) in the definition of values and to encourage the idea that there would be as many definitions as there are individuals. In addition, again with regard to the international component, the interviewee considers that at the group level, "you could not find a different definition of integrity or implementation of integrity in Germany or France" (E).

A Differentiated Cultural Understanding
of Ethical Risk Management

Ethical risks may not be perceived in the same way in different national cultures. Whether it is the country where the company operates (case C), or the different employee culture (case A), cultural differences seem to lead to a different understanding of ethical risks.

Some managers have highlighted the evolution of their organization's risk profile (C). The HRD interviewed pointed out that before the independence/merger and establishment of the group, the company was a subsidiary and reasoned in terms of "pooling risks, sheltered from a large company with a senior management," and could therefore be less ethical (provided that "big" scandals were avoided). The use of intermediaries to obtain contracts, to "subcontract these ethical issues" in countries in the South, Asia or Africa was rather opaque. Since becoming independent, the company must fully assume the risks (the HRD speaks of "awareness") and must therefore equip itself with ethical tools to prevent them.

128   Hamza Asshidi

Table 7.2 Key elements related to the ethics of the multinationals studied

	Case A	Case B	Case C	Case D	Case E	Case F	Case G
THE DESIGN: TAKING INTO ACCOUNT CULTURAL DIVERSITY IN THE OVERALL DEVELOPMENT OF THE ETHICAL SYSTEM							
Existence of precise values for the entire group	YES	YES	YES	YES	YES	YES	YES
Existence of a very detailed ethical charter for the whole group	YES	NO	YES	NO	NO	NO	YES
THE TRANSPOSITION: MODALITIES FOR TAKING INTO ACCOUNT CULTURAL DIVERSITY							
Consideration of the different countries of implementation for the development of ethical tools	YES	NO	YES	YES	NO	NO	NO
Existence of ethics-related training for staff from different countries	YES	YES	NO	YES	NO	YES	YES
Possibilities for adaptation margin for field actors	YES	YES	NO	YES	YES	NO	YES
THE RECEPTION: FROM THE POINT OF VIEW OF EMPLOYEES							
Existence of an ethical charter specific to a country of location	NO	NO	NO	NO	NO	NO	YES (ongoing)
Existence of a behavioral reference framework specific to a country of location	NO	NO	NO	NO	YES	NO	NO
Differentiated cultural understanding of ethical risk management	YES	NO	YES	NO	NO	NO	NO

The *Ethical Tools of Multinationals* 129

Whether it is corruption, conflicts of interest or otherwise, ethics can help to avoid abuses.

Clearly legal risks are also mentioned regarding the need for its employees to have work visas when travelling for professional purposes.

One of the main consequences of ethical risks, beyond the legal dimension, is measured in terms of the company's image and the way it suffers from it. Indeed, image and reputation are a precious asset for the multinationals studied.

Thus, the unavoidable nature of the impact of ethical behavior on reputation and brand image was highlighted (A). In the form of questions, the interviewees (A) ask themselves: "What will be the brand image I will give to the whole world as an international company?" "What will I lose as a business if my business is not ethical today?" The idea is that this must be taken into consideration, in an invariable and systematic way, even in countries where ethics are different or simply less important. It is therefore necessary to take care to preserve its ethical image, even if the ethical standards of the culture of the country where the company works may appear less demanding. In this respect, cultural differences should not be an excuse or a reason to diminish the need to act ethically; on the contrary, the idea of exemplarity and the importance of reputation are clearly defended by several of the people interviewed.

Discussion

Ethical Tools for Strategic Risk Management

Generally, the resources allocated to ethics vary greatly depending on the companies studied. This is independent of the size or structure of the company. This clearly raises the question of the strategic dimension of ethics for companies, which is difficult to assess in itself.

Yet several studies have clearly shown the validity of and even the need to make business ethics a strategic focus (Hosmer, 1994; Key and Popkin, 1998). It was also highlighted that much of the business ethics literature considers that ethics must be clearly and substantially integrated into the company's overall strategy, not only to contribute to its success but also to allow positive impacts on all stakeholders (Noland and Phillips, 2010). Other research, such as that conducted by Martinuzzi and Krumay (2013), has also focused on providing guidance on the different steps that can be taken to gain comparative advantages in ethics and to introduce organizational transformations that can improve business performance.

This strategic dimension of ethics lies in the way multinationals understand risk. The literature has shown that ethical charters can sometimes in reality follow a logic of control and risk management rather than a logic of human resources management. By mixing legal, ethical and corporate interests, in particular, we can manage to generate situations within a group where it is difficult to discern what is exclusively ethical and what concerns risk issues. This type of configuration implies that any misconduct from an ethical point of view leads to misconduct from a risk management point of view, generating potential power effects that could be sanctioned (Adelstein and Clegg, 2016). This shows how ethical charters can have real implications for employees and represent tools that are binding and that must be respected. This can already be difficult to integrate into a site with the same national culture as the parent company but can be even more complicated when it is a subsidiary located in another country, with another culture. More generally, risks must lead to an understanding of ethics as a field in its own right; ethics should be recognized as concrete, precise and effective, and not simply cosmetic, because the demands of consumers and stakeholders in general are pressing and must be satisfied in the interest of multinationals (Flipo, 2007).

The study also shows that the strategic dimension of risk also deals with the concern for image expressed by multinationals. Thus, and the literature has often highlighted this (Fombrun et al., 2000; Bartlett and Preston, 2000; Tian and Slocum, 2016), the company's reputation is essential, and it must be protected at all costs because the consequences of a scandal, of whatever nature, can be disastrous.

Managing People With Cultural Diversity

The engagement survey as a tool shows how employee engagement can play an essential role in the proper functioning of the company and in compliance with its ethical principles. This shows that ethics facilitate a better adherence to the company's operations while allowing it to evolve according to the feedback that management, both local and global, receives from employees. By seeking to give a voice to employees who are sometimes geographically distant from the parent company, which does not share their national culture and which does not know them except through the company's ethical tools and values, we can give them a voice and generate concrete changes that will lead to better integration into the organization.

In addition, training is also of crucial importance in the implementation of ethical tools. Thus we have clearly shown how important training is in the ethical arrangements of some of the multinationals studied. The idea of training is discussed in the literature, which shows that it is the best way to give a concrete dimension to principles that may seem distant. This is what D'Iribarne et al. (2010) assert by analyzing the Chinese subsidiary of the Lafarge group, which showed how the multinational Lafarge implemented its corporate values while adapting them to the Chinese context, in particular through investment in training.

This has made it possible to give substance to these values and to generate a good image of the company and its ideals and practices in a Chinese

The Ethical Tools of Multinationals 131

context that is often difficult to understand in this respect (D'Iribarne et al., 2010).

Ethics, a Translation of Parent Company/Subsidiary Relationships

In all our cases, the first impulse and the development of ethical measures follow a vertical logic from the parent company to the subsidiaries, with real importance consecrated to the will of the group's management to equip itself with these tools. What differs, however, is the degree of autonomy or the flexibility left by the parent companies to their subsidiaries in terms of ethics.

Overall, little work has been undertaken showing in general terms the means used by multinationals to effectively control their subsidiaries abroad, despite the fact that this issue remains central (Jaussaud and Schaaper, 2006). The latter have generally shown how difficult it is to strike a balance between the various possible control instruments and the countries where multinationals operate (Jaussaud and Schaaper, 2006). Our chapter focuses on ethical instruments, which have been even less studied in the literature and which, surprisingly, do not appear at all in Jaussaud and Schaaper (2006), despite their desire to encompass all the instruments that would allow a parent company to control its subsidiaries. However, important works exist on this subject. Barmeyer and Davoine (2013) have shown in particular that even if parent companies strive to develop and disseminate their ethical measures throughout their subsidiaries, the interpretation of the latter may differ according to the cultures of the countries where they operate.

Moreover, even if the ethical tools of the multinationals studied do not always reflect this, management clearly has in mind the importance of cultural differences and the need to better understand them. Not only does management know, as it regularly faces the difficulties cultural differences can generate, but managers also perceive the impact on the proper functioning of the company. Whether operating in poor countries where ethics are not always the primary concern or simply in national cultures radically different from the parent company, the confrontation of cultures often generates difficulties that are imposed on human resources representatives and managers. This is why the idea of ethical tools, such as a dedicated ethical charter, especially designed by the parent company for subsidiaries located in culturally different countries, is relevant. An ethical code adapted to a given national culture may indeed seem to be in line with the ideas developed by D'Iribarne (2003a, 2003b), who insists on the fact that there are moral communities within multinational corporate subsidiaries that are based in particular on the national culture of the site, and which generate concepts of good and evil clearly identified and shared by

132   *Hamza Asshidi*

employees. By taking into consideration the cultural context, decision makers within the company can succeed in developing a strong corporate culture where ethics are understood by all employees and applied by them with good will. These examples fully illustrate the actors' awareness of ethics, human resources and management, which is that cultural differences, beyond being a potential constraint, can be understood in such a way as to become a constructive and enriching contribution for companies internationally.

We have seen that in each of the companies, the degree of adaptation of ethical measures varies. Some have the same tools everywhere and apply them in the same way, whereas others allow subsidiaries, willy-nilly, a real margin for adaptation. The management sciences literature can give us some insights into these different cases. Perlmutter's work in this area can be enlightening. Perlmutter's (1969) ERPG (ethnocentric, regiocentric, polycentric and geocentric) model provides us with an analytical framework to understand the different options available to multinationals in their international development. The three main configurations (ethnocentric, polycentric and geocentric) can provide us with a relevant framework for understanding the ways in which multinational companies develop ethical tools in their various subsidiaries. A company may choose to keep the same ethical standards for all subsidiaries, regardless of their country of implantation, considering, for example, that the corporate culture must be the same for all (ethnocentric logic). On the other hand, the multinational may consider that cultural differences are so strong that ignoring them would be counterproductive. It can thus move toward a polycentric configuration, leaving much more flexibility in terms of CSR to its subsidiaries, to better adapt to cultural realities on the ground (polycentric logic). But whatever the configuration, it must be said that the diffusion of corporate ethical standards is not obvious, and that these different ethical outlooks are theoretical and never absolutely present in a company.

Other authors, following Perlmutter, distinguish three possible configurations of strategic international human resources management (Taylor et al., 1996): a global strategy through the export of human resources management and universal ethical standards; multi-domestic strategies through the adaptation of human resources management; and a transnational strategy through the integration of human resources management and cosmopolitan ethics (Kolk and Van Tulder, 2004).

The two theories are quite similar and show that the literature can help to better identify the most appropriate and balanced ethical configurations between parent company and subsidiaries. This shows the need to study in a detailed and interactive way the parent company/subsidiary relationships, which is the only way to understand how and to what extent cultural differences exist, and especially how this improves the performance of these companies.

Conclusion

In several of the cases studied, real efforts or at least a real willingness have been expressed to take better account of the different countries and national cultures in which companies operate. Whether this consideration is already implemented or only for the time being desired and under development, cultural diversity is a reality that managers, human resources executives or ethical managers are confronted with and wish to respond to as effectively as possible. This chapter provides a rather detailed description of the mechanisms by which ethical tools can be developed, disseminated, and implemented in the multinationals studied.

Due to its exploratory nature, this study gives only a small insight into the field reality in this area. Indeed, each time, only one or two interviewees were solicited. In addition, they may have been in different positions, ranging from human resources responsibility to managerial or ethical responsibility. These elements are inherent in any exploratory study, which in no way claims to be exhaustive but which allows us to glimpse new and subtle elements regarding the implementation of ethical tools. Another limitation is the fact that some interviewees work at the headquarters or in the same country (and therefore have the same culture) as the latter, whereas in other interviews the interviewees work in a subsidiary, and therefore in a different cultural environment from that of the parent company.

In the future, it would be necessary to carry out in-depth case studies to clearly understand the different ways in which ethical tools are implemented in all subsidiaries of multinationals. This exploratory study has highlighted different scenarios that need to be better defined, detailed and analyzed to understand how cultural differences hinder, or on the contrary, help to define a global corporate culture.

References

Adelstein, J., Clegg, S. (2016). "Code of ethics: A stratified vehicle for compliance." *Journal of Business Ethics*, 138(1), pp. 53–66.

Adler, N. (2002). *International Dimensions of Organizational Behavior*. Cincinnati: South-Western.

Allhoff, F. (2011). "What are applied ethics?" *Science and Engineering Ethics*, 17(1), pp. 1–19.

Allhoff, F., Vaidya, A. J. (eds.). (2008a). *Business Ethics*. Calgary: Broadview Press.

Barmeyer, C. I., Davoine, E. (2007). "Les résistances européennes aux codes de conduite nord-américains: une étude de cas franco-allemande." *Revue Sciences de Gestion*, 60, pp. 51–74.

Barmeyer, C. I., Davoine, E. (2013). "'Traduttore, Traditore'? La réception contextualisée des valeurs d'entreprise dans les filiales françaises et allemandes d'une entreprise multinationale américaine." *Management International/International Management/Gestión Internacional*, 18(1), pp. 26–39.

134 *Hamza Asshidi*

Bartlett, A., Preston, D. (2000). "Can ethical behaviour really exist in business?" *Journal of Business Ethics*, 23(2), pp. 199–209.

Bergadaa, M., Nyeck, S. (1992). "Recherche en marketing, un état des controverses." *Recherche et Applications en Marketing*, 7(3), pp. 23–44.

Buller, P. F., McEvoy, G. M. (1999). "Creating and sustaining ethical capability in the multi-national corporation." *Journal of World Business*, 34(4), pp. 326–343.

Callaghan, M., Wood, G., Payan, J. M., Singh, J., Svensson, G. (2012). "Code of ethics quality: An international comparison of corporate staff support and regulation in Australia, Canada and the United States." *Business Ethics: A European Review*, 21(1), pp. 15–30.

Canary, H. E., Jennings, M. M. (2008). "Principles and influence in codes of ethics: A centering resonance analysis comparing pre- and post-Sarbanes-Oxley codes of ethics." *Journal of Business Ethics*, 80(2), pp. 263–278.

Cox, T. H. (1993). *Cultural Diversity in Organizations: Theory, Research and Practice*. San Francisco: Berrett-Koehler.

D'Iribarne, P. (2002). "Motivating workers in emerging countries: Universal tools and local adaptations." *Journal of Organizational Behavior*, 23(3), pp. 243–256.

D'Iribarne, P. (2003a). "Des pratiques de gestion modernes enracinées dans les cultures du tiers-monde." *Présence Africaine*, 167/168, pp. 27–35.

D'Iribarne, P. (2003b). "The combination of strategic games and moral community in the functioning of firms." *Organization Studies*, 24(8), pp. 1283–1307.

D'Iribarne, P. (2009). *L'épreuve des différences, l'expérience d'une entreprise mondiale*. Paris: Seuil.

D'Iribarne, P., Taillefer, G., Tréguer-Felten, G. (2010). "In China, between Guanxi and the celestial bureaucracy." *Annales des Mines—Gérer et comprendre*, 100, pp. 37–47.

Doh, J., Husted, B. W., Matten, D., Santoro, M. (2010). "Ahoy there! Toward greater congruence and synergy between international business and business ethics theory and research." *Business Ethics Quarterly*, 20(3), pp. 481–502.

Fernando, M., Moore, G. (2015). "MacIntyrean virtue ethics in business: A cross-cultural comparison." *Journal of Business Ethics*, 132(1), pp. 185–202.

Flipo, J.-P. (2007). "L'éthique managériale peut-elle n'être qu'un facteur stratégique?" *Revue Française de Gestion*, 180, pp. 73–88.

Fombrun, C. J., Gardberg, N. A., Barnett, M. L. (2000). "Opportunity platforms and safety nets: Corporate citizenship and reputational risk." *Business and Society Review*, 105(1), pp. 85–106.

Freeman, R. E. (1984). *Strategic Management: A Stakeholder Approach*. London: Pitman.

Freeman, R. E. (1994). "The politics of stakeholder theory." *Business Ethics Quarterly*, 4(4), pp. 409–421.

Friedman, M. (1970). "The social responsibility of business is to increase its profits." *New York Times Magazine*.

Geertz, C. (1973). *The Interpretation of Cultures: Selected Essays*. New York: Basic Books.

Hambrick, D. C., Canney Davison, S., Snell, S. A., Snow, C. C. (1998). "When groups consist of multiple nationalities: Towards a new understanding of the implications." *Organization Studies*, 19(2), pp. 181–205.

The Ethical Tools of Multinationals 135

Helin S., Sandström J. (2008). "Codes, ethics and cross-cultural differences: Stories from the implementation of a corporate code of ethics in a MNC subsidiary." *Journal of Business Ethics*, 82(2), pp. 281–291.

Holtzhausen, D. R. (2015). "The unethical consequences of professional communication codes of ethics: A postmodern analysis of ethical decision-making in communication practice." *Public Relations Review*, 41(5), pp. 769–776.

Hosmer, L. T. (1994). "Strategic planning as if ethics mattered." *Strategic Management Journal*, 15(2), pp. 17–34.

Jaussaud, J., Schaaper, J. (2006). "Control mechanisms of their subsidiaries by multinational firms: A multidimensional perspective." *Journal of International Management*, 12(1), pp. 23–45.

Kaptein, M., Wempe, J. (2002). *The Balanced Company: A Theory of Corporate Integrity*. Oxford: Oxford University Press.

Key, S, Popkin, S. J. (1998). "Integrating ethics into the strategic management process: Doing well by doing good." *Management Decision*, 36(5), pp. 331–338.

Kirchmeyer, C., Cohen, A. (1992). "Multicultural groups." *Group & Organization Management*, 17(2), pp. 153–170.

Kolk, A., Van Tulder, R. (2004). "Ethics in international business: Multinational approaches to child labor." *Journal of World Business*, 39(1), pp. 49–60.

Luetge, C. (2015). "Business ethics." In *International Encyclopedia of the Social & Behavioral Sciences* (2nd ed.), 3, pp. 15–20.

Martinet, A. C., Payaud, M. A. (2007). *Stratégies de Responsabilité Sociale de l'Entreprise (R.S.E.) et Entreprise Sociale*. Formes et limites de coopérations hybrides. Première Conférence Mondiale de Recherche en Economie Sociale du CIRIEC, Canada (hal-00363813).

Martinet, A. C., Payaud, M. A. (2013). *RSE: Le foisonnement des pratiques commande un retour sur les fondamentaux*. (halshs-00806999), 1–25.

Martinuzzi, A., Krumay, B. (2013). "The good, the bad, and the successful—How corporate social responsibility leads to competitive advantage and organizational transformation." *Journal of Change Management*, 13(4), pp. 424–443.

Maznevski, M. L., Canney Davison, S., Jonsen, K. (2006). "Global virtual team dynamics and effectiveness." In G. K. Stahl and I. Björkman (eds.), *Handbook of Research in International Human Resource Management*. Cheltenham: Edward Elgar, 364–384.

Mele, D. (2015). "Religious approaches on business ethics: Current situation and future perspectives." *Ramon Llull Journal of Applied Ethics*, 6, pp. 137–160.

Mercier, S. (2002). "Une typologie de la formalisation de l'éthique en entreprise: l'analyse de contenu de 50 documents." *Revue de Gestion des Ressources Humaines*, 43, pp. 34–49.

Moon, C. J., Williams, P. (2000). "Managing cross cultural business ethics." *Journal of Business Ethics*, 27(1/2), pp. 105–115.

Noland, J., Phillips, R. (2010). "Stakeholder engagement, discourse ethics and strategic management." *International Journal of Management Reviews*, 12(1), pp. 39–49.

Perlmutter, H. (1969). "The tortuous evolution of the multinational corporation." *Columbia Journal of World Business*, 4(1), pp. 9–18.

Pesqueux, Y. (2009). "La responsabilité sociale de l'entreprise: un dialogue sans interlocuteur?" *Vie sociale*, 3, pp. 137–154.

136 Hamza Asshidi

Piekkari, R., Welch, C. (eds.). (2011). *Rethinking the Case Study in International Business and Management Research*. Cheltenham: Edward Elgar.

Stajkovic, A. D., Luthans, F. (1997). "Business ethics across cultures: A social cognitive model." *Journal of World Business*, 32(1), pp. 17–34.

Talaulicar, T. (2009). "Barriers against globalizing corporate ethics: An analysis of legal disputes on implementing U.S. codes of ethics in Germany." *Journal of Business Ethics*, 84(3), pp. 349–360.

Taylor, S., Beechler, S., Napier, N. (1996). "Toward an integrative model of strategic international human resource management." *Academy of Management Review*, 21(4), pp.959–985.

Thorne, L., Sanders, S. B. (2002). "The socio-cultural embeddedness of individuals' ethical reasoning in organizations (cross-cultural ethics)." *Journal of Business Ethics*, 35(1), pp. 1–14.

Tian, X., Slocum, J. W. (2016). "Managing corporate social responsibility in China." *Organizational Dynamics*, 45(1), pp. 39–46.

Watson, W. E., Kumar, K., Michaelsen, L. K. (1993). "Cultural diversity's impact on interaction process and performance: Comparing homogeneous and diverse task groups." *Academy of Management Journal*, 36(3), pp. 590–602.

8 The Long March of the CSR in China

From Confucius to the Teachings of Business Schools

Gildas Lusteau and Isabelle Barth

Introduction

This chapter describes and interprets the challenges and evolution of corporate social responsibility (CSR) in China. As the basis of CSR theory is nowadays clear in western societies, we decided to turn our attention to the case of China. Between attachment to traditional Confucian thinking, the political transition from the Maoist era to the opening up to the West advocated by Deng Xiaoping from the end of the 1970s that gave multinational firms access to the country, we begin by examining how Chinese society has evolved over the course of its history and the emergence of the concept of corporate social responsibility.

In the second part of the chapter, we examine the premise of a generational split in China. We show that the post-'80s generation, known as the "ME generation," the result of the one-child per family policy initiated by Deng Xiaoping in 1978, is often considered by older generations as individualistic and arrogant. Interacting through social media and exposed to change, these young people nonetheless show signs of being open to the world, displaying the entrepreneurial skills essential to the transformation of the country's economy.

In the final section, we review the values of Chinese students through an online survey. Our study compares some of our findings with those obtained from young French people.

From Confucius to Xi Jinping, a Political/Cultural Concept of CSR in China

Confucian Influence on Modern Chinese Society

Confucianism is a long-established tradition in Chinese society. Confucius (551–479 BC), a government official famous for his immense wisdom, passed on his teachings to his many disciples throughout his life. He is considered as China's most important philosopher and the person who has had the biggest influence on Chinese civilization. His

138 *Gildas Lusteau and Isabelle Barth*

doctrine, which became the state religion under the Han dynasty (206 BC–AD 220), has been linked to other schools of thought, such as Taoism, the school of nominalism, Legalism during the Warring States period (403–256 BC) and then Buddhism from the 1st century AD. Under the Song dynasty (960–1279), there was a resurgence of interest in Confucianism—which was called neo-Confucianism and was based on a Taoist and Buddhist-inspired model—while at the same time criticizing them (Wang 2011:18:69–67).

Linked to Taoism and Chan Buddhism, Confucianism had an influence on the trading practices of traditional Chinese society (Li-Wen, 2010). During the 16th and 18th centuries, under the Ming and Qing dynasties, these aspects of Chinese philosophy helped to establish a culture of honesty and charity in the business world and prompted a desire to contribute to the development of society. Many businessmen, mainly from the provinces of Shanxi and Anhui, set aside part of their wealth to build roads, shelters and schools for the poorest in society and began to take up social functions that had previously been discharged by local governments.

During the nationalist movement of May 4, 1919, mainly directed against the Japanese Empire, and during the Cultural Revolution led by Mao from 1966 to 1976, Confucianism became taboo and was harshly repressed across the country (Chan, 2008).

The doctrine made a remarkable recovery in the 1980s and the beginning of the 1990s before once again being disparaged during the economic crisis that affected some Asian countries in the middle of the 1990s and being blamed for its role in cases of cronyism and nepotism (Chan, 2008). Despite this, at the beginning of the 21st century Confucianism remained deeply entrenched in Chinese society, especially within the family, and Hu Jintao went so as far as to couch the slogans of his presidency (2002–2012) in Confucian vocabulary when expressing his determination to build a "harmonious society."

The notion of *benevolence*, or *ren* in Chinese (仁), is at the heart of Confucian thinking (Redfern and Crawford, 2004). In the translation of the *Analects* of Confucius by Anne Cheng (1981), the concept of *ren* holds a central place.

According to Faure and Fang (2008), "Chinese society has been governed by the primacy of man as opposed to the primacy of law." In their study on the relationship between culture and management in China, Child and Warner (2003) note the importance of Confucian thinking and the idea that moral education supersedes the notion of law.

Thus, the West opted for governance by law, a model previously praised by Aristotle, whereas China chose governance by man. In today's China, the importance given to trust forged by interpersonal relations between people (*guanxi*) remains very strong, as opposed to the primacy of contracts in the West.

The Long March of the CSR in China 139

From Mao to Deng Xiaoping: Precepts of a Chinese Style CSR

The Maoist Era

In contrast to the traditional Confucian hierarchy of relationships, Mao opted for an egalitarian ideology: "There where Confucianism instilled loyalty to the family, the father and the emperor, Maoism turned it towards the people, the Party and the leader" (Fairbank and Reischauer, 1978, cited by Whitcomb, Erdener and Li, 1998). This view was particularly prevalent during the Cultural Revolution (1966–1976), when power was given to individuals who criticized their superiors and denounced their friends and members of their family who failed to respect the political thinking of the time. During this major event in Chinese history, the only legitimate objective of every organization was to "serve the people."

After coming to power in 1949, Chairman Mao introduced a policy that could be qualified as xenophobic (Global Alliance, 2004), aimed at gradually moving away from the western world and the Soviet model in order to construct a "third path," a unique model between liberalism and state control (Séhier, 2010). After the fiasco of the Great Leap Forward (1958–1960) and the misery caused by the proletarian Cultural Revolution launched by Mao in a bid to destroy traditional Chinese culture and values (Child and Warner, 2003), the People's Republic of China, then totally isolated economically (Darigan and Post, 2009), subsequently became one of the fastest growing economies in the world, quickly catching up with other nations to become a major economic driving force.

In Maoist China, work and private life were controlled by the place of employment alone (*danwei*), in respect of which every employee had to prove themselves both loyal and irreproachable (Faure and Fang, 2008). The *danwei* unit, which held a vital place in the country's economic and social decisions, partially explains why, for many years, the right to work was "virtually non-existent" and unnecessary given that "all professional—and personal—relations were subject to administrative rules applied within the framework of *danwei*" (Huchet, 2007).

It is interesting to link the context of *danwei* with the precept of corporate social responsibility via the system of the "iron rice bowl," introduced in 1949 when the communists came to power and proclaimed the People's Republic of China on October 1 of the same year. Implemented under Mao in the newly nationalized enterprises, this guaranteed workers and employees "a job for life, free healthcare, and a pension or free education for everyone for real social protection" (ORSE, 2006), as well as "special access to rice" for peasants within the "People's Commune" (Séhier, 2010)."

140 Gildas Lusteau and Isabelle Barth

Transition and Opening to the World of Capitalism Under Deng Xiaoping

Following the death of Mao (the "Great Helmsman") on September 9, 1976, Deng Xiaoping gained the trust of his peers and became the new leader of China at the 11th Central Committee Congress of the Chinese Communist Party in December 1978. Admitted to the United Nations Organization in October 1971, the People's Republic of China, led by its new leader, was finally recognized by the United States in 1979. After UNESCO, the International Labour Organization (ILO) opened its first office in Peking in 1984, although in a climate of distrust with regard to foreign institutions. Between 1978 and 1993, its reforms allowed the country to multiply the amount of its foreign capital by a factor of 15 (Global Alliance for Workers and Communities, 2004). The culmination of this economic and diplomatic strategy was finally celebrated when on December 11, 2001, China became the 143rd member of the World Trade Organization (WTO) (Séhier, 2010).

Considered as the great reformer of China, Deng Xiaoping opened the doors of the country to the global market and foreign investment from the West. This "great economic leap forward," with firms entering the country with foreign capital, the partial or total privatization of a large number of enterprises and the emergence of a private sector (ORSE, 2006), meant the country went from a "planned" economy to a so-called socialist market economy (Darigan and Post, 2009).

During this period of economic reform, Maoist ideology was heavily criticized. In companies, the incentive system that helped them to achieve a certain level of productivity was entirely revised (Whitcomb, Erdener and Li, 1998). From then on, instead of putting moral pressure on employees, the leaders introduced material rewards in order to boost motivation and performance. Pursuit of profit became the main goal, creating a "new ethic market" that ran counter to the former principles dictated by Confucian values and Maoist thinking.

For Faure and Fang (2008), the new leader was an incarnation of the Chinese paradox and its people's unique capacity to juggle endless contradictions: learning and adapting to open up to the world, while simultaneously resistant and asserting its culture and strong values. Faure and Fang liken it to the yin/yang philosophy still found in contemporary society. Deng Xiaoping regularly played with these paradoxes during his years in power, promoting, as the authors note, "one state, two systems," "the socialist market economy" and "stability and development."

Among the adverse effects of the reforms introduced by the "Little Helmsman," this sudden desire for wealth by individuals in the 1990s was built on a short-term view "in complete contradiction with sustainable development and a 'harmonious society'" (ORSE, 2006).

Western Influence on Chinese organizations

Whereas the reforms embraced in the 1970s lifted several hundreds of millions of individuals out of poverty, the 1980s were characterized by "first development, then environment." In China, some saw CSR as a western concept that would weaken the country's productivity by increasing production costs and creating non-tariff barriers following its membership of the WTO in December 2001.

Cramer and Westgaard (2005) point out that American and European companies developed in the last two centuries without having to face any real obstacles, and often benefited from circumstances that served them well, like colonialism. Now they could focus on Asia, the true "El Dorado of the East," the land of "cheap, abundant labour, malleable regulatory and enforcement regimes, and new markets," citing Walmart as an example.

According to Li-Wen (2010), for consumers, "Made-in-China" products are synonymous with low price, poor quality and questionable production processes at a time when western consumers, especially Europeans and Americans, are increasingly turning to products made in a socially and environmentally responsible way. Added to the problems of pollution and the many scandals recently published in the media, Li-Wen considers that these factors constitute the main driver for the development of CSR in China, and that state-owned enterprises have to learn from the experience and draw inspiration from the actions of foreign entities in the field. However, while suppliers need to understand and engage in CSR in order to win tenders from international groups, the pressure that multinational firms put on them is reversed to some extent by the media spotlight they receive. The author gives several examples to illustrate this: Häagen-Dazs was criticized for its unhygienic kitchens, Kentucky Fried Chicken (KFC) for the use of an illegal red food coloring, and Nestlé for a dangerous application of iodine in its infant food preparations.

Jaussaud and Liu consider that "the aims of multinationals that invest in China vary, but generally combine the search for cheap labour and access to a high potential market" (2006). The two authors note the challenges that foreign firms have to contend with in terms of human resources, especially given the specific "cultural and institutional" factors and the challenges in recruiting qualified managerial staff.

In this context of diversification of direct investment flows, Jaussaud and Mayrhofer (2013) examined the inherent "global-local tensions." Faced with the disparity of environments in which organizations choose to develop their activities, the authors stress the importance of taking local peculiarities into account, "including when a business strives to promote a global approach to its markets."

142 *Gildas Lusteau and Isabelle Barth*

Evolution of the Chinese Legislative Framework

Jean-François Huchet (2007) conducted a study on changes to labor laws and social rights in China. For him, China has significantly developed its legal system since the beginning of the 1990s. Huchet notes that "since the labour laws and unions were introduced in 1995 and 2002, Chinese workers have benefitted from theoretical protection that, while not yet up to international standards, is by no means insignificant." However, he regrets the severe shortcomings in the application of these laws, linked in particular to the Chinese Communist Party (CCP), which is omnipresent "at every stage of the law-making process and monitoring of its application, the lack of independence of the legal system, local cronyism, the absence of independent unions, as well as the authoritarian nature of the political regime." Since the advent of the communist regime, the legal situation has moved slowly in line with changes to the political and economic framework.

The Labour Law of July 5, 1994, which came into force on January 1, 1995, is an example of the "desire for unification of the law" (Huchet, 2007). Seen by many as a unique Labour Code consistent with the constitution, it "protects the legitimate rights and interests of workers, realigns labour relations, develops and defends a labour system adapted to a socialist market economy, and promotes economic development and social progress" (article 1). According to the author, by 2002 the Labour Law of 1994 only helped to protect 36.5% of the working Chinese population, excluding various, often large categories, like migrant workers (*mingongs*) and agricultural workers.

The Labour Law of 1994 also called for an employment contract to be drawn up between the employer and the employee (articles 16 and 19) to include seven mandatory elements (article 19): "the length of the contract, the position, the conditions, the salary, the firm's field of business, termination of the contract, and responsibilities in the event of breach of contract."

Li-Wen (2010) discussed at length the link between the "Company Law" Act of 1994 and the development of CSR in China. According to the author, the country's traditional socialist ideology was supported by the workers, whereas "the Constitution of the People's Republic of China establishes that the country is governed by the proletariat and founded on the alliance between workers and peasants." These workers formed a large political group, highly influential at the national level, especially in decisions relative to salaries and social benefits in factories. While it does not specifically mention the concept of CSR, the Labour Law of 1994 strengthened the legitimacy of employees in Chinese organizations.

Li-Wen (2010) mentions article 15 of the Labour Law relative to workers' rights that closely reflects the socialist ideology of the Chinese Communist Party, where firms must protect the legal interests of employees, strengthen safeguards at work and contribute to safe production. They

The Long March of the CSR in China   143

can also adopt several measures to support education and employee training, and thus improve the quality of employees.

While the notion of "social responsibility" is not explicitly mentioned in the law, Li-Wen sees an allusion to CSR in article 14 and to the idea that companies must pursue activities that go beyond simple legislative requirements: "Companies must act in accordance with the law and with business ethics, reinforcing the construction of a socialist civilisation, and submit to the government and to public scrutiny in their business dealings."

We should also note that a law passed in 2008 made some additions to the Labour Law of 1994, especially regarding how to deal with disputes and employment contracts. This law of January 2008 compelled companies to draw up employment contracts and to address the sensitive issue of overtime payments (Jaussaud and Liu, 2011).

Civil Society and CSR Under the Reign of Xi Jinping

The NGO Community in China

In becoming the "workshop of the world," Chinese firms attracted the attention of the international community and NGOs (Ip, 2009). The latter pushed them to become more ethically minded with regard to workers, more environmentally friendly, and to address the scourge of corruption in particular. The role of NGOs was thus crucial in the social responsibility movement (Li-Wen, 2010). While the presence of these "critical players" has increased significantly in China since the early 2000s, the formation of NGOs depends on the goodwill of the administration, and the "NGOs' CSR programme must act within the environmental policies established by the government." This aspect of state control thus gives NGOs operating on Chinese soil a certain legitimacy, but nonetheless calls into question the CSR movement itself, given that its content and basis is, to a large extent, determined by the authorities. Thus, we can see that NGOs working on environmental issues have far more room for maneuver than organizations working in areas such as human rights or labor rights.

According to Li-Wen, Chinese NGOs are more likely to use *non-confrontational tactics* in order to get their CSR message across. The author gives the example of the different means used, like education and communicating information to the public, the organization of forums and field visits.

While the number of NGO-company partnerships is increasing, there is often a lack of expertise and funding in these local organizations, due in particular to their recent creation. Although NGOs have made a major contribution to the development of CSR across the globe, "they're still in the very early stages in China, and so company-civil society relations are still weak" (Moon and Shen, 2010).

144 *Gildas Lusteau and Isabelle Barth*

Internet, Social Networks and Media: New Tools for Protest

On September 25, 2005, the Information Office of the State Council and the Ministry of Industry and Information introduced new legislation to control the Internet, called the "11 commandments" of the Internet by Reporters without Borders. This law intensified "the fight against cyber-crime and cyber dissidence and applied to website editors and bloggers" (ORSE, 2006). In total, this legislation includes a list of 11 interdictions, including two new ones related to "any mention of strikes, riots or other forms of social disorder that disrupt the country" as well as "the organisa-tion of illegal activities or associations via the Internet." Any infringement of the regulations may result in the website being closed down and a fine of up to RMB 30,000 (about EUR 3,800).

The ORSE also mentions the complicity of foreign firms in the surveillance of cyber dissidents, quoting findings from the Human Rights Watch orga-nization according to which Yahoo! China contributed to the arrest of the journalist Shi Tao, despite its confidentiality obligations. He faced a ten-year prison sentence for sending an internal circular from his Yahoo! account to a foreign website. The circular was given to his paper by the Party and called on people not to commemorate the 15th anniversary of the Tiananmen Square demonstrations because of the risk of creating "social destabilization." His sentence was finally reduced, and he was released from prison on September 5, 2013. Other major firms were also involved in monitoring Internet use, like Google, which excluded "some news headlines and some links to sources of information that the Chinese leaders consider objectionable."

We cannot investigate the role of the Internet in Chinese society without mentioning social media, now widely used across the country. Among these websites, Weibo, the equivalent of Twitter, strikes fear in Chinese leaders. This "scoop machine" has seen its use evolve considerably over the last few years, and Internet users have begun considering Weibo as a useful tool to denounce the abuses of officials and their entourages.

In September 2013, the authorities stepped up the fight against Internet users who launch "rumours" by publishing new directives regarding the limits they should not overstep. Thus, the author of a note posted on a microblog and containing "fake news" whose impact is judged "serious" if it is viewed over 5,000 times or forwarded over 500 times is liable to prosecution and could face up to three years in prison if a complaint is lodged. Paradoxically, "government and party organizations are famous for regularly employing their own agents of influence" called *wumaodang*, or the "five mao band," as they were previously paid 5 mao (0.6 cents) to spread propaganda-based opinions.

Chinese Youth and Its Relationship With Ethics

The "Me-Generation": A Mixed Portrait of Chinese Youth

In this chapter, we decided to focus on the post-'80s (*Balinghou*) and post-'90s (*Jiulinghou*) generation, also called the "Me generation" (Wang and

Juslin, 2011). This generation, considered individualist and arrogant by its elders, also demonstrates solid entrepreneurial skills that are crucial to helping the country's economy to modernize. Buoyed up by Deng Xiaoping's 1978 social reforms (Egri and Ralston, 2004) and immersed in Chinese consumer society, it is connected to social media, open to the world and experiencing a shift in its basic values.

Wang and Juslin (2011) describe them as "second-generation rich" who are ill-perceived and stir up outrage in the rest of the population as they flaunt their wealth without restraint or decency. Accused of living in "hyper-consumption, the cult devoted to luxury and extreme irresponsibility," the Chinese media love describing the town center races these young people indulge in at the wheels of powerful cars, which sometimes end tragically. To both authors, "the Chinese Me generation is unquestionably a product of the period of transition, having grown up in specific conditions." They believe that the transition toward a Chinese socialist market economy has led to profound social changes, with the young generation being the main beneficiary of the resulting economic boom: "unlike the older generation, they haven't experienced hardship and for them a material life is characterised by abundance and consumerism."

In addition, it is the first generation since the introduction of the 1979 one-child policy in China, making these young people real "little emperors" within their families, especially in urban areas (Wang and Juslin, 2011). Following the opening-up policy, this young generation grew up in a society that was far more outward-looking toward the world and trade relations, and was therefore exposed to change as well as an enormous amount of information and pluralist values: "the values of these young people thus consist not only of traditional values that feature a strong Confucian dynamism and a strong long-term orientation, but also diverse value systems."

Despite the positive economic climate, Lu Jie (2012) noted that the young generation has had to deal with a series of major events in recent years, including the Sichuan earthquake in 2008, the eventful journey of the Olympic torch relay in some European capitals, as well as many territorial conflicts between China and its Japanese, Vietnamese and Philippine neighbors. These events led to very strong nationalist feeling in the Chinese population and in young people in particular, which is noticeable on social media sites and led to the emergence of "liberal public opinion leaders." Apart from the political aspect, the economic crisis of 2008 also had repercussions across the country, especially on jobs.

Chinese Teaching and Ethics

Apart from citizenship and academic skills, UNESCO's special China dossier on the World Data on Education (2011) detailed the employability criteria of teaching staff with state-fixed objectives, such as to "provide educational activities that promote patriotism, collectivism and socialism

146   *Gildas Lusteau and Isabelle Barth*

as well as ideals, ethics, discipline, legality, national security and ethnical unity in learners."

Despite the numerous positive repercussions made possible by the opening up of the Chinese economy in the 1990s, there were also many negative impacts in social terms, like the corruption reported by Au, Chan and Tse (2006). Describing this corruption as "social practice," the authors believe that time is needed to correct such behavior and that the role of teachers, especially in management studies, is crucial. They thus attempt to determine the ethics of university professors with the difficult task of "building the nation's future" and ask the following question: "How ethical are business teachers?" For Au, Chan and Tse, the ethical decision-making mechanism hinges on factors related to the individual on the one hand, and to factors that form and define the environment in which decisions are taken on the other hand (2006).

For business schools, it is crucial to obtain recognized international accreditations. The AACSB (Association to Advance Collegiate Schools of Business) guidelines emphasize the ethical dimension that must "ensure an understanding of business perspectives by including ethics, globalisation, the business world and demographic diversity" (Premeaux 2005).

While the teaching of ethical principles is well established in western business schools, especially in France, as are the issues of equality/discrimination/diversity advanced by Isabelle Barth and Christophe Falcoz (2009), here we explore the situation in China. De Bettignies and Tan examine how ethics is taught to the prospective leaders of tomorrow in Chinese business schools, and the inclusion of China's traditional philosophy in this discipline for potential solutions to the challenges facing the country: "environment, intellectual property, safety and labour treatment, corruption and human rights" (2007).

The authors first reflect on assumptions regarding traditional Chinese values, especially Confucian values, as factors of change. They evoke the country's old relationship with leadership, beginning with the world's first treatise on military strategy, *The Art of War*, the famous book by Sun Tzu (Sunzi, 孙子), written over 2,500 years ago. The book lists the five qualities that all good leaders should have, namely, wisdom, integrity, humanity, courage and discipline. As noted earlier, Confucius is still the most influential philosopher in modern Chinese and many other Asian societies, including Hong Kong, Singapore, South Korea, Japan and Taiwan. We will not dwell here on the many characteristics of his doctrine or the arguments of his defender Mencius that De Bettignies and Tan also detail in their study: "Confucius identifies virtue, benevolence, generosity and the example of a leader as someone who keeps his promises" (2007).

De Bettignies and Tan examine the pertinence of Confucian values with regard to the education of leaders and managers (2007). Confucius advocates altruism rather than personal gain: an individual "helps others to achieve what he would wish to achieve for himself." Leaders are also expected to

The Long March of the CSR in China 147

take care of the people under their orders, encouraging them to adopt morally acceptable behavior and to be generous. Perseverance and hard work are also basic qualities required for a leader to obtain the trust of others.

With the increase in international business programs across the globe since the beginning of the 2000s, it was felt that training in ethics would be complementary and crucial to the success of all good future managers who have to deal with individuals from different cultures, different religions, different political systems and with distinct values. Referring to recent studies, Whitla believes that understanding "ethical issues is a key condition for multinationals when they hire international business school graduates, as is cultural understanding, considered as even more important than technical and functional knowhow in international trade" (2011).

Earlier we mentioned the importance and influence of values, especially Confucian ones, on society. We thus attempted to gain more insights into the values of young Chinese people through an analysis of the latter.

Survey on the Values of Chinese Students

To understand the role of CSR and ethics for young Chinese adults, we decided to analyze the values of students. To this end, we posted a questionnaire online that adopted the values of Schwartz in line with the Portrait Values Questionnaire (PVQ) method. We decided to focus on values, especially the model proposed by Shalom Schwartz for whom "values have been a central concept of social sciences since their origin" (2006). As Table 8.1 shows, he identified ten basic values that differ in terms of motivation, and he describes the dynamic of opposition and compatibility between them. In other words, whereas some basic values like benevolence and power contrast with one another, others like conformity and security go hand in hand. According to the author, if a similar structure is observed in groups from different cultures, while we may believe that there is a "universal organisation of human motives," groups differ from each another by the relative importance given to different values. Here we speak about "hierarchies" or "priorities" of values. In order to validate his hypothesis, Schwartz gathered data from over 70 countries. The professional values questionnaire thus measures the respondents' *hierarchy* of values rather than their *importance* in order to correct the bias inherent in individual answers: "in effect, it's the

Table 8.1 Theoretical model of relationships between the ten basic values

Self-transcendence	*Universalism, benevolence*
Conservation	*Conformity, tradition, security*
Self-enhancement	*Power, achievement, hedonism*
Openness to change	*Stimulation, self-direction*

Source: Schwartz (2006).

148   *Gildas Lusteau and Isabelle Barth*

relative ranking of values and not the importance of a single value in the absolute that influences behaviour and attitudes" (Schwartz, 2006).

Between January 2014 and May 2015, more than 600 students from different higher education institutions across China received an email with a brief explanation of the research project. In total, 234 people registered on the purpose-built platform and 88 answered the questions.

Taking the average of the dates of birth, we calculated that the typical (average) student who took part in the study was born on January 5, 1992. Of the 88 students, there was a much larger number of women (66, or 75%) and a lower number of men (22, or 25%). Of the participants, 69% identified as bachelor's degree students, and 18% were in master's programs or above. Finally, it was impossible for us to determine the academic level of 11 of the participants (around 13%) as the information they provided was not specific enough.

Of the respondents, 48% were students in management, 35% in languages, 7% in computer science and technology, 3.5% in the arts, and 7% in a range of other disciplines (psychology, machinery, light chemicals, landscaping and education).

We realize that this sample population is not representative of all Chinese higher education students but simply a small proportion of them because many of them come from prestigious universities on the Chinese coast or from large cities like Beijing and Chengdu. Their foreign language skills give them a gateway to the world, and most of them expressed a wish to go and study in France or in an Anglo-Saxon country, with the aim of returning to China in order to work for public or private companies, large multinationals or small family businesses so as to stay close to their families. We believe that they represent the future decision makers, leaders, managers and entrepreneurs of a globalized China, a China looking to grow beyond its borders, and in this respect our sample seems particularly relevant.

We asked the participants to express their degree of agreement or disagreement using a 5-point Likert scale (from *Not at all like me* to *Exactly like me*) by replying to the following question: "To what point is this person like you?" Among the 40 items proposed by Schwartz, we selected 20, which can be seen in Table 8.2.

Each of the items listed above corresponds to a specific motivational area:

- Universalism: items 1, 7 and 14
- Conformity: items 2 and 9
- Tradition: items 3 and 11
- Security: items 4 and 12
- Power: items 5 and 18
- Benevolence: items 8 and 15
- Hedonism: item 10
- Stimulation: items 16 and 20
- Self-direction or autonomy: items 17 and 19
- Success, or achievement: items 6 and 13.

The Long March of the CSR in China 149

Table 8.2 Questionnaire of values by portraits

---

1. It is important to respect different people's opinions. Even if you don't agree with them, you still want to understand their points of view and be able to get along with them.
2. Always being polite is important. One should always respect one's parents and elders.
3. It is important to behave the way one has been brought up in order to respect one's family values.
4. The country's security and being protected from its enemies is important.
5. One likes responsibilities and giving orders. One wants others to do as one says.
6. Success, standing out and impressing others is important.
7. This person is convinced that people should do their part for the environment.
8. A person always wants to help the people who are close to him/her. Taking care of the people he/she knows and loves is very important.
9. A person tries to live up to other people's expectations. It is important to follow orders and be self-disciplined.
10. A person takes every opportunity to have fun. It is important to do things that please one.
11. Religion is very important. He/she follows his/her religious beliefs.
12. This person is very cautious, avoiding anything that could put him/her in danger.
13. It is very important to show off one's abilities and to want people to admire one's work.
14. This person wants everyone to be treated with justice, even those he/she doesn't know. Protecting the weak is important.
15. It is important to feel trustworthy, wanting others to know that they can always rely on this person.
16. This person believes it is important to do a variety of different things in life.
17. It is important to have innovative ideas, to be creative and to like being original.
18. Being rich, having lots of money and buying expensive things is important.
19. This person is self-reliant. He/she wants to be able to cope on his/her own whatever the situation.
20. This person thrives on adventure and likes taking risks. He/she wants a life filled with excitement.

Based on the participants' answers to the survey, the results for each motivational area were obtained according to the following calculations:

- Universalism = (Schwartz_1 + Schwartz_7 + Schwartz_14)/3
- Conformity = (Schwartz_2 + Schwartz_9)/2

Gildas Lusteau and Isabelle Barth

- Tradition = (Schwartz_3 + Schwartz_11)/2
- Security = (Schwartz_4 + Schwartz_12)/2
- Power = (Schwartz_5 + Schwartz_18)/2
- Benevolence = (Schwartz_8 + Schwartz_15)/2
- Hedonism = Schwartz_10
- Stimulation = (Schwartz_16 + Schwartz_20)/2
- Self-direction, or autonomy = (Schwartz_17 + Schwartz_19)/2
- Success, or achievement = (Schwartz_6 + Schwartz_13)/2

According to Schwartz, "each portrait describes the goals, the aspirations or the wishes of a person and simply refers to a basic value" (2006). For instance: "He/she really wants to get the most out of life. It is important for this person to have fun" describes a person who values hedonism. "He/she is convinced that people should protect nature. Preserving the environment is important for this person" describes someone who values universalism.

Our ranking of motivational areas (benevolence, universalism, conformity) partially confirms that of Schwartz (benevolence, universalism, autonomy) and Schaaper and Zhen (conformity, benevolence, security) (2013).

Two of the top three values in our study ranking are Confucian and collectivist by nature, the third being both collectivist and individualistic (universalism). We note that more western and individualist personal values, like hedonism, achievement and power, come nearer the bottom of the ranking. Paradoxically, tradition is in ninth place (eighth for Schwartz and tenth for Schaaper) as it serves individual interests.

The motivational areas that serve personal interests are also important, like the values of autonomy and hedonism, respectively ranked in fourth and fifth place. Schaaper and Zhen explain this by the one-child policy, which heightened individualism and the desire for success in young Chinese people (2013).

Schaaper and Zhen note that Chinese women place more importance on personal values attached to the motivational areas of benevolence, conformity, security and universalism. Given that 75% of Chinese participants in our study were women, our results confirm this tendency. However, we want to once again underscore the over-representation of women among the participants in our study population.

We share with Schwartz the fact that benevolence comes in first position. According to the author, the importance of benevolence "arises from the central nature of positive and cooperative social relations within the family, which is the main place where we learn and acquire values" (2006).

In second position, in both our study and that of Schwartz, and still with regard to social relations, universalism is very useful, "especially when the group members must relate to others with whom they do not easily identify, at school, at work, etc."

The Long March of the CSR in China 151

Conformity, a value ranked third in our study and fifth by Schwartz, positively influences the harmony of social relations by contributing "to avoiding conflict and ensuring that the group norms are not violated." Here again, we can see the importance of Confucianism and the sense of cooperation in Chinese society of the past and present.

Autonomy, the fourth value that emerged from our study, and third in Schwartz's ranking, is more individualist. It develops "creativity, innovation and encourages people to confront the challenges that groups may encounter in times of crisis." These autonomy values no doubt enable the young people questioned, once out in the business world, to use their skills to serve business and help create a China based on innovation. Moreover, Schwartz observed that it is rare for autonomy to threaten "the harmony of social relations."

Based on our findings, we calculated the average of the ten motivational areas in order to identify which dimensions young Chinese adults tend to follow:

- Surpassing oneself (self-transcendence)[1]
- Self-affirmation (self-enhancement)[2]
- Openness to change[3]
- Continuity (conservation).[4]

We thus observe a tendency among the young Chinese questioned to try to surpass themselves. In effect, the participants wish to ensure the preservation and improved well-being of the people around them (*benevolence*). The sample population placed importance on loyalty and honesty, wished to be seen as indulgent and responsible, and wanted to take count for others. The recognition and protection of the well-being of all and of nature were also basic elements for these young people who envisaged surpassing themselves and transcendence (*universalism*). Equality, social

Table 8.3 Average scores of Chinese students for the ten motivational areas

Self-transcendence	Universalism	4.05
	Benevolence	4.22
Conservatism	Conformity	3.86
	Tradition	3.18
	Security	3.56
Self-enhancement	Power	2.76
	Achievement	3.19
	Hedonism	3.27
Openness to Change	Stimulation	3.73
	Self-Direction	3.83

152 Gildas Lusteau and Isabelle Barth

justice, peace, protecting the environment and relating to nature were all values shared by the respondents.

On the other hand, the students were less inclined toward *self-affirmation*. Authority, wealth and social power (power over others) are a key channel for this power. The individuals inclined toward self-affirmation place more importance on their image and on social recognition.

If the vertical trend is clear on the Schwartz circumplex model, in other words, the people under study mainly strive to surpass themselves, it is more difficult to see a clear trend on the horizontal dimension (i.e., openness to change—conservatism).

We nonetheless observe a slight preponderance of openness to change, characterized as valuing autonomy (fourth motivational area in our ranking), otherwise reflected through creativity, freedom, curiosity, independence and the right to a private life. Stimulation (fifth motivational area) is also valued. This involves enthusiasm when confronted with novelty and enjoying taking up challenges. Stimulation also corresponds to the quest for an exciting and varied life and a taste for adventure and risk. Hedonism is also taken into account in openness to change and corresponds to the search for pleasure and personal gratification (seventh motivational area in our ranking).

To the left of the graph, the sphere of continuity (or conservatism) takes the values of conformity (third in the ranking) and tradition (ninth) into account. Individuals who value these dimensions generally respect the norms and expectations of the environment, which sometimes involve the acceptance and appropriation of customs, culture and/or religion, but also respect for elders and moderation, especially by avoiding emotions and extreme behaviors. Individuals geared toward continuity also find security (sixth motivational area) important and seek out social order.

The same questionnaire was sent to 411 French students at the same time. We briefly present the results of the young French adults' values in Table 8.4. As the table shows, benevolence, universalism, conformity,

Table 8.4 Average scores of French students for the ten motivational areas

Motivational area	Average score	Orientation
Benevolence	3.88	Collectivism
Universalism	3.45	Collectivism/individualism
Conformity	3.37	Collectivism
Autonomy	3.36	Individualism
Stimulation	3.23	Individualism
Achievement—success	3.04	Individualism
Hedonism	2.94	Individualism
Security	2.77	Collectivism/individualism
Power	2.44	Individualism
Tradition	2.01	Collectivism

The Long March of the CSR in China   153

autonomy and stimulation top the French ranking, which is the same as for the Chinese students. The second part of the ranking changes a little, however. It is thus interesting to note that Schwartz's so-called universal values present substantial similarities between France and China.

The questionnaire of values by portraits presents young Chinese adults as being split between individualist tendencies, surpassing oneself and open to change (like the French respondents), combined with an attachment to Confucian thinking and collective values. In addition, these results show a somewhat positive facet of a Chinese youth that is demanding yet nonetheless aware of the social challenges.

Conclusion

The main aim of this study was to explore an emerging and complex issue, with increasing importance placed on the international economic and scientific aspects of it. The complexity of corporate social responsibility in China can be explained by the theoretical reasons arising from multiple dimensions detailed in the first section.

On the one hand, there is the philosophical concept with the contribution of Confucianism to modern society, and on the other hand, there is the political concept based on the decisions of the main 20th- and 21st-century leaders, as well as the economic concept, with the country opening up to foreign organizations. Finally, there is the social concept, in other words, evolving social rights and the emergence of an increasingly demanding civil society that have all contributed to the development of a CSR model specific to China. In the absence of trade union freedoms and collective negotiations in the present context, the social dimension still has plenty of room for improvement with regard to the future of social responsibility in the country.

Despite considerable effort being made in recent years, China still has a long way to go in terms of CSR. The country must deal with the global economic slowdown and also be more open to a civil society that no longer hesitates to call out abuses of authority or of Chinese and foreign organizations on social media.

In our study of the younger Chinese generation, we believe that the term "ME generation," used at times to describe it, while emphasizing the generational split, is exaggerated. On the contrary, we saw that these young people born in the 1980s and 1990s display entrepreneurial skills that are vital to the country's economic adaptation. Our study shows that young Chinese adults have many strong similarities with young French adults with respect to attitudes and values. We observed a tendency to want to surpass oneself, and the particular importance given to the motivational areas of benevolence and universalism, thereby confirming in part Schwartz's theory of universal values as well as an openness to change. Whereas globalization plays a role in this tendency to openness and the development of more individualistic values, the young Chinese adults we

154 *Gildas Lusteau and Isabelle Barth*

studied remain strongly rooted in collective and Confucian values. We hope that these evolving values and attitudes will foster the adoption of responsible behaviors in the organizations of the future, helping to make China an ethical superpower that is more competitive on the world market and more attentive to the country's internal challenges.

Notes

1. (Universalism + Benevolence)/2 = (4.05 + 4.22)/2 = 4.13.
2. (Achievement + Power)/2 = (3.19 + 2.76)/2 = 2.98.
3. (Autonomy + Stimulation + Hedonism)/3 = (3.83 + 3.73 + 3.27)/3 = 3.61.
4. (Tradition + Conformity + Security)/3 = (3.18 + 3.86 + 3.56)/3 = 3.53.

References

Au, A.K.M., Chan, A.K.K., Tse, A.C.B. (2006). "How ethical are university students in the People's Republic of China—A preliminary analysis." *International Indigenous Journal of Entrepreneurship, Advancement, Strategy and Education,* 2(1), p. 47.

Barth, I., Falcoz, C. (2009). "Quels enseignements des thématiques Égalité/Discrimination/Diversité à dispenser aux futurs managers en France?" *Humanisme et Entreprise,* 2009/5, 295, pp. 41–56.

Chan, G.K.Y. (2008). "The relevance and value of Confucianism in contemporary business ethics," *Journal of Business Ethics,* 77, pp. 347–360.

Cheng, A. (1981). *Entretiens de Confucius,* Paris: Éditions du Seuil.

Child, J., Warner, M. (2003). "Culture and management in China." In *Culture and Management in Asia,* London: Routledge Curzon, chapter 2.

Cramer, A., Westgaard, G. (2005). "CSR with Chinese characteristics," *Leading Perspectives, Business for Social Responsibility (BSR),* Fall.

Darigan, K. H., Post, J. E. (2009). "Corporate citizenship in China—CSR challenges in the 'harmonious society.'" *Journal of Corporate Citizenship,* 35, Autumn.

De Bettignies, H.-C., Tan, C. K. (2007). "Values and management education in China." *International Management Review,* 3(1).

Egri, C., Ralston, D. (2004). "Generation cohorts and personal values: A comparison of China and the United States." *Organization Science,* 15(2), pp. 210–220.

Fairbank, J. K., Reischauer, E. O. (1978). *China: Tradition and Transformation.* Boston: Houghton Mifflin.

Faure, G. O., Fang, T. (2008). "Changing Chinese values: Keeping up with paradoxes." *International Business Review,* 17, pp. 194–207, January 30.

Global Alliance for Workers and Communities. (2004). *Corporate Social Responsibility in China: Mapping the Environment.* GA Publication Series, en partenariat avec Impactt Limited, April.

Huchet J.-F. (2007). *La Responsabilité Sociale des Entreprises Étrangères en Chine.* CGT-FO, Institut de Recherches Économiques et Sociales (IRES), June, 153 pp.

Ip, P. K. (2009). "Is Confucianism good for business ethics in China?" *Journal of Business Ethics,* 88(3), pp. 463–476.

The Long March of the CSR in China 155

Jaussaud, J., Liu, X. (2006). "La GRH des personnels locaux dans les entreprises étrangères en Chine—une approche exploratoire." *Revue de Gestion des Ressources Humaines*, January–March, p. 59.

Jaussaud, J., Liu, X. (2011). "When in China... The HRM practices of Chinese and foreign-owned enterprises during a global crisis." *Asia Pacific Business Review*, 17(4), pp. 473–491.

Jaussaud, J., Mayrhofer, U. (2013). "Les tensions global-local: l'organisation et la coordination des activités internationales." *Management International*, 18(1), pp. 18–25.

Li-Wen, L. (2010). "Corporate social responsibility in China: Window dressing or structural change?" *Berkeley Journal of International Law*, 28(1), March, pp. 64–100.

Lu, J. (2012). "The Me-Generation or agent of political change? Democratic citizenship and Chinese young adults." Institute of Political Science, Academia Sinica (IPSAS), September 20–21, Taipei.

Moon, J., Shen, X. (2010). "CSR in China research: Salience, focus and nature." *Journal of Business Ethics*, 94, pp. 613–629.

ORSE, Observatoire sur la Responsabilité Sociétale des Entreprises. (2006). "La responsabilité sociétale des entreprises en Chine," ORSE en partenariat avec CSR Europe, étude no. 9, September.

Premeaux, S. (2005). "Undergraduate student perceptions regarding cheating: Tier 1 to Tier 2 AACSB accredited business schools." *Journal of Business Ethics*, 62, pp. 407–418 (cited by Hilliard, Crudele, Matulich, McMurrian, 2009).

Redfern, K., Crawford, J. (2004). "An empirical investigation of the ethics position questionnaire in the People's Republic of China." *Journal of Business Ethics*, 50, pp. 199–210.

Schaaper, J., Zhen, J. (2013). "Valeurs Confucéennes en Chine mesurées par les valeurs personnelles et domaines motivationnels de Schwartz." *Management International*, 17(4), Spring, pp. 58–82.

Schwartz, S. H. (2006). "Les valeurs de base de la personne: théorie, mesures et applications." *Revue française de sociologie*, 2006/4, vol. 47, pp. 929–968.

Séhier, C. (2010). "La transition institutionnelle chinoise au prise de la Responsabilité Sociale des Entreprises—Influence et pratiques des firmes multinationales." Université de Lille 1, mémoire de Master 2, Commerce et Management des Affaires Internationales.

UNESCO. (2011). "World date on education—People's Republic of China" (7th ed.), 2010/11 (updated version), June.

Wang, F., (2011). "Le confucianisme et la Chine actuelle: l'héritage de Zhang Dainian (1909–2004)." *Histoire et Missions Chrétiennes*, 18, pp. 69–87.

Wang, L., Juslin, H. (2011). "The effects of value on the perception of corporate social responsibility implementation: A study of Chinese youth." *Journal of CSR and Environmental Management*, 18(4), pp. 246–262.

Whitcomb, L. L., Erdener, C. B., Li, C. (1998). "Business ethical values in China and the U.S." *Journal of Business Ethics*, 17, pp. 839–852.

Whitla, P. (2011). "Integrating ethics into international business teaching: Challenges and methodologies in the Greater China context." *Journal of Teaching in International Business*, 22(3), pp. 168–184.

9 "Islamic Ethics and the Spirit of Capitalism"

The Case of MÜSİAD in Turkey

Laure Dikmen

Introduction

At a time when dogmas prevail, we are witnessing a rapprochement between religions and the business world. In the early 20th century, Max Weber had already highlighted the overlap between religious order and economic order in his book *The Protestant Ethic and the Spirit of Capitalism*. Does being more religious and more practicing improve performance? Does religion influence business behavior, and its ethical dimension, in particular? Many authors have examined the relationship between religion and business in an attempt to answer these questions (Kennedy and Lawton, 1998; Mitroff and Denton, 1999; Agle and Van Buren, 1999; Giacalone and Jurkiewicz, 2003; Worden, 2005; Angelidis and Ibrahim, 2004), while the specific relationship between Islam and business has been studied by Greif (1994) and Kuran (2002, 2003).

A study titled "The Future of the Global Muslim Population" showed that Muslims are expected to number 2.2 billion by 2030, compared with 1.6 billion in 2010, and that they will represent 26.4% of the global population by 2030 compared to 23.4% in 2010. The preponderant place of Islam in the world calls for a profound reflection on ideological, sociological, economic, strategic and political issues. Tammâm and Haenni (2007) used common characteristics to define the *ideal type* of Islamic entrepreneur: ambitious and entrepreneurial, with a desire for oneself and for the Muslim community. Our objective is to study the link between Islam and business performance. Graafland et al. (2006) regret that few studies to date have focused on the impact of Islamic entrepreneurs' religious beliefs in European countries. Yousef (2001) argues that few studies have been conducted on the effects of ethical Islamic work. Arslan (2001) enjoins researchers to deepen the links between the Muslim religion and capitalism. "Market Islam" combines ambition, wealth, success, imagination and efficiency (Holtrop and Haenni, 2002). Our study aims to answer the question, "What is the impact of market Islam on the performance of MÜSİAD member firms?" We first study the concept of "market Islam" before examining the relationship between religion and firm performance.

Islamic Ethics and the Spirit of Capitalism 157

We then use 119 completed questionnaires from members of MÜSİAD, the Turkish employers' association, to analyze the interpenetration of religious order and economic order. We conclude with a discussion of our results and the potential avenues for future research.

The Theoretical Foundations

From Islam to "Market Islam"

Definitions of religion are abundant (Spiro, 1966). Whereas some authors have studied the transcendental relationship, others have emphasized the social or philosophical character of religion. Bell (1980, p. 333) proposes a definition that combines the social and philosophical aspects of religion:

> Religion is a set of coherent responses to the main existential questions facing each human group, the codification of these responses into a form of belief that is important to its adherents, the celebration of rites that provides an emotional bond for those who participate and the establishment of an institutional body to bring into the congregation those who share the creed and celebration and provide for the continuity of these rites from generation to generation.

Religion can be defined as a particular institutionalized system of beliefs, values and practices linking the divine, a level of reality or power that is like an imminent transcendent "source" or the "ultimate" in the human experience. Worden (2005) defends a positivist vision where the items would belong to religion and where religion would enrich the crucial elements of charismatic leadership, such as strategic choices of values, vision, ethics and credibility. The content of beliefs may influence cognition, which is in turn involved in the strategic choice process (Prancer et al., 1995).

According to Islam, a person must live his or her life in submission and obedience to Allah. It is assumed as a commitment to the ethics dictated by Allah. Islamic morality is seen as a factor conducive to the ethics of trade. This morality is reflected in the distinction between the allowed (*halal*) and the prohibited (*haram*). The fundamental values in business life are freedom and justice (Ahmad, 1995). The condition for justice in business is mutual consent, which requires the contracting parties to be in full agreement regarding their transaction. Muslims must be honest, sincere, and true in their business. Islam condemns deceit and lies. Justice prohibits the unequal payment of wages (Ahmad, 1995). Hiring should be based on merit and skills for the job. Although inequity in terms of wealth is justified, every member of society has the same rights regardless of race, religion, language, color, sex, age, health and status. The distribution system depends on charitable acts: *infaq* means "to meet financial needs";

158 *Laure Dikmen*

zakat is one of the five pillars of Islam that states that every Muslim must give a percentage of his or her earnings to people in need.

Graafland et al. (2006) mention three main "virtues" relating to Islam and business: (1) clemency refers to the notion of politeness, which is considered a necessary condition for establishing relationships of goodwill and mutual trust between partners; (2) servitude is associated with services to the community; and (3) conducting business in the name of Allah means that the businessman must be constantly aware of His presence and not let business commitments interfere with his spiritual duties. This implies, for example, that he should interrupt his activity during prayer time.

According to Rice (1999, p. 379), "Muslims behave in a particular way because they believe that their actions implement God's commands." Muslims believe that the Koran (*Qur'an*, God's revelation to Muhammad), Sunnah (the Prophet Muhammad's sayings and practices), and Shari'ah (Islamic law) provide the answers to all ethical questions (Rice, 2006). Abbasi et al. (1989) argue that Islam provides guidance in ethical behavior. The Koran, Sunnah, and Shari'ah propose ethical behavior through the concepts of unity (*wehda*), justice (*adalah*), and guardianship (*kilafah*) (Rice, 2006). The concept of "unity" implies equality and fraternity among people, leading to cooperation and equal sharing of transactions. The concept of "justice" prohibits usurious operations and forbids Muslims from defrauding, lying, or supporting transactional promises. The concept of "guardianship" is a similar idea to sustainable development in that luxurious and ostentatious consumption is discouraged.

Islam considers business to be a useful social function, and the Prophet Muhammad was himself involved in trade (Rice, 1999). However, unlike capitalism, individual profit is not the main motivation in Islamic law. Entrepreneurs should also be guided by social concerns. According to Rice (1999), Islam condemns the evils of greed, unscrupulousness, and disregard for the rights and needs of others. Unlike most western cultures, ethics dominate the economy in Islam. This means that Muslims pass their business actions through "a moral filter of Islamic values."

Religiosity is not incompatible with managerial efficiency. In the case of Islam, Haenni (2005) notes the emergence of "market Islam," articulated around three principles: openness to market culture and to self-realization, moral rigor and mistrust of the welfare state. Market Islam is an ideological current based on religious cultural values and the attraction of western management. This new Islamic movement fully adheres to the ethical values that Islam promotes in daily life but also in business (Saeed et al., 2001). Islam promotes the values of brotherhood, equity, justice, honesty and sincerity (Rice and Al-Mossawi, 2002; Zainul et al., 2004). The practice of Islam goes beyond individual belief and is part of a collectivist culture in which individuals are interdependent and obey common rules and norms.

The Relationship Between Religion and Business

Graafland et al. (2006) show that managers develop their own standards in a relatively autonomous manner. For most managers, the standard of good and evil is set by both God and humans. The interviewees had a relatively positive view of human nature, with the majority believing that humans are inclined to do "good." Most managers did not believe in a (completely) predestined life and emphasized personal responsibility in their lives. Consistency between personal belief systems, internalized standards, and current behavior in organizations is not only important for the psychological well-being of individuals, but can also improve organizational performance.

Barnett and Schubert (1992) and Viswesvaran and Deshpande (1996) have shown that spirituality improves productivity and reduces absenteeism and staff turnover (Giacalone and Jurkiewicz, 2003). Rest et al. (1986), Treviño (1986), and Jones (1991) showed that the relationship between religious beliefs and behaviors is moderated by (1) individual factors such as ego strength, field dependence and place of control; and (2) situational factors including organizational culture, work characteristics and work context.

Our research aims to answer the question, "What is the impact of market Islam on the performance of MÜSİAD member firms?" To do this, we analyzed the interpenetration of religious order and economic order using the case of Turkish entrepreneurs, commonly referred to as "Anatolian tigers." We then created a conceptual model (see Figure 9.1) based on our review of the literature.

Our main research hypotheses are as follows:

> H1. A firm's adoption of Islamic values is positively correlated with its performance.
>> H1.1. A firm's adoption of moral values is positively correlated with its performance.
>> H1.2. A firm's adoption of ethical values is positively correlated with its performance.
>> H1.3. A firm's adoption of religious values is positively correlated with its performance.
>> H1.4. A firm's redistribution of its profits is positively correlated with its performance.

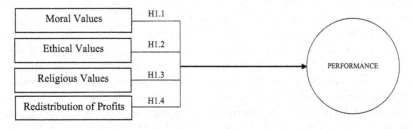

Figure 9.1 Conceptual model

Research Method

The Study Context

Turkey has a population of 80,745 million people and is ranked the 17th biggest economy in the world, with a GDP of USD 852.466 billion and a GDP growth rate of 7.42% in 2017 (UNCTAD, 2018). In the same year, the country hosted USD 10.864 billion in foreign direct investment (FDI). The private sector is dynamic and mature, with USD 157.020 billion in exports (UNCTAD, 2018). Turkey has a young, dynamic, well-trained and multicultural population. The country is strategically located between the east-west and north-south axes, making it an effective and lucrative access point to key markets. The country could provide a gateway to 1.6 billion consumers in Europe, Eurasia, the Middle East and North Africa. Despite its economic attractiveness, Turkey nonetheless faces national and geopolitical instability and is heavily reliant on external borrowing and imports (Coface, 2018). The official unemployment rate exceeds 11% and the inflation rate is more than 11% (World Bank, 2018). Furthermore, since summer 2011, the country has welcomed 2.5 million refugees from Syria. Syrian refugees accounted for 3.5% of the population in 2015 (IMF, 2015). We do not yet know the impact of these refugees on the Turkish labor market.

Field of Study: The MÜSİAD

Since the Ottoman era, Turkey has had a tradition of placing political supremacy over Islam. Unlike Muslim countries adopting Shari'ah law, Turkey adopted *Kanun* lawin public, administrative, criminal and financial spheres. However, since 2002, the Party of Justice and Development, or AKP (*Adalet ve Kalkınma Partisi*), has represented political Islam in Turkey. The Turkish model has advocated economic growth and the emergence of a new bourgeois class that has benefited from globalization, capitalism and democratic openness (Taspinar, 2011). Economic liberalization and new communication technologies have provided an opportunity for Islamic movements to set up their own economic institutions, media and education facilities (Kuru, 2005).

Turkey has witnessed the development of a new class of small- and medium-sized entrepreneurs, commonly referred to as "Anatolian tigers" or "Islamic Calvinists" (McDonald, 2011, p. 529). These entrepreneurs created a new association, the MÜSİAD (Yavuz, 1999), bringing together entrepreneurs from the Anatolian region (Konya, Gaziantep, Denizli, Eskişehir, and Kayseri) (Kutluay, 2011, p. 76). The expression "Anatolian tigers" was coined by the European Stability Initiative (ESI) think tank. The ESI aimed to define the social changes within religious conservatism in Central Anatolia by conducting a study with the leaders of the largest companies in the Kayseri Province, described as "Islamic Calvinists."[1] This

Islamic Ethics and the Spirit of Capitalism 161

latter expression comes from the Turkish sociologist Hakan Yavuz, who observed the emergence of a "Protestant Islam." This hypothesis suggests a growing parallelism between Islamic ideals and the material interests of the new pious social classes since 1980 (Yankaya, 2013). Hakan Yavuz sees this movement as the march of a silent Islamic reform in Turkey. "To name the members of the new Islamic bourgeoisie" Islamic Calvinists "or to consider the new manifestations of Islam in the market society as the emergence of a 'Protestant Islam'" would mean "Weberizing Islam."[2] Among the Muslim middle class, there has been a visible growth in Muslim entrepreneurs who pursue Islamic precepts and capitalist aspirations (Adas, 2006; Osella and Osella, 2009; Sandikli, 2011). Max Weber (1905) presents Islam as a warrior religion that has produced an ethic fundamentally incompatible with the spirit of capitalism. This notion has been refuted by studying the influence of religion on Muslim communities in its historicity and contextuality.

This entrepreneurial profile reflects the new Anatolian bourgeoisie, which is geographically and culturally close to the countries of the Middle East and Central Asia. Anatolian SMEs apply the precepts of Islam literally. For the *zakat*, Anatolian entrepreneurs donate 1/40 of their fortune to help build religious schools, finance universities and help the poorest members of society. Founded in Istanbul in 1990, by 2013 MÜSİAD had more than 7,000 members and represented more than 35,000 companies that employed about 1.5 million people.[3] These firms are highly integrated into the international economy through trade, especially with Europe, Central Asia, the Middle East and the Maghreb. MÜSİAD brings together pious Muslim entrepreneurs around an Islamic conception of work ethics. The economic liberalization of the 1980s and the entry into force of the Customs Union in 1996 have led MÜSİAD-member SMEs to develop trade relations with European Union member countries. They export building materials, machinery, furniture, packaging products, and food products. They import high-tech machinery, including construction equipment for their own firms or European items to be resold.

Sample Description

The objective of our study is to analyze the link between the practice of market Islam and the performance of MÜSİAD member firms. In other words, do firms that adopt Islamic values in their business perform better? To answer this question, we distributed a research questionnaire to MÜSİAD members at the *MÜSİAD Fuar Expo* biannual fair held November 9–12, 2016, in Istanbul. We determined our base population in function of the most important sectors of activity in Turkey: construction, industrial production and services (Turkstat, 2015). We therefore reduced our investigations to three of the fair's halls (2, 6 and 7), and 150 companies were

162   *Laure Dikmen*

present. We only selected companies that were members of the MÜSİAD organization. Our final sample comprises 134 companies. We collected 119 usable questionnaires (a return rate of 88.81%). Of our respondent companies, 73.03% were located in Istanbul compared to 26.97% in Anatolia; 52.94% were created more than 20 years ago and most companies were in the industrial sector (85.71%). The companies had between 10 and 250 employees (68.91%). In 78.15% of cases, the companies had a board of directors. On the other hand, 82.35% of companies did not have a union. We note the very low presence of women, who represented only 7.56% of respondents. In addition, 63.87% of respondents had little seniority in the company (i.e., 1 to 5 years). This may produce an informational bias (see Table 9.1).

Table 9.1 Sample description

	Modalities	*Respondents*	*%*
Firm location	0-Istanbul	75	73.03
	1-Anatolia	44	36.97
Creation date	1–5 years	15	12.61
	6–10 years	10	8.40
	11–20 years	12	10.08
	> 20 years	63	52.94
	NA*	19	15.97
Sector	1-Industry	102	85.71
	2-Service	17	14.29
Number of employees	< 10	11	9.24
	10–250	82	68.91
	> 250	26	21.85
Union	1-Yes	21	17.65
	2-No	98	82.35
Board of directors	1-Yes	93	78.15
	2-No	26	21.85
Gender of respondent	1-Male	110	92.44
	2-Female	9	7.56
Seniority in the firm	1–5 years	76	63.87
	6–10 years	7	5.88
	10–15 years	17	14.29
	15–20 years	4	3.36
	> 20 years	4	3.36
	NA*	11	9.24

* NA = Not available.
Source: Author.

Research Results

Dependent Variable

Our dependent variable is "firm performance since joining MÜSİAD." Its measurement scale initially comprised 14 items, including both objective measures and subjective measures. The eight objective measures were turnover, profitability, market share, productivity, export sales, quality production, research and development efficiency, and budget. We also mobilized six subjective measures: global integration, bureaucratic skills, product quality, respect of fixed objectives, relations with partners and compliance with delivery dates. Examination of the communalities revealed that all items had a Cos^2 above 0.5. We therefore performed a confirmatory factor analysis (CFA) on all items. This led us to delete two items to improve the absolute and relative indices (PerfRela, "performance related to relationships with partners," and PerfExpo, "performance related to export sales"). In the end, the performance variable comprises 12 items with an excellent Cronbach's alpha (α = 0.984) (see Table 9.2).

Independent Variables

We analyze Islamic values using four independent variables: moral values, ethical values, religious values and the redistribution of profits.

Table 9.2 Dependent variable

Scale measure (5-point Likert scale)	Items	SPSS items	Authors
Performance since joining MÜSIAD 5-point Likert scale ("*Highly lowered*" to "*Strongly increased*")	Turnover	PerfTurn	Beamish (1984) Geringer and Hebert (1991) Mohr and Spekman (1994)
	Profitability	PerfProf	
	Market share	PerfShar	
	Productivity	PerfProd	
	Export sales	PerfExpo	
	Quality production	PerdProQ	
	R&D efficiency	PerfRD	
	Budget	PerfBudg	
	Global integration	PerfInteg	
	Bureaucratic skills	PerfBure	
	Product quality	PerfQual	
	Respect of the fixed objectives	PerfRObj	
	Relations with partners	PerfRela	
	Compliance with delivery dates	PerfRDat	

Source: Author.

164 *Laure Dikmen*

We first operationalized the "moral values" scale using ten items. Following our review of the communalities, we removed four items whose Cos^2 was below the minimum required (0.5) (ValEAmbi, ValEWeal, ValE-Succ, and ValEMone). The items relating to monetary value and ego were therefore removed: ambition, wealth, success and money. The CFA, performed on the six items retained, shows that the deletion of two items (ValEEffi and ValEWork) improves the absolute indices and the relative indices. Nevertheless, the RMSEA index is poor (0.147). In the end, we retained only four items: vision, ethics, credibility and respect. The Cronbach's alpha is high ($\alpha = 0.856$) (see Table 9.3).

Second, the "ethical values" scale initially included six items. After examination of the communalities, we removed one item with a Cos^2 below 0.5: honesty (VEthicHo). The CFA performed on the five items retained shows that all items have a correlation exceeding 0.5. The absolute indices and the relative indices are satisfactory. However, the RMSEA index is mediocre (0.187). The "ethical values" scale is composed of five items: solidarity, justice, integrity, benevolence and mutual trust with a high reliability index ($\alpha = 0.877$) (see Table 9.3).

Third, the "religious values" scale has 12 items. Examination of the communalities revealed that all items have a Cos^2 above 0.5. We therefore performed a CFA on all items. The absolute indices and the relative indices are satisfactory. Nevertheless, the RMSEA index is poor (0.187). The "religious values" scale is composed of six items: services to the community, respecting prayers, following *zakat*, respecting Ramadan, going to Mecca (*Haj*) and not drinking alcohol. The Cronbach's alpha is high ($\alpha = 0.962$) (see Table 9.3).

Fourth, the "redistribution of profits" scale initially comprised 11 items. Analysis of the communalities required us to remove three items with a Cos^2 below 0.5 (RedReli, RedArti, and RedMora). We removed items relating to redistribution for religious actions, artistic actions, and "moral" actions. The CFA performed on the eight items retained shows that the removal of the three items improves the absolute and relative indices. In the end, only five items were retained: charitable actions, corporate development, redistribution to employees, redistribution by MÜSİAD members and investing in real estate. The reliability index after purification is satisfactory ($\alpha = 0.847$) (see Table 9.3).

Multiple Linear Regression

We used the multiple linear regression method. Our dependent variable, "firm performance since joining MÜSİAD" was regressed on four independent variables ("moral values," "ethical values," "religious values" and "redistribution of profits"). Table 9.3 reveals that ethical values and religious values do not contribute significantly to the regression. Nevertheless, the moral values and the redistribution of profits explain 38.8% of the

Islamic Ethics and the Spirit of Capitalism   165

Table 9.3 Independent variables

Scale measures	Items	SPSS items	Authors
Moral values *5-point Likert scale* *("Not at all* *important" to "Very* *important")*	Ambition Wealth Success Efficiency Vision Ethics Credibility Respect Work Money	ValAmbi ValWeal ValSucc ValEffi ValVisi ValEthi ValCred ValResp ValWork ValMone	Rice (1999) Holtrop and Haenni (2002) Worden (2005) Yankaya (2013)
Ethical values *("Not at all* *important" to "Very* *important")*	Solidarity Justice Integrity Honesty Benevolence Mutual trust	VEthiqSo VEthiqJu VEthiqIn VEthiqHo VEthiqBe VEthiqMu	Rice (1999) ESI (2005) Graafland et al. (2006) Yankaya (2013)
Religious values *("Not at all* *important" to "Very* *important")*	Honesty Transparency Fair wage payment Community services Respecting prayers Following *zakat* Respecting Ramadan Going to Mecca (*Haj*) Managing spending rationally Using financial profitability Not using interest rates Not drinking alcohol	VRelHonn VRelTrans VRelPaym VRelServ VRelPray VRelZaka VRelRama VRelMecc VRelMana VRelProf VRelRate VRelAlco	Ahmad (1995) Tropman (1995) Graafland et al. (2006) Yankaya (2013)
Redistribution of **profits** *("Not at all" to* *"Strongly")*	For moral actions For educational activities For religious activities For societal actions For artistic actions For charity actions For the development of the company For wage redistribution To members of MÜSİAD Investment in real estate Investments in shares	RedAmora RedAEduc RedAReli RedASoci RedAArti RedAChar RedDevCo RedWage RedMÜSİAD RedInvIRe RedInvSh	Ahmad (1995) Yankaya (2013)

Source: Author.

166 Laure Dikmen

performance of MÜSİAD member firms (R^2). The results of the analysis of the variance (ANOVA) show that the model is significant (sig. = 0.000). The collinearity test indicates that tolerances and variance inflation factors (VIF) are close to 1, that is, within the recommended limit (tolerance > 0.3 and VIF < 3.3). There is therefore little correlation between the independent variables "moral values" and "redistribution of profits." Moral values and the redistribution of profits are thus the two determinants of performance for MÜSİAD member firms. MÜSİAD firms' adoption of moral values (β = 0.262) and their redistribution of their profits (β = 0.197) are positively correlated with improved performance (see Table 9.4).

Discussion and Conclusion

The objective of this chapter was to understand the link between market Islam and the performance of firms belonging to MÜSİAD, an employers' organization in Turkey. Fervent believers and practitioners, the members of this organization invoke the practice of Islam in the success of their businesses. We therefore wanted to examine the link between the adoption of the principles of Islam and firm performance. In our study, we analyzed 119 MÜSİAD member firms. The originality of our work lies in the fact that few studies have examined the relationship between the religious beliefs of Islamic entrepreneurs and capitalism (Arslan, 2001; Graafland et al., 2006).

Our hypothesis H1 (a firm's adoption of Islamic values is positively correlated with its performance) is partially validated. Our study shows that ethical values (e.g., solidarity, justice, integrity, benevolence and mutual trust) and religious values (e.g., community services, respecting prayers, following the *zakat*, respecting Ramadan, going to Mecca (*Haj*) and not drinking alcohol) are not significantly related to the performance of MÜSİAD member firms. Hypotheses H1.2 and H1.3 are thus not validated. However, moral values and the redistribution of profits account for 38.8% of the performance of MÜSİAD member firms (R^2). The moral values of the company are apprehended through vision, ethics, credibility and respect. They are positively and significantly related to firm performance (β = 0.262; sig. = 0.000). Hypothesis H1.1 is validated. In addition, firms redistribute profits to charitable actions, business development, wages, MÜSİAD members and real estate. The redistribution of profits is positively and significantly related to firm performance (β = 0.197; sig = 0.000). Hypothesis H1.4 is thus validated.

Our research question examines the impact of market Islam on the performance of MÜSİAD member firms. The five pillars of Islam are the foundation of the Islamic way of life. These pillars are the profession of faith, to respect prayer, to follow the *zakat* (financial support to the poor), to fast during the month of Ramadan, and to make a pilgrimage to Mecca once in a lifetime for those who can afford it. The results of our research show that four of the five pillars of Islam are not significantly related to firm performance. Our results reveal that the practice of Islam, through

Islamic Ethics and the Spirit of Capitalism   167

Table 9.4 Multiple linear regression analysis (dependent variable: performance)

Analysis of variance

Multiple R	0.388
Sum of squares	17.743
Df	2
Mean square	8.872
F	10.265
Sig.	0.000

Models	Standardized coefficient	Statistical significance		Collinearity statistics	
	Beta	t	Sig.	Tolerance	VIF
Moral values	0.262	2.779	0.006	0.826	1.211
Redistribution of profits	0.197	2.091	0.039	0.826	1.211

Excluded models

	Beta	Statistical significance		Partial Correlation	Collinearity Statistics	
		T	Sig.		Tolerance	VIF
Ethical values	−0.048	−0.454	0.651	−0.042	1.510	0.606
Religious values	0.045	0.460	0.646	0.043	1.305	0.704

Source: Author.

religious values (H1.2) and Islamic values (H.1.3), has no significant link with firm performance. Being more devoted and practicing the Muslim faith does not therefore appear to promote economic performance. We are instead witnessing the intertwining of moral and economic orders. Moral order manifests itself through the moral values conveyed by the firm, such as vision, ethics, credibility and respect. Economic order is reflected in the redistribution of profits for the company and its real estate, employees and business network—in other words the members of MÜSİAD. We are firmly in the capitalist spirit, where redistribution is conducted primarily within the company.

Our results corroborate the works of Mullin Marta et al. (2004, p. 55): "There is a degree of divergence between the Islamic teachings (the ideal) and the business practices (the reality) in the economic world of the majority of Islamic countries." Dilemmas in business can be seen as a conflict

168 Laure Dikmen

between different values, ideas (Railton, 1996), duties (Donagan, 1996) or interests (Donaldson and Dunfee, 1999). Graafland et al. (2006) distinguished three types of standards: moral, religious and practical. Solidarity, justice, integrity and honesty are considered moral standards. Religious standards meet the criteria of moral standards. For example, justice is an important standard in many religions, but it has also become a moral standard. Practical standards include all other standards (non-moral and non-religious). The spirit of the work of the new Islamic bourgeoisie in Turkey thus comes from the articulation of its Anatolian conservative culture and Islamic morality with capitalist rationality. Capitalism and Islam do not appear to be contradictory phenomena; these two "morals" are intertwined, complementary and reinforcing. This reflects the uniqueness of this bourgeoisie. Finally, our study shows that firms are more sensitive to moral values than to religious values. We wish to continue our investigations on the moralization of the business world in Turkey (ethical, social and societal dimensions, firm managers, etc.) in future studies.

Notes

1. ESI, "Islamic Calvinists. Change and Conservatism in Central Anatolia," Berlin-Istanbul, September 19, 2005.
2. This means studying Islam independently of structural factors and instead studying the social, economic, political, regional, territorial and cultural features of Muslim countries through a Weberian Orientalist lens. See A. Y. Saribay (2006). "*Weberlestirilmis Islam*" ("Weberized Islam"), Birikim, February, pp. 86–92.
3. www.musiad.org.tr/tr-tr/musiadla-tanisin.

References

Abbasi, S. M., Hollman, K. W., Murrey, J. H., Jr. (1989). "Islamic economics: Foundations and practices." *International Journal of Social Economics*, 16(5), pp. 5–17.

Adas, E. B. (2006). "The making of entrepreneurial Islam and the Islamic spirit of capitalism." *Journal for Cultural Research*, 10(2), pp. 113–125.

Agle, B. R., Van Buren, H. J., III. (1999). "God and mammon: The modern relationship." *Business Ethics Quarterly*, 9, pp. 563–582.

Ahmad, M. (1995). *Business Ethics in Islam*. Islamabad: IIIT and IRI Press.

Angelidis, J., Ibrahim, N. (2004). "An exploratory study of the impact of degree of religiousness upon an individual's corporate social responsiveness orientation." *Journal of Business Ethics*, 51(2), pp. 119–128.

Arslan, M. (2001). "The work ethic values of Protestant British, Catholic Irish, and Muslim Turkish managers." *Journal of Business Ethics*, 31(4), pp. 321–339.

Barnett T., Schubert E. (1992). "Perceptions of the ethical work climate and covenantal relationships." *Journal of Business Ethics*, 36, pp. 279–290.

Beamish, P. W. (1984). *Joint Venture Performance in Developing Countries*. PhD dissertation, University of West Ontario, Canada.

Bell, D. (1980). *Sociological Journeys: Essays 1960–1980*. Cambridge, MA: ABT Book.

Islamic Ethics and the Spirit of Capitalism 169

COFACE Handbook: Country & Sector Risks (2018). https://www.coface.com/content/download/160155/2633137/file/COFACE-HANDBOOK-CR2018.pdf

Conroy, S. J., Emerson, T.L.N. (2004). Business ethics and religion: Religiosity as a predictor of ethical awareness among students." *Journal of Business Ethics*, 50(4), pp. 383–396.

Donagan, A. (1996). "Moral dilemmas, genuine and spurious: A comparative anatomy." In H. E. Mason (ed.), *Moral Dilemmas and Moral Theory*. Oxford: Oxford University Press, pp. 11–22.

Donaldson, T., Dunfee, T. W. (1999). *Ties that Bind: A Social Contracts Approach to Business Ethics*. Boston, MA: Harvard Business School Press.

European Stability Initiative. (2005). "Chapter 1. New challenges facing the Turkish economy." In *Islamic Calvinists: Change and Conservatism in Central Anatolia*, September.

Geringer, J. M., Hebert, L. (1991). "Measuring performance of international joint venture." *Journal of International Business Studies*, 22(2), pp. 249–263.

Giacalone, R. A., Jurkiewicz, C. L. (2003), "Toward a science of workplace spirituality." In R. A. Giacalone, C. L. Jurkiewicz (eds.), *Handbook of Workplace Spirituality and Organizational Performance*. New York: M. E. Sharpe, pp. 3–28.

Graafland, J., Mazereeuw, C., Yahia, A. (2006). "Islam and socially responsible business conduct: An empirical study of Dutch entrepreneurs." *Business Ethics: A European Review*, 15(4), pp. 390–406.

Greif, A. (1994), "Cultural beliefs and the organization of society." *Journal of Political Economy*, 102(5), pp. 912–950.

Haenni, P. (2005), *L'Islam de marché*. Paris: Le Seuil.

Holtrop, T., Haenni, P. (2002). "Mondaines spiritualité . . . Amr Khâlid, shakyh banché de la dorée cairote." *Politique Africaine*, 87, pp. 45–68.

IMF Annual Report (2015). https://www.imf.org/external/pubs/ft/ar/2015/eng/index.htm

Jones, T. M. (1991). "Ethical decision making by individuals in organizations: An issue-contingent model." *Academy of Management Review*, 16(2), pp. 231–248.

Kennedy, E. J., Lawton, L. (1998). "Religiousness and business ethics," *Journal of Business Ethics*, 17, pp. 163–175.

Kuran, T. (2002). "The Islamic commercial crisis: Institutional roots of economic underdevelopment in the Middle East," Research Paper C03–1, Islamic Commercial Crisis Center for Law, Economics and Organization, Los Angeles.

Kuran, T. (2003). "Islamic redistribution through Zakat: Historical record and modern realities." In M. Bonner, M. Ener, and A. Singer (eds.), *Poverty and Charity in Middle Eastern Contexts*. New York: State University of New York Press, pp. 275–293.

Kuru, A. T. (2005). "Globalization and diversification of Islamic movements: Three Turkish cases." *Political Science Quarterly*, 120(2), pp. 253–274.

Kutluay, M. (2011). "Economy as the 'practical hand' of 'new Turkish foreign policy': A political economy explanation." *Insight Turkey*, 13(1), pp. 67–88.

McDonald, D. B. (2011). "The AKP story: Turkey's bumpy reform path towards the European Union." *Society and Economy*, 33(3), pp. 525–542.

Mitroff, I. I., Denton, E. A. (1999), "A study of spirituality in the workplace." *Sloan Management Review*, 40, pp. 83–92.

170 *Laure Dikmen*

Mohr, A. T., Spekman, R. (1994). "Characteristics of partnership success: Partnership attributes, communication behaviour and conflict resolution techniques." *Strategic management Journal*, 15(2), pp. 135–152.

Mullin, M., Janet, K., Singhapakdi, A., Attia, A., Vitell, S. (2004). "Some important factors underlying ethical decisions of Middle-Eastern marketers." *International Marketing Review*, 21(1), pp. 53–67.

Osella F., Osella C. (2009). "Muslim entrepreneurs in public life between India and the Gulf: Making good and doing good." *Journal of the Royal Anthropological Institute*, pp. S202–S221.

Prancer, M. S., Jackson, L. M., Hunsberger, B., Pratt, M. W., Lea, J. (1995). "Religious Orthodoxy and the complexity of thought about religious and non-religious issues." *Journal of Personality*, 63, pp. 213–232.

Railton, P. (1996). "The diversity of moral dilemma." In H. E. Mason (ed.), *Moral Dilemmas and Moral Theory*. Oxford: Oxford University Press, pp. 140–166.

Rest, J. R., Thoma, S., Moon, Y. L., Getz, I. (1986). "Different cultures, sexes and religions." In J. R. Rest (ed.), *Moral Development: Advances in Research and Theory*. New York: Prager.

Rice, G. (1999). "Islamic ethics and the implications for business." *Journal of Business Ethics*, 18(4), pp. 345–358.

Rice, G. (2006). "Pro-environmental behavior in Egypt: Is there a role for Islamic environmental ethics?" *Journal of Business Ethics*, 65, pp. 373–390.

Rice, G., Al-Mossawi, M. (2002). "The implications of Islam for advertising messages: The Middle Eastern context. *Journal of Euromarketing*, 11(3), pp. 71–97.

Saeed, M., Ahmed, Z. U., Muktar, S. (2001), "International marketing ethics from an Islamic Perspective: A value-maximization approach." *Journal of Business Ethics*, 32(2), pp. 127–142.

Sandikli, Ö. (2011). "Researching Islamic marketing: Past and future perspectives." *Journal of Islamic Marketing*, 2(3), pp. 246–258.

Spiro, M. (1966). "Religion: Problems of definition and explanation." In M. Banton (ed.), *Anthropological Approaches to the Study of Religion*. London: Tavistock.

Tammâm, H., Haenni, P. (2007). "Le management, nouvelle utopie islamiste: Une lecture managériale des textes." *Revue Française de Gestion*, 2(171), pp. 175–193.

Taspinar, Ö. (2011). "The Turkish model and the Arab world." *Zaman*, July 11.

Treviño, L. K. (1986). "Ethical decision making in organizations: A person-situation interaction model." *Academy of Management Review*, 11(3), pp. 601–617.

Tropman, J. E. (1995). *The Catholic Ethic in American Society: An Exploration of Values*. San Francisco, CA: Jossey-Bass.

Turkish Statistical Institute (TURKSTAT), Annual Industry and Service Statistics (2015). http://www.turkstat.gov.tr/PreHaberBultenleri.do?id=30911

UNCTAD (2018). Annual report; https://unctad.org/en/PublicationsLibrary/dom2019_en.pdf

Viswesvaran, C., Deshpande, S. P. (1996). "Ethics, success and job satisfaction: A test of dissonance theory in India." *Journal of Business Ethics*, 15(10), pp. 1065–1069.

Weber, M. (1905). *L'Éthique protestante et l'esprit du capitalisme*. Traduction en français 1967. Paris: Plon.

World Bank (2018). *The World Bank Annual Report 2018 (English).* Washington, D.C.: World Bank Group. http://documents.worldbank.org/curated/en/630671538158537244/The-World-Bank-Annual-Report-2018.

Worden, S. (2005). "Religion in strategic leadership: A positivistic, normative/theological, and strategic analysis." *Journal of Business Ethics, 57,* pp. 221–329.

Yankaya, D. (2013). *La nouvelle bourgeoisie islamique.* Paris: Presses Universitaires de France.

Yavuz, H. M. (1999). "Towards an Islamic liberalism? The Nurcu movement and Fethullah Gülen." *Middle East Journal, 53*(4), pp. 584–605.

Yousef, D. A. (2001). "Islamic work ethic: A moderator between organizational commitment and job satisfaction in a cross-cultural context." *Personnel Review,* 30(2), pp. 152–169.

Zainul, N., Osman, F., Mazlan, S. H. (2004), "E-commerce from an Islamic perspective." *Electronic Commerce Research & Applications,* 3(3), pp. 280–293.

Part III

The Challenges of Cross-Cultural Issues in International Management

Part I of this book analyzes the cultural and societal challenges of international management through strategic decision-making, whereas Part II deals with issues of ethics and social responsibility. Part III is devoted to the study of the ever-changing challenges of interculturality in international management.

In Chapter 10, John Eustice O'Brien and Josiane Martin-O'Brien examine the limits of classical managerial approaches in the Indian context. These approaches, of western origin, are rooted in a form of rigid techno-instrumental rationality (Weber, 1992 [1905]). On the basis of field studies in India, the authors point out, from an institutionalist perspective, the difficulties that may be encountered in deploying these classical managerial approaches in a non-western context.

In Chapter 11, Nathalie Touratier-Muller and Dan Andersson analyze the management of transport service purchases by shippers, for example, the criteria for selecting transport organizations and suppliers in Sweden and France. The authors show that environmental concerns have more influence on the choice of carrier for Swedish shippers than for French shippers.

In Chapter 12, Anne Bartel-Radic and Marie-Estelle Binet explore under what conditions and in what contexts international student mobility increases intercultural competence. Study visits abroad have been introduced in many student study programs with the aim of developing students' intercultural competence through a meaningful international experience.

In Chapter 13, Sophie Wodociag, Axelle Lutz and Chiara Ghislieri examine the extent to which intercultural competencies can be at the heart of labor market expectations. As companies become more international and globalization increasingly integrates economies, employers increasingly value intercultural competences in recruitment and subsequently in career management. The authors seek to better identify the expectations of the labor market and to better understand the place that different actors give to these intercultural competences.

174   *The Challenges of Cross-Cultural Issues*

Reference

Weber, M. (1992 [1905]). *The Protestant Ethic and the Spirit of Capitalism*. New York: Routledge.

10 The Limits of Managerialism for International Enterprise in India

John Eustice O'Brien and Josiane Martin-O'Brien

Introduction

The managerial role depends on an interplay of structural and interpersonal forces. Particularly in countries of diverse cultural disposition and linguistic capacities, it is hardly surprising that international managerial responsibilities are difficult to assure. Conduct must be consistent with limited positional authority, accord with the techno-administrative requirements of its formal function and fit with the human dynamics of workers, clients and the operative world of an enterprise. Ensuring respect for standards and effective action with those in subordinate or higher positions, as well as external agents, is a further demand. This tension is intensified when a managerial logic of foreign origin is imported by training into non-western countries. Focusing on the case of India, in this study we examine the resulting institutional confrontation and how it is resolved by industrial managers.

As practiced in the United States, extreme managerialism is the teleological endpoint of the scientific management project initiated by Frederick Taylor (1903). The action it underwrites is often practicable for managing monocultural, monolinguistic companies, or even in non-western areas, for companies in depersonalized, high-tech sectors. However, when applied in enterprises from major industrial sectors, founded and operating in non-western countries, one might question the limits of this western logic for worldwide managerial action. We explore this issue, using data gathered by interviewing engineer managers, who were back on the job at least two years after completing a yearlong study program that resulted in an advanced management diploma equivalent to the Harvard model MBA.

Under the Washington Consensus, integrating western managerial practices is generally a necessary condition, imposed by international agencies for investments in less developed countries. These constraints are tied in turn with international markets, operating under rules and institutions that have been established in keeping with the US approach to business. Consequently, over the 20th century, managerialist principles driven by a form of techno-administrative automatism came to dominate industrial

176 *John Eustice O'Brien et al.*

management. Now in the 21st century, broadly accepted as if natural, this is an ideology that merits reconsideration. The observation of sociologist Pierre Bourdieu highlights the dilemma of criticism of any dominant practice:

> It is a general property of specialized fields [i.e., Western managerialism] that the competition for what is at stake conceals collusion concerning the very principles of the game. The struggle for the monopoly of legitimacy contributes to reinforce the legitimacy in the name of which it is conducted. Participation in the constitutive interests of belonging to the field (which presupposes and produces them by its very functioning) implies the acceptance of a set of presuppositions and postulates which, being the undeniable condition of the discussion, are by definition safe from debate."
>
> (Bourdieu, 1996 [1992], 167)

Our study challenges managerialism from a critical perspective. Having proliferated in the United States and diffused worldwide by business schools and consulting firms, it is anchored in a form of rigid techno-instrumental rationality (Weber, 1992 [1905]). Executive order-giving imposes conformity that is often out of fit with local circumstances. Justified by the demand for the efficiency of the result for investors, this managerial strategy has taken on an ideological force, resulting in the treatment of employees, including managers, as abstract goods. As illustrated by our work in India, this practice is poorly suited to the historical determinants of non-western peoples.

Managerialism: Results Measured by Profit

Managerialism is a profit-maximizing perspective that focuses on enterprise unit outcomes rather than individual behavior, emphasizing control and accountability. It is radically pragmatic: the end justifies the means. But only one "end" counts: profitability for investors. Works by Elton Mayo (2003 [1933]), Peter Drucker (1954) and others explored more complex modes of management aimed at balance between internal technical, organizational and symbolic processes with environmental demands. Managerialism as ideology implies commitment to action that is inconsistent with this bouquet of larger responsibilities.

This distinction, between the narrow focus of managerialism and other management strategies, is exemplified in Table 10.1.

The diverse content presented in Table 10.1 highlights the complexity of the management task: to balance participation with delegation; to foster pedagogical advancement; to encourage institutional adaptation; to minimize conflict; to encourage sensitivity to the operational environment; to enhance negotiating skill; to facilitate team evolution in

The Limits of Managerialism in India   177

Table 10.1 Popular models of management

1. Situational leadership (Hersey and Blanchard, 1977): Balance and timeliness of leadership in four key activities: (a) telling, (b) selling, (c) participating and (d) delegating.
2. Build Your Own Model (Birkinshaw, 2010): An educational approach designed to help managers of an organization to collectively establish what for them is a best-fit management approach.
3. SWOT analysis (Osita et al., 2014): Evaluate organizational . . . (a) forces, (b) weaknesses, (c) opportunities and (d) threats; modify the strategy to adapt to institutional processes or conflict with the operating environment.
4. PEST analysis (Lemaire, 2003 [1997]): An institutional radar to analyze the international environment; assess influences: (a) policy, (b) economy, (c) social, (d) technical and (e) environmental.
5. Porter's Five Forces scheme (Porter, 1979): Evaluate five forces for micro-environmental analysis, with adjustment of strategy as needed: (a) threat of new entrants to one's domain, (b) threat of market substitutes, (c) bargaining power of buyers, (d) bargaining power of suppliers and (e) industry rivalry.
6. Project management (Kerzner, 2003): Develop prospective planning cycles, based on logical-linear assumptions, with team participation, aimed at maximizing competition at each stage of the specification to action, and with managers having a sense of the whole process and project to facilitate each functional unit through time.
7. Schein on culture (Schein, 2010): Identify the objective thread of the company's cultural context as an institution and adapt or modify it as much as possible; since the 1980s, focusing on three levels in organizational culture: (a) artifacts and behaviors, (b) values adopted and (c) business assumptions.

fit with cycles of action; and to foster agreement between corporate and national cultures. As practice, managers must balance technical objectives with social-cognitive factors, human and cultural, internal and external. Managerialism identifies these non-technical dimensions of managerial competence as sources of inefficiency to be overlooked, if not eliminated.

Managerialism: Foundations

The managerialist strain in corporate operations dates from Frederick Taylor a century ago (Hsu, 2003; Bendix, 1947), which when followed would transform managers into labor manipulators serving capital, overshadowing other approaches that stress more holistic approach to organizations (Fayol, 1916; McGregor, 1960).

In the United States, continuing the logic of wartime production after World War II, the strategy developed to consider organizations as semi-organic entities in need of skilled "operators" trained in regulating

178   *John Eustice O'Brien et al.*

"organizational behavior" for a maximum of productivity. A study by Phillip Selznick (1949) of the Tennessee Valley Authority (TVA) provided the case exemplifying this approach. As summarized in his "TVA and Grassroots" (1949), this giant industrial enterprise had been nationalized for military purposes. Thereafter the intention was to transform it into a domestic service while maintaining its depersonalized logic of project management. This ambition to use a private enterprise for managing public enterprises was gradually generalized, facilitating the eventual elimination of public ownership in favor of private investors.

As summarized by Lilienthal (1941)—a famous consultant to General Motors, Selznick's study exposed a new ambiguity that was then arising in the domain of management:

> [The TVA illustrated] a social revolution which was then encompassing the land, . . . elevating leaders of . . . big corporations, to the heights of social power; [but] might this new class [of leader] become an exploitive group, using their specialized skills and social position for their own class benefit; [thus posing in turn] a threat to democracy?"
>
> (Selznick, 1949, 27)

He warned:

> We can choose, between an exploiting ruling class versus managers bound by the principles of public service and democratic methods. . . . Every wise leader knows that tyranny and exploitation feed on excessive centralization of the administration; . . . [how might] the risks of managerial exploitation be diminished?
>
> (Selznick, 1949, 27)

While awareness of the exploitive potential of management is general (Getz, 2009; Verrier and Bourgeois, 2016), there is disagreement on what should be done to solve it. As Clegg (2014) points out, the managerialist initiative represents a hardening of Taylorism, about which management professors are not passive bystanders. Managerialist logic fits with the contemporary mandates of rational science. Rather than treating managerialist tactics with a critical eye of humanist inspiration, many management professors are committed to the epistemological logic of the natural, which is to say non-humanized sciences. As a result, "this positivist model has come to define the ascendancy for the science of management and its associated theories" (Deroy and Clegg, 2011).

Managerialism: Institutional Perspective

We use a neo-institutional model (see Table 10.1) for our analysis of the power and limitations of managerialism in action (O'Brien, 2014b). We

The Limits of Managerialism in India   179

draw attention to the dynamics beyond the formal boundaries of an enterprise that influence its internal dynamics, both structurally and interpersonally. The importance of local community and culture for enterprise action become evident, framing our discussion of Indian cultural distinctions in the structuring of businesses.

We postulate that quality management is intended to contribute to the sustainability of the organization in which managers work. Rather than "anything goes," sustainability requires normative regulation, accepted as legitimate by participants and reinforced by behavioral conformity (Robertson and Crittenden, 2003). Norms come in complex packages, such as those that define appropriate behavior for teachers and students in schools. Such packages define every social institution. A company is a large and formalized social institution of this nature, that is, a symbolic-cultural community of meanings as well as a technical, instrumental and economic machine (Alexander, 2011a, 2011b; Powell, 2007; Lounsbury, 2007, 2001; Powell and DiMaggio, 1983).

Still, as Scholz and Stein point out,

> Many students (in business schools) consider culture almost as a necessary evil, to learn about only on the basis of the need to know, so as not to steal learning time from economics; as if the real subject of the studies were commercial.
> (Blasco, 2009, 181, referring to Scholz and Stein, 2012)

To increase interest about institutional problems among management researchers in this complex problem, Roy Suddaby organized a special forum for the 2003 conference of the Association of Management on the theme "Organizations and their Institutional Environments: Bringing Meaning, Values and Culture" (Suddaby et al., 2010). In subsequent work, he discussed how attention to institutional dynamics reveals the otherwise hidden concern that he labeled that of "two worlds":

> Institutionalist theory suggests that organizations exist simultaneously in two worlds—a technical world with a focus on the material resources of work, and a social world where they have to deal with symbolic resources such as legitimacy and status.
> (Suddaby, 2013, 381)

This led him to favor "reclaiming the symbolic in institutional theory" (Suddaby, 2013), requiring first-order attention to the symbolic forces of organization in order to find meaning in technical action:

> [Such] analysis is historically concentrated in the symbolic rather than the material domain; [revealing] why organizations adopt behaviors that conform to normative requirements, which often conflict with the

180   *John Eustice O'Brien et al.*

rational realization of economic goals or that purely technical or productive objects, which acquire meaning far beyond their utility value.

(Suddaby, 2014)

The neo-institutional perspective on enterprises is more open to the environment (Suddaby, 2013; Boli and Thomas, 1999). It offers a view of the company's processes or events, which fits the position of other specialists, from Pettigrew (1992) to Mintzberg (2003) and Weick (2009). All in all, an institutional perspective for organizational study is implicitly a "critique of rationality" (O'Brien, 2016d), that opposes the all-technical approach that might otherwise serve as a basis for managerial operations:

> The central contribution of institutional theory to the understanding of organizations is, to a large extent, an obstacle to economic rationality. As Lincoln stated, the central idea of the institutional tradition is the observation that "social structures and processes tend to acquire meaning and stability as such rather than as instrumental tools for attaining specialized goals".
>
> (Lincoln, 1995; Suddaby, 2013)

Suddaby observes that "modern organizations reflect the intensive cultural rationalization of the contemporary world in their constituent structures." A western strategy driven by a managerialist logic may succeed in the West because it corresponds to the dominant mode of its cultural organization. But what about India? (Said, 2005).

Open System Model—Institutional Analysis of Managerial Context

To frame the institutional forces of managerial action, we draw on an open-systems (PETOS) model developed by one of the authors (O'Brien, 2015b). Attention is balanced, to both the technical and symbolic facets of organizational action, as well as between the internal and external forces and constraints. As depicted in Figure 10.2, the forces at play in enterprise action are partitioned into five domains of opportunity and resources: (1) population of social agents that bear on the enterprise (P); (2) environment in which enterprise operates (E); (3) technological core that makes the identity of the enterprise (T); (4) organizational dimensions that structure the enterprise; and (5) symbolic normative/communication domains of routinized action (S).

To exemplify application of the model, consider an innovative enterprise, called NEW. It emerges thanks to the conjuncture of forces from population (P) demand as potential market and the competitors, regulators, resource constraints and opportunities that constitute its dynamic business *environment* (E). NEW then serves markets of individuals,

The Limits of Managerialism in India 181

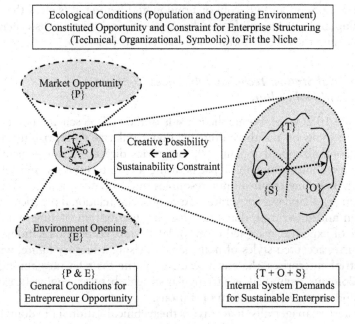

Figure 10.1 Five domain (PETOS) enterprise model (O'Brien, 2014a)

institutions or other organizations but is buffeted by social-political agents and socio-cultural structures, legal-political actors including nation-state apparatus (e.g., the EU, UN, World Bank, IMF, WLO—World Labour Organization—and international agencies like UNO—United Nation Organizations) and financial institutions. This results in a set of friendly and hostile external factors that must be overcome if NEW is to succeed. The same mix of forces are open to others as well, such that direct competition quickly arises.

Although "managing the environment is vital," management action is principally concerned with the internal dynamics of the firm. We indicate the three major domains under direct corporate control: technical (T), organizational (O) and symbolic (S).

While focus here is on the business-service-regulative environment, this is not to suggest indifference to the natural environment on which life itself ultimately depends. This is not the place to debate the nature of responsibility in regard to the natural environment that ought to be borne by business or public service enterprises.

Taken together, the forces that define enterprise opportunity and thus managerial responsibility are local for peoples and societies. This points to the importance of the national-cultural variable: both the nature of demand of a population and of the operating environment are culturally

182 John Eustice O'Brien et al.

framed by the rules and norms of societies. Given the evident differences between London and Nairobi or London and Beijing, it is clear that recognizing and not being blocked by cross-cultural mistakes is crucial in determining the success of international enterprise.

Managerial Strains: Technical Objectives Confront Organizational Culture

In Figure 10.2, we elaborate the left side of the PETOS schema (see Figure 10.1) to focus on the three domains that regularize enterprise functioning: an organizational domain (O), configuring direction, management and labor; a technical domain (T), structuring a core technology and related factors including input-output resources and practices; and a symbolic domain (S), shaping a corporate culture of social-relational practices, both written and unwritten, that prescribe the distribution of functions, the nature of expertise, accepted forms of leadership, corporate relations, and of course, accepted styles of management. Using a literary figure, within industrial enterprises, there is a recurrent battle for relevance among the TOS domains, embodied by a triangular struggle between engineers, executives and managers about firm operations.

Western managerialist logic favors the technical-rational (T) domain as a determinate force over organization factors (O) with the content of the symbolic domain (S)—which directly touches the human dimension of

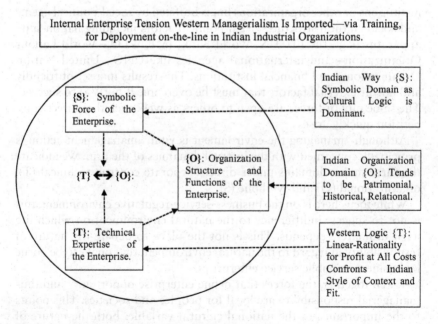

Figure 10.2 Managerial tension within Indian enterprise

The Limits of Managerialism in India   183

organized labor and management alike, as of secondary concern. India is quite different, with the symbolic domain (S) governing collective activity, for business, pleasure, education, family and other. Examples drawn from our field study in India illustrate how these cultural differences play themselves out when managerial training "made in America" is imported into India via MBA-type training for Indian industrial engineer managers. This tension is visually represented by the schema in Figure 10.2, depicting how forces issue of the technical (T) domain, battle those anchored in the symbolic (S) domain for control of organizing structures (O) of enterprise.

Managerialism: An Unquestioned Ideology?

The difficulty when attempting to avoid cross-cultural issues of this nature is that each national group assumes the unquestioned rightness of its approach to strategy. For example, former *Harvard Business Review* editor Magretta (2012, 3) has said, "We all learn to think like managers, even if it's not what we are called." Whereas this may be valid for Wall Street personnel, even in the United States, large swaths of the population do not stress monetary reward and technical efficiency as primary values. For India, this is clearly not a valid claim, because other values constantly intrude to modify the blind pursuit of economic advantage.

According to Thomas Klikauer (2015), managerialism is primarily an ideology rather than a model or theory of modern management. Applied as a meta model, in all modes of ordinary management, it explains both its strength and its danger. As he points out, not all organizations are alike, and thus no single style of performance can optimize action. "Managerialism justifies the application of unidimensional managerial techniques to all fields of work, society and capitalism on the basis of the superior ideology . . . [as if] necessary to direct public institutions and society as enterprises" (Klikauer, 2015, 1105).

Ideologies are cultural constructs that contribute to the foundation of every culture group. Accepted without conscious analysis, the content varies considerably from one national group to the next, generating conflicts that defy facile negotiation. High-ranking business schools and journals are a fertile ground for its diffusion, and the American Way is favored.

Enveloped in ideology, broader human concerns—such as the meaning of participation in work, or commitment to duty—are treated as exogenous to the "pure" act of managerial rationality: "[These schools] . . . make[] [managerialist] ideology appear as common sense requiring no other explanation, e.g. competitive advantage" (Klikauer, 2015, 1106). As Bourdieu (1979, 1992) points out, the potential of strong ideas that take on ideological power is not peculiar to the field of management. Nonetheless, due to the particular quality of business activity, the ideological self-promotion of managerialism diffuses to the surrounding operating environment and seduces uncritical categories of the population:

184   *John Eustice O'Brien et al.*

For managerialism, politics and democracy are simply an obstacle to efficiency and competitive advantages. . . . There are no democratic solutions to problems, only management problems. . . . Managerialism does not concern the general will of Rousseau's people, but a managerial approach to the engineering of societal problems transformed into technicalities.

(Klikauer, 2015, 1107)

Shih-wei Hsu (2010) considers the possibility that managerialist rigidity might be softened in practice. The distortion of managerialism is that it "results directly from the marriage of capitalism and managerialism" (Hsu, 2003, 14), raising issue at the ethical rather than technical level. Rather than assuming that technical rationality aimed at profit on capital be the end justifying any managerial means, he proposes a "paradigm revolution." Doing so would require altered pedagogy in management training, providing students with the broader education needed to assume a critical stance about political-economic forces, with the rightness of managerial action balanced by attention to human and societal consequences.

Hsu envisions nothing less than "the creation of a new subjective consciousness," accepting that management entails knowledge at many levels. Since "all knowledge is interconnected," management practice "can never be free of ethics" (Hsu, 2003, 14). The next part of this text draws on our research work in India to exemplify the difficulties when managerialist action, based on western business culture, is carried into the Indian industrial sector via training for engineer managers.

Managerial Particularities in Indian Enterprises

The lack of fit of western managerialism with the Indian Way is due to cultural differences that frame enterprise action and are taken in without question by the majority of Indian citizens. (Capelli et al., 2010). In brief, the symbolic domain of Indian culture is overdetermined by a generic spiritual attitude (Gopalan and Rivera, 1997). Supernatural forces are part of everyday life, as evidenced by the innumerable gods, goddesses and animals that are constantly solicited for the protection of individuals, including those at work. The theory of karma makes everyone accept his fate and his place.

Unlike Americans, the natural order is considered dominant among Indians, with human authority—such as might be asserted by managers, promoting only minor variations in pregiven dispositions. Establishing valid evidence of these Indian opposites as they are materialized in practice depends on the use of qualitative, ethnographic methods of study (Suddaby, 2006).

The dense symbolic climate penetrating all the facets of Indian society cannot be "algorithmized." Accepting the technical, symbolic and ideological differences between the western business culture and the Indian Way

The Limits of Managerialism in India 185

is not to justify extremism. One must not assert that the American/western way of business management is bereft of the symbolic content related to human meanings and values, nor that Indian nationals are culturally indifferent about resource rationality or labor efficiency. It is a matter of value hierarchies, such that in the West—or at least for Americans—the symbolic issues are sacrificed in favor of technical considerations, which is the other way around for Indians. The following are five examples of this in reference to managerial action.

Devaluing Taylorism

As principle, Indian management is a team activity. The individualist work motive is foreign to them. Whether in reference to subordinates, superiors or immediate colleagues, to use the sports metaphor, force is team outcome oriented rather than the seeking of star recognition. Interdependence is fundamental, developed early and reinforced constantly by family, the local community and education. This links corporate motivation with the history of castes and *jatis*, which are universally identified in reference to specific occupations, dispositions and skills. Most of the managerial undertakings associated with planning, programming, budgeting, execution and quality control occur in operational teams, linked in elaborate networks that are largely opaque for westerners. For example, from field work we found that, after advanced training, even if a proposed innovation of a technical nature is attractive, it will be treated as unwelcome if not canceled, if there has been insufficient consultation and agreement with the members of implementing teams (Martin-O'Brien, 2017). Negotiation is mandatory.

The managerial challenge is the coordination, communication and resolution of the conflicts, framed temporally in agreement with the operational objectives of the company. However, teamwork takes time, which can be misinterpreted (by westerners) as a sign of incompetence, confusion, insolence or stupidity. Moreover, the Indians are masters of passive resistance. When their participation in work is vilified, they thwart without aggression, in the spirit of Gandhi's historical image. For example, an American expatriate director launched a standard marketing program for the entire Indian territory indifferent to regional cultural diversity. His Indian deputy director reported watching this exercise begin and fail, because opposing one's boss is also taboo. He knew that the result would be replacement of the boss by another westerner who was likely to confront the same deception.

This contradiction between Indian values and the tradition of Taylorism is particularly evident for industrial production. The western managerialist fetish favoring performance over skill rests on the principle of depersonalization of labor, touted as if a sign of moral equanimity. Accordingly, labor action is reduced to a series of fine, repetitive acts, with workers constrained by robot-like job descriptions.

186   John Eustice O'Brien et al.

In foreign settings such as India, the attempt is made to apply the same standards for local managers, extending to the middle manager level (Holmes, 2013). Indians abhor depersonalized treatment not as a personality issue as it might be understood in the West but in relation to the identity of each one who has his own determined role (*moksha*) and his duty to perform (*dharma*) as negotiated within a given group.

Human Resources: Development or Management?

In large Indian companies, human resources must be developed and not simply managed. In New York, the top personnel function would be identified as DHR (director of human resources) whereas in India it would be HRD (human resources development). The distinction in referents is intentional and important, extending to the central government's Ministry of Human Resources Development (MHRD India, 2010), which includes both labor and education.

HRD involves a career-oriented treatment of each manager with promotion and privileges based on categorical qualities of role rather than details of execution or personal relationship with a boss. This does not mean that Indians are insensitive to differences in performance but that performance ratings are used more for self-improvement rather than as a basis for differentiation and sanction between positions of similar experience (Singh, 2013).

Historically, in the United States, under Fordist philosophy, industrial corporations prospered in part because of the care taken to cultivate an internal labor market. Personnel began at entry positions and, with continued investment in training, advanced toward greater responsibility and compensation. This promoted loyalty and positive motivation that linked employees to companies in a way that benefited both parties.

A similar logic pertains for large Indian companies, particularly in the very important public sector. Managers must complete seven days of management training per year, which for a company employing 6,000 executives demands organization of 42,000 training days a year. Significant changes in managerial grade are formalized by training programs whose acronyms are known by everyone: AMP (advance management program); SMP (senior management program). This is done for entire batches of similarly trained and experienced managers, whereupon they are treated with new levels of respect and deference as a sign of their collectively attributed competence. Whether this practice will be preserved under globalization, with western managers prone to individual action for selection, promotion and demission, remains to be seen.

Authority Is Honored, Action Is Pragmatic

Whatever the rule or authority, when faced with problem incidents that impede orderly action, Indian managers are disposed to adopt idiosyncratic

The Limits of Managerialism in India   187

solutions of a type labeled *Système-D* in France, known as *Jugaad* (Radjou et al., 2012). This is a Hindi term meaning "an ability to manage somehow, in spite of lack of resources" (Capelli et al., 2010).

Each company has a history, which includes ways to solve recurring operational problems, to define the normative rules of which many remain unwritten. Invariably, problems arise, which implies either that the normal operating procedure has failed or that it has been made dysfunctional by circumstances.

Rather than arrest productive processes, Indian managers take initiatives to create an emergency solution, involving people, materials and actions that are brought together in a way that requires a major weakening of rules. Once initiated, when effective, such an unusual practice may endure, because infrastructural reliability is lower than in more developed countries. This form of spontaneity, involving complex action, organized on an ad hoc basis, is a major transgression of the principles of standardization associated with the managerial ideology.

Historically Established Priorities Are Preferred

In India, history speaks loudly: the location of a community, the nature of the work for a particular caste, the logic that explains the origin of this or that enterprise, the intellectual matter that constitutes one or another academic discipline—for everything of this nature, there is an obligation in the present to preserve the past. From a managerial point of view, this leads to a form of resistance to the technical improvements that threaten the traditional central mission of a company or the definition of the assigned roles (Martin-O'Brien, 2018). With European cultures somewhat in the middle, the United States is at the other extreme, where action unrolls as if history never existed. This may explain why technical innovation is well received in the United States, possible when negotiated in Western Europe, but extremely difficult in India.

One practical example is that traditional industrial organization is a unitary, internal problem that reduces enthusiasm for outsourcing, centralizing vendors or shifting distribution routines in the name of streamlining, efficiency and globalization. Americans criticize this as a form of crony favoritism.

Another example: a new director appointed at TATA Inc. accepted western consultant advice to reorganize the holding model. This generated disharmony throughout the company, carried by new managerial priorities (profitability, rationalization and priority on the stock market) that threatened the sustainability of jobs. After less than two years, the new director was abruptly replaced by the board of directors and the previous CEO was recalled from retirement, which effectively returned the enterprise to the status of a multinational family business (Times of India, 2016).

188 *John Eustice O'Brien et al.*

Under foreign pressure, the Security Exchange Board of India (SEBI) has issued standards of compliance with the US Sarbanes-Oxley Act of 2002. This includes the requirement that the boards of enterprises traded on Wall Street are composed of a mix of members with international experience that is not dependent on an Indian career. To date, compliance with that mandate is limited, with uncertain consequences for global finance (Martin-O'Brien, 2016).

Vigilance Day—Respect of Public Interest

The ethical considerations for Indian managers extend well beyond their own work unit, to the level of the enterprise as framed within the national culture. This is a historical derivation, unreducible symbolically to a formula, with right and wrong defined by practice. To sharpen attention for this, during what is known as Indian national week, each major Indian enterprise schedules a Vigilance Day. The aim is to raise awareness and educate all employees about the internal and external regulations in force regarding forms and practices of corruption that threaten the public service. As one respondent summarized, ignorance of the rules and illiteracy, rather than a desire to cheat, often leads to their transgression.

On that day, managers arrive at the office ready to contribute to vigilance workshops. Via diverse collective activities, including role play and staging, employees are grouped into teams to deal with ambiguous regulatory situations. They are corrected when they fail to find an honorable solution to handle equivocal circumstances in a manner that meets regulatory requirements. This may seem anachronistic to foreigners, who often complain about the corruption experienced in India, but such an initiative would benefit from being extended by the IMF.

Summary and Conclusion

Based on a careful study of western managerial strategy, we explored some of the strengths and weaknesses of its deployment in practice in India. This study was designed from an institutionalist perspective to focus on the contextual and cultural forces that affect the internal management of the business. The Indian situation has been examined in turn to illustrate how the peculiarities of its culture alter the position of the company and the conditions of management in that country. This work shows the importance of considering the macro-cultural characteristics of countries like India, for the deployment of an effective and sustainable management strategy.

On the surface, managerial principles seem to facilitate the deployment of international projects; however, we show that in India, when the project begins, the reality is often quite different because of the explicit power of the cultural differences discussed earlier.

The Limits of Managerialism in India   189

Our study clarifies the major challenge of adaptability of westerners to India due to cultural differences that define the common context of Indian companies. Hopefully, the examples from our research of the workings of these hazy symbolic forces will aid western managers to engage more effectively with local personnel in Indian companies.

Acknowledgment

Appreciation is acknowledged for the helpful comments of two anonymous reviewers of the original version of this chapter, prior to its acceptance for delivery at the 2017 meeting of the Association Francophone of International Management, Madagascar.

References

Alexander, J. C. (2011a). "Fact-signs and cultural sociology: How meaning-making liberates the social imagination." *Thesis Eleven*, 104, pp. 87–93.

Alexander, J. C. (2011b). "Market as narrative and character: For a cultural sociology of economic life." *Journal of Cultural Economy*, 4(4), pp. 477–488.

Bendix, R. (1947). *Work and Authority in Industry: Ideologies of Management in the Course of Industrialization*. Berkeley: University of California Press.

Birkinshaw, J. (2010). "What is your management model?" www.managementexchange.com/blog/what-your-management-model.

Blasco, M. (2009). "Cultural pragmatists? Student perspectives on learning culture at a business school." *Academy of Management Learning & Education*, 8(2), pp. 174–187.

Boli, J., Thomas, G. M. (1999). *Constructing World Culture: International Non-governmental Organizations since 1875*. Stanford University Press.

Bourdieu, P. (1979). *La Distinction. Critique sociale du jugement*. Paris: Éditions de Minuit.

Bourdieu, P. (1996 [1992]). *The Rules of Art: Genesis and Structure of the Literary Field*. Cambridge: Polity Press.

Capelli, P., Singh, H., Singh, J., Unseem, M. (2010). "The India way: Lessons for the US." *Academy of Management Perspective*, 24(2), pp. 7–23.

Clegg, S. R. (2014). "Managerialism: Born in America." *Academy of Management Review*, 39(4), pp. 566–585.

Deroy, X., Clegg S. R. (2011). "When events interact with business ethics." *Organization*, 18, pp. 637–653.

DiMaggio, P. J., Powell, W. W. (1983). "The iron cage revisited: Institutional isomorphism and collective rationality in organizational fields." *American Sociological Review*, pp. 147–160.

Drucker, P. (1954). *The Principles of Management*. Harper & Brothers, New York.

Evans, C., Holmes, L. (2013). *Re-Tayloring management: Scientific management a century on*. Farnham: Grower.

190   *John Eustice O'Brien et al.*

Fayol, H. (1916). *Administration industrielle et générale.* Paris: Dunod.

Getz, I. (2009). *L'entreprise libérée.* Paris: Vuibert.

Gopalan, K. S., Rivera, J. B. (1997). "Gaining a perspective on Indian value orientations: Implications for expatriate managers." *International Journal of Organizational Analysis,* 5(2), pp. 156–179.

Hersey, P., Blanchard, K. H. (1977). *Management of Organizational Behavior: Utilizing Human Resources.* Princeton, NJ: Prentice Hall.

Hsu, S. W. (2003). "Beyond managerialism." Lancaster, UK: Proceedings annual conference Critical Management Studies.

Hsu, S. W. (2010). *Towards a Critical Approach to Knowledge Management.* London: Lambert Academic.

Kerzner, H. (2003). *Project Management: A Systems Approach to Planning, Scheduling, and Controlling.* New York: Wiley.

Klikauer, T. (2015). "What Is Managerialism?" *Critical Sociology,* 41(7–8), pp. 1103–1119. www.laviedesidees.fr/Le-capitalisme-indien-a-la.html.

Lemaire, J-P. (2003 [1997]). *Stratégies d'internationalisation: développement international de l'entreprise.* Paris: Dunod.

Lilienthal, D. E. (1941). "Management—responsible or dominant?" *Public Administration Review,* 1(4), 91–99.

Lincoln, J. R. (1995). "Book review—Walter W. Powell & Paul DiMaggio (Eds.): The new institutionalism in organizational research." *Social Forces,* 73, pp. 1147–1148.

Lounsbury, M. (2001). "Institutional sources of practice variation: Staffing college and university recycling programs." *Administrative Science Quarterly,* 46, pp. 29–56.

Lounsbury, M. (2007). "A tale of two cities: Competing logics and practice variation in the professionalizing of mutual funds." *Academy of Management Journal,* 50(2), pp. 289–307.

Magretta, J. (2012). *What Management Is: How It Works and Why It's Everyone's Business.* London: Profile Press.

Martin-O'Brien, J. (2016). *L'internationalisation du management en Inde par la formation: les effets du "PGPMX" sur des managers indiens de grandes entreprises industrielles publiques.* Thèse de doctorat, Sorbonne Université Librairie.

Martin-O'Brien, J. (2017). "International management language: Negotiating action in Indian MNCs." Milan: *Proceedings annual conference European International Business Association.*

Martin-O'Brien, J. (2018). "Age, gender, and cast in ethnographic research in India: The intersectional challenge of managerial language and meaning across cultures." Toronto: *Proceedings International Sociological Association World Congress.*

Mayo, E. (2003 [1933]). *The Human Problems of an Industrial Civilization.* New York: Routledge.

McGregor, D. (1971 [1960]). *La Dimension humaine de l'entreprise.* Paris: Gauthier-Villars.

MHDR—Ministry of Human Resources Development India Annual report (2010). https://mhrd.gov.in/sites/upload_files/mhrd/files/document-reports/AR2010-11.pdf.

Mintzberg, H. (2003). *Managers Not MBAs: A Hard Look at the Soft Practice of Managing and Management Development.* San Francisco: Berrett-Koehler.

The Limits of Managerialism in India   191

O'Brien, J. E. (2014a). *Critical Practice from Voltaire to Foucault and Beyond*. Leiden: Brill.

O'Brien, J. E. (2014b). "Enterprise strategy in global perspective: A systems-institutional approach." Marseille: Proceedings Annual Conference of Atlas/ Association Francophone for Management International.

O'Brien, J. E. (2015a). "Piketty's capital: 21st-century gravitational force?" *Critical Sociology*, 41(2), pp. 385–400.

O'Brien, J. E. (2015b). "Charismatic leadership: A structural perspective on institutional authority for international management." Hanoi, Vietnam: Proceedings Annual Conference Atlas/Association Francophone for Management International.

O'Brien, J. E. (2015c). "Democracy with leadership: The political dialectics of Maurice Merleau-Ponty." Lausanne: Proceedings Biannuel Congrès des Associations Francophones des Sciences Politiques.

O'Brien, J. E. (2016a). "Global political-economy as capitalist hyperspace: Progressive utopia or otherwise?" *Critical Sociology*, 42(1), pp. 167–175.

O'Brien, J. E. (2016b). "Train factories in India? Cross-cultural challenges for Western entry in an Eastern world." Nice: Proceedings annual conference Atlas/ Association Francophone for Management International.

O'Brien, J. E. (2016c). "India's over-determined precariat: Caste & class between tradition & modernity." Vienna: *Proceedings Biannual Forum of International Sociological Association*.

O'Brien, J. E. (2016d). *Critique of Rationality from Walter Benjamin to Maurice Merleau-Ponty*. Leiden: Brill.

Osita, I. C., Idoko, O. R., Nzekwe, J. (2014). "Organization's stability and productivity: The role of SWOT analysis." *International Journal of Innovative and Applied Research*, 2(9), pp. 23–32.

Pettigrew, A. M. (1992). "The character and significance of strategy process research." *Strategic Management Journal*, 13(2), pp. 5–16.

Porter, M. (1979). "How competitive forces shape strategy." *Harvard Business Review*, March/April, pp. 78–93.

Powell, W. W. (2007). "The new institutionalism." In *The International Encyclopedia of Organization Studies*. Thousand Oaks, CA: Sage.

Radjou, N., Prabhu, J., Simone, A. (2012). *L'innovation Jugaad*. Paris: Ed. Diateino.

Robertson, C. J., Crittenden, W. F. (2003). "Mapping moral philosophies: Strategic implications for multinational firms." *Strategic Management Journal*, 24, pp. 385–392.

Said, E. (2005[1978]). *L'Orientalisme*. Paris: Editions du Seuil.

Schein, E. H. (2010). *Organizational Culture and Leadership*. San Francisco, CA: Jossey-Bass.

Scholz, C., Stein, V. (2012). "From cultural chameleons to competitive acceptance: Teaching cross-cultural management in the real world." Boston, MA: Proceedings annual conference of Academy of Management.

Selznick, P. (1949). *TVA and the Grass Roots: A Study in the Sociology of Formal Organization*. Los Angeles: University of California Press.

Singh, A. K. (2013). "HRM practices and managerial effectiveness in Indian business organizations." *Delhi Business Review*, 14(1).

192 *John Eustice O'Brien et al.*

Suddaby, R. (2006). "What grounded theory is not." *Academy of Management Journal*, 49(4), pp. 633–642.

Suddaby, R. (2013). "Institutional theory." In Kessler E. H. (ed.), *Encyclopedia of Management Theory-I*. Los Angeles, CA: Sage.

Suddaby, R. (2014). "Editor's comments: Why theory?" *Academy of Management Review*, 39(4), p. 407.

Suddaby, R., Elsbach, K. D., Greenwood, R., Meyer, J. W., Zilber, T. B. (2010). "Organizations and their institutional environments—Bringing meaning, values and culture back." *Academy of Management Journal*, 53(6), pp. 1234–1240.

Taylor, F. W. (1903). *Shop Management*. New York: American Society of Engineers.

Times of India. (2016). "Tata sons replaces Cyrus Mistry as TCS chief," October 24. https://timesofindia.indiatimes.com/business/india-business/Tata-Sons-replaces-Cyrus-Mistry-as-TCS-chief/articleshow/55345362.cms.

Verrier, G., Bourgeois, N. (2016). *Faut-il libérer l'entreprise?* Paris: Dunod.

Weber, M. (1992 [1905]). *The Protestant Ethic and the Spirit of Capitalism*. New York: Routledge.

Weick, K. E. (2009). "The impermanent organization." In *Making Sense of the Organization*. New York: Blackwell.

11 Environmental Considerations When Purchasing Transport Services

A Comparison of Management Approaches Between Swedish and French Shippers

Nathalie Touratier-Muller and Dan Andersson

Introduction

The transport sector, which accounts for almost a quarter of Europe's greenhouse gas emissions (GHG),[1] generates much debate, study and discussion regarding how to decrease this impact. All the countries that ratified the Kyoto Protocol, which meet once a year to evaluate the application of the United Nations Framework Convention on Climate Change (UNFCCC), continuously refer to its negative effect on the environment. When the United Nations Climate Change Conference (COP21), held in 2015 in Paris, concluded an agreement committing 195 states to reduce their greenhouse gas emissions, it also launched a strong call to action for the transport sector, The following COPs, held in Marrakech in November 2016 (COP22), Bonn in November 2017 (COP23) and Katowice in December 2018 (COP24), consequently addressed the transport emissions problem through a "transport thematic day." Recognizing the improvements and successful sustainable urban mobility actions initiated by some cities, it also highlighted the urgent need to reduce carbon emissions at a broader level, which could be accomplished by a mix of policies and governmental measures.

The majority of greenhouse gas emissions (GMG) from transport are caused by CO_2 emissions (Piecyk and McKinnon, 2010). In Sweden, approximately 30% of all GHG emissions come from transport, and of this about 30% are emissions from trucks (both heavy and light).[2]

Initiatives to reduce the negative impact from transport can be observed in many countries. Within Europe, France and Sweden are examples of quite proactive countries while applying different policies. France has set the objective to reduce CO_2 emissions from the transport sector by 29% from 2015 to 2028,[3] whereas Sweden has as the objective to reduce emissions from domestic transport by at least 70% by 2030 compared with 2010.[4] On its side, France has introduced various transport initiatives, for instance, carriers that voluntarily adhere to a specific charter of commitments (*Charte Objectif CO2*) since 2008, can obtain compliance certification after three years if they have achieved a high environmental performance. In response to this measure, a new voluntary charter has been agreed for shippers (*Charte FRET 21*). It has been on trial with ten proactive shippers since May 2015 and should be open to 1,000 other French companies by 2020 (Touratier-Muller and Jaussaud, 2017). Under a different heading, since October 2013 a mandatory scheme (decree no. 2011–1336) obliges all French carriers to calculate and inform their customers about their CO_2 impact. There are, however, four different official calculation methods resulting in difficulties in centralizing and comparing the real environment performance of carriers. An example of voluntary action in Sweden is the organization KNEG, an acronym meaning "climate neutral goods transport on road," which was formed in 2006. This organization includes vehicle manufacturers, fuel producers, logistics companies, academics and governmental authorities. It aims to show how the climate impact from road transport can be reduced by different voluntary actions. The members implement different actions that should lead to concrete results, which are followed up and documented. Each year all the results are compiled, analyzed and presented in a yearly report showing the extent of the progress.

The European Union has prioritized the reduction of CO_2 emissions from transport, adopting a roadmap of 40 concrete initiatives outlined in a white paper in 2011.[5] However, behaviors influencing emissions, such as how freight transport services are purchased, have been scarcely explored, and even less research has been undertaken on comparisons between countries. Scrutinizing how shippers (i.e., transport purchasers who own the goods to be shipped) select their transport providers (suppliers in charge of the transportation service) could provide insights facilitating the development of appropriate national or European environmental freight transportation measures.

There are some national studies that have highlighted how sustainable development can be better taken into account during the transportation procurement process, for instance, in Sweden (Rogerson et al., 2014), in Germany (Large et al., 2013) and in France (Touratier-Muller et al., 2017). However, to the best of our knowledge, there are no extant studies analyzing and comparing transport procurement practices between European countries. Such management studies might provide knowledge and support when developing sustainable European policies. Consequently, as a first step, the purpose of this chapter is to shed light on transportation purchasing processes in two different European countries. The starting point is Sweden and France, both of which could be considered as progressive with respect to their ambitions to curb the negative consequences of transport emissions. In order to find relevant comparable transport services buyers in each country, it was decided to focus only on transport services buyers for whom the environmental aspects of transport are of very high importance. As a consequence, this research provides an

Considerations When Purchasing Transport   195

overview regarding the features of transportation purchasing practices, highlighting some specificities inherent to each country context. The main priority of our study is not to test or generate theory but to use some industrial purchasing concepts of the IMP group (Cova and Salle, 1992) to investigate the buying purchasing process in both countries.

This chapter is organized as follows. An overview of the extant literature provides the starting point for the work and the formulation of three research questions. The subsequent section presents the methodology deployed, and thereafter the main results of our research are presented and discussed. A final section presents the conclusions and suggests areas suitable for future research.

Literature Review

Academic studies on the road freight sector provide a broad spectrum of information. We decided to conduct a literature overview divided into two main sections: (1) shippers' influence in the adoption of sustainable transportation and (2) shippers' "perspective" when purchasing transportation services. This work enables us to identify the research gap, which is delineated by the three main research questions.

Shippers' Influence in Adopting Sustainable Transportation Practices

While cultural values seem to shape certain processes within supply chains (Walker et al., 2008; Marshall et al., 2015), relating to positively sustainable cultural and entrepreneurial practices, the work of Thornton et al. (2013) reveal that socially responsible supplier selection is more encouraged and rewarded in developed countries. Other surveys conducted specifically on the transportation purchasing process in Sweden (Pålsson and Kovács, 2014) highlight company cultural weight to retaining environmental criteria in the process. Although the culture of the shipper seems to play a key role, no work has been undertaken scrutinizing these cultural differences according to country specificities.

Additionally, we investigate the role played by the size of the company. Whereas Björklund (2011) suggests that the size has no correlation, contributions from Lammgård (2012) and Pålsson et al. (2014) find a correlation showing that the bigger the company, the more proactive it is in integrating environmental issues. In line with these findings, Rogerson (2016) and Van den Berg and De Langen (2017) underline that larger companies are more inclined than small companies to implement green transport practices. This could be explained by the willingness of large companies to deploy financial resources in order to achieve environmental improvements, whereas small companies need to be more focused on costs (Lammgård, 2012).

196 *Nathalie Touratier-Muller et al.*

In another vein, industry sectors seem to exert a substantial influence, as highlighted by Isaksson (2012, p. 47): "customers from the industry sector are considered to have fewer and lower green requirements than customers from the food industries." This is particularly relevant because specific industry sectors (such as the food sector) involving direct consumer products are believed to induce more detailed green demands. This argument, raised by Isaksson (2012), could be explained because green requirements coming from final customers are higher. Product characteristics (Björklund, 2011) as well as material flow characteristics (Rogerson, 2012) also seem to exert an influence to green the transportation flows. In this sense, the transport of hazardous substances, fresh or frozen food products, seems to require special attention or targeted measures. These different findings lead us to formulate the first research question:

> *RQ1.* Are there any specific patterns among environmentally proactive shippers surveyed in France and Sweden when purchasing transportation services?

Shippers' Perspective When Purchasing Transportation Services

The purchase of services that include logistic services as well as transport are intangible by nature. As a consequence, the selection process is far different from the purchase of goods, as underlined by Jackson et al. (1995). In order to explore shippers' perspective regarding the transportation purchasing process, the core elements of the interaction model (Håkansson, 1982) as well as the activity-resource-actor (ARA) model, established by IMP researchers (Cova and Salle, 1992; Håkansson and Snehota, 1995; Håkansson, 2009) could be used. The interaction model (Håkansson, 1982), which constitutes the very foundations of the network perspective, depends on four basic elements: (1) the interaction process, (2) the participants, (3) the environment and (4) the atmosphere. The interaction process involves several exchanges (product, service, information, financial, social), that contain many different characteristics. These characteristics induce a significant effect on the relationship between the buying firm and the supplier as a whole, represented as "the participants." Third, the interaction environment is represented by "governmental pressures as well as general cultural patterns in the particular countries of the parties" (Håkansson, 1982, p. 46). We can then wonder if environmental norms or environmental culture can shape the shippers' behaviors when purchasing transport services. In this respect, as is underlined by Håkansson (1982), a particular country includes individuals' perceptions that influence the interaction process as a whole. The fourth element, represented by "the atmosphere," consists of detecting the level and nature of conflict or cooperation between the companies. It can take a number of forms, such as power or dependence, trust or opportunism, closeness or distance, cooperation or conflict and different expectations. We can then wonder if environmental requirements can constitute a key element of the atmosphere within the shipper and carrier relationship.

Håkansson's (1982) interaction model also draws our attention to explore the specificity of business-to-business (BtoB) relationships. According to him, relationships between buying and selling firms have a stability that derives from the length of the relationship. They look for "stability" rather than "change," "long-term relationship" rather than "short-term business transactions," and "closeness" rather than "distance." We can then observe if this particularity is noticeable among environmental proactive shippers surveyed in France and Sweden.

This interaction model was gradually refined by IMP researchers in the 1980s, pointing out that the more a company invests in interaction, the more it perceives its effects on its "activities," its "resources," and itself as an "actor." Therefore, we decided to make use of the ARA model, which relies on three main network components: (1) the actors (involved in the business interaction), (2) the resources (physical, financial, human and technical assets) and (3) the activities. In our case, we decided to adopt the lenses of the ARA model in order to examine how different layers (activity, resource and actor) are interconnected and linked together between the buying firms (shippers) and their transportation suppliers (carriers).

Studies investigating the transportation purchasing process among shippers established various behavioral perspectives. Bardi (1973) seems to be one of the first authors that tries to identify the key factors determining the carrier selection. This author identifies five factors of influence: transit time reliability, transportation rates, total transit time, willingness to negotiate and financial stability. Additional studies confirm that service quality (Govindan et al., 2013; Rogerson et al., 2014) and price (Lammgård and Andersson, 2014; Rogerson, 2016) remain the two most important criteria when selecting a carrier. In this perspective, carriers' environmental performance is frequently cited but does not seem to constitute a selection criterion (Large et al., 2013; Gonvindan et al., 2013). However, Björklund and Forslund (2013) noticed that shipping companies that include environmental performance in transport contracts do not necessarily consider how to measure the environmental performance and how to handle noncompliance. In this perspective, Evangelista (2014) adds that the lack of a standard methodology for environmental performance measurement prevents companies from sharing the costs and benefits of environmental initiatives. As a consequence, in line with these findings, we could formulate the second and third research questions:

RQ2. What are the transportation criteria used by these 20 environmental proactive shippers in France and Sweden?

RQ3. How is the transportation purchasing organized?

198 *Nathalie Touratier-Muller et al.*

Methodology

The purpose of this research is to explore transport purchasing practices in two progressive European countries (France and Sweden) in order to understand how environmental aspects are taken into account. We conducted a comparative study in order to estimate and highlight similarities or dissimilarities between environmentally proactive shippers in both countries.

Sample and Data Collection

The data used has been collected from 20 shippers that have demonstrated high levels of interest in environmental aspects of transport: ten companies in Sweden (Table 11.1) and ten companies in France (Table 11.2). In France, the ten companies selected are committed to a voluntary environmental program called FRET 21. The data are the results from a case-based methodology, providing rich descriptions and allowing examination of numerous factors as underlined by Boyer and Swink (2008). In Sweden, the companies claiming very high levels of attachment to environmental aspects of transportation were chosen out of a random sample of 151 surveyed companies. This survey is part of the work of the Swedish Transport Procurement Panel (Andersson et al., 2016). The data from the two countries were collected at the same time in 2016.

The 20 companies included provide a field study group showing geographical diversity and heterogeneity in size and industry sector. These characteristics are presented in Table 11.1 and Table 11.2; however, for reasons of confidentiality, details and names of the companies cannot be shown.

Table 11.1 List of the Swedish shippers interviewed

Companies in Sweden			
Industrial sector	*Size*	*Country of origin*	*Respondent*
Hygiene	Medium	Sweden	Warehouse manager
Forest industry	Large	Sweden	Transport manager
Manufacturing	Large	Japan	Purchaser
Wholesale	Medium	Sweden	Transport manager
Manufacturing	Large	Sweden	Purchasing manager
Manufacturing	Medium	Sweden	Purchaser
Wholesale	Medium	Sweden	Logistics manager
Manufacturing	Large	United States	Purchasing manager
Food industry	Medium	Sweden	Logistics manager
Chemicals	Large	Sweden	Transport coordinator

Considerations When Purchasing Transport   199

Table 11.2 List of the French shippers interviewed

Companies in France

Industrial sector	Size	Country of origin	Respondent
Petrochemical	Large	United States	Supply chain manager
Mass distribution	Large	France	Sustainable supply chain and transportation manager
Food industry	Large	United States	Sustainable supply chain manager
Food industry	Large	Italy	Transportation purchasing manager
Food industry	Large	France	Transportation purchasing manager
Food industry	Medium	France	Transportation purchasing manager
Chemical	Medium	France	Transportation purchasing manager
Hygiene	Large	Sweden	Supply chain director
Building material	Large	France	Supply chain director and two transportation buyers

The Swedish survey instrument included questions divided into 34 main categories with several sub-questions for each. In France, an interview guide was developed addressing the same topics. Various categories emerged, such as (1) motivation and resources to develop sustainable transportation procurement, (2) purchasing process and environmental sensitiveness, (3) CO_2 information utilization and (4) environmental collaboration between shippers and carriers. Each interview with the French shippers was fully recorded, transcribed and codified by the researchers. This method of typing and organizing handwritten field notes offers a great opportunity to obtain verbatim transcriptions (Patton, 2002).

Data Analysis

The coding process has been made on the basis of the extant literature review as well as emergent theme categories identified in all responses that we had collected. We decided to use a cross-case analysis, involving an exploration of similarities and differences across cases. This technique, recommended by Yin (2009), can be especially relevant and effective, particularly when the studies "reflect subgroups or categories of general cases—raising the possibility of a typology of individual cases that can be highly insightful" (p. 160). Using this method, the cross-case analysis offers a way to group together answers from different respondents to

200   *Nathalie Touratier-Muller et al.*

similar questions (Patton, 2002, p. 440). This process allowed researchers to centralize and synthesize key answers to the research questions. Based on data from the two data collections, a selection of variables has been displayed in comparative tables that have been designed to respond to the three research questions.

Findings and Discussions

French and Swedish Shippers' "Characteristics" to Integrate Sustainability in Their Transportation Purchasing Process

Comparing Table 11.1 and Table 11.2, we can notice that although shippers' countries of origin are diversified, their parent company comes from developed countries. This first examination may rely on cultural backgrounds. The findings of Pålsson and Kovács (2014) suggest that the cultural weight of developed countries seems to exert an influence committing companies to integrate sustainability into their purchasing process. This observation may tie up with the idea that socially responsible supplier selection might be more encouraged and rewarded in developed countries, as has been suggested by Thornton et al. (2013). From a theoretical perspective, these cultural patterns can constitute the "environment," underlined by the IMP's theoretical concept, and more precisely the interaction model, in which the interaction takes place. In this way, companies coming from developed countries may have a more environmentally conscious behavior influenced by cultural motives.

In relation to size, there is no link between proactivity and size because large companies as well as small and medium-sized companies interviewed in our sample wish to incorporate sustainability into their transportation purchasing process. A French company, for instance, with a staff of 40 employees showed great proactivity and a strong desire to change its transport purchasing method despite its small size. Whereas Rogerson (2016) and Van den Berg and Wan De Langen (2017) highlight that larger companies are more inclined to implement green transport practices than small companies, our results underscore that small and medium-sized companies may be also be highly involved.

Moreover, as we can see in Table 11.2, industry sectors where proactive French and Swedish shippers are active are diversified: food industry, chemical industry, hygiene sector, building materials, petrochemicals, automotive, mechanical manufacturing and so forth. Consequently, there is no industry sector in particular that seems to emerge more than another. In addition, our cases seem to differ from the results of Isaksson (2012), who highlighted that companies that are closer to the end consumers have more detailed green requirements than other industry sectors. Very few of the cases in our study interacted directly with the end consumers: in Sweden only one, and in France only two.

Considerations When Purchasing Transport 201

According to the IMP model, some characteristics impact the actor interactions such as social systems in particular countries that "surround a particular industry or market" (Håkansson, 1982, p. 29). Because the countries of origin of the environmentally proactive companies are developed countries, we could interpret that it is in line with previous research, even if we have not been able to compare it with companies of other origin. However, the size of the company or industry sector do not seem particularly relevant in our studies. These first findings, highlighting specific patterns among 20 environmentally proactive shippers, provide relevant elements answering research question 1. However, a larger-scale analysis would be needed to confirm these results.

Transport Provider Selection Criteria Used by 20 Environmentally Proactive Shippers in France and Sweden

We explored and compared the transportation selection criteria among these 20 proactive companies in France and Sweden (Table 11.3).

From the French side, a primary carrier selection criterion is the price for half of the companies interviewed. Nevertheless, the other half of French shippers mentioned that service quality (punctuality, reactivity, truck availability) and the safety of the vehicles (especially for transportation of dangerous materials) remain the primary criterion. Despite the fact that these ten environmentally proactive French shippers are committed to a voluntary program to reduce their transportation impact, and half of them view environmental aspects as important, none of them stressed the environmental criteria in their decision process. Five of them took into account carriers' environmental performance, awarding points regarding their fleet of vehicles, their fuel consumption, their truck standards, their truck consumption or their signing up to the voluntary carrier commitment charter (*Charte Volontaire CO2*) launched by the French government in 2008. They also take into consideration where carriers use lighter trucks and those who set up financial benefit sharing and provide fronthauling/ backhauling services. Nonetheless, although environmental awareness is

Table 11.3 Some of the criteria used when selecting carrier/transport provider

		French Shippers										Swedish Shippers									
		F1	*F2*	*F3*	*F4*	*F5*	*F6*	*F7*	*F8*	*F9*	*F10*	*S1*	*S2*	*S3*	*S4*	*S5*	*S6*	*S7*	*S8*	*S9*	*S10*
Transport criteria	Price	○	○	○	○	○	○	○	○		○	○	●	●	●	●	●	●	●	●	●
	Punctuality/quality of service	○		○	○	○		○				○	●	●	●	●	●	●	●	●	●
	Safety	○						○													
	Environmental			○		○	○	○			○	●	●	●		●	●	●	●	●	●
	Good collaboration in the past		○			○						●			●		●	●	●	●	●
	Certification, ISO											●	●	●	●	●	●	●	●	●	●

rising, these elements as well as certifications or ISO standards do not yet weigh heavily in the decision process.

From the Swedish side, all of the ten proactive shippers had high marks on most of the provider selection criteria in Table 11.3. All the Swedish shippers regarded punctuality as being of highest importance when selecting a service provider; this was not the case in France. In a similar way as in France, half of the companies view price as a primary carrier selection criterion and, with one exception, the rest of them view price as an important criterion. The exception, shipper S10, did not view price as important at all. This company listed instead an array of service aspects such as punctuality and reliability as the most highly rated criteria, with the environment also being considered a more important criterion than price. The remaining nine Swedish companies listed the environment as the most or second most important provider selection criterion. This observation contrasts sharply with the response of the ten proactive French shippers.

However, none of the Swedish companies stressed the importance of previous experience very much when selecting a carrier, and three of them even gave this criterion very low scores. However, the interpretation of this should be done with care, because two of these companies have long (4 and 12 years, respectively) relationships with their most important service provider (the length of the third relationship is not known, but they have a two-year contract).

Analyzing these observations through the ARA model perspective, we notice that Swedish shippers have a certain impact on their carriers introducing environmental standards. The "activity structure" is then conditioned to some changes from an environmental point of view. These new patterns can change the network progressively as a whole, requiring by a cascade effect new capacities and resources.

Finally, among the ten French shippers interviewed, only two of them operating in the chemical industry mentioned safety as a determining selection criterion in the tender process. However, this point has not been investigated deeply among Swedish companies. As a consequence, although this observation provides rich insight, we are being cautious not to make any general statement about this first observation, which needs to be further investigated.

We noticed that in both countries, a solution "at the same price, but less polluting" is favored. In this way, Swedish shippers highlight their efforts to select the most environmentally friendly solution "if it works from a service point of view and is not too expensive."

Björklund and Forslund (2013) as well as Evangelista (2014) have highlighted the lack of a standard methodology for environmental performance measurement, and we note that the French government introduced various programs to assess carriers' environmental performance. Decree 2011–1336, which has to be respected by all French carriers, could be a selection criterion, for example. However, French shippers' attitudes regarding decree 2011–1336 are not favorable. Having four separate official calculation methods seems to largely affect its credibility. Surprisingly, French shippers value carriers more when they are involved in voluntary programs and do not give any weight at all whether carriers comply with the law (i.e., respecting decree 2011–1336). However, in contrast to this observation, most of the Swedish companies believe that laws and regulations will have a very important impact on the future transport system. These contrasting reactions in both countries can amount to the "environment characteristics" being one of the key elements in the IMP interaction model. In this way, and as reactions from these countries can be observed, governmental pressures do not generate the same impact across different cultural patterns.

Looking at all statements obtained through this cross-case analysis, this investigative and comparative work answers research question 2, drawing up an inventory of the transportation criteria favored in both countries.

Transportation Purchasing Organization

In addition to transport selection criteria, the purchasing process from a managerial point of view has been scrutinized. In this perspective, comparisons are used to indicate which department inside the company participates in the choice of the transport provider. The contract length and the call for tenders are also examined.

Comparing results in both countries, it has been observed that both the purchasing department and the supply chain department play a key role among the French proactive shippers; this is also the case in Sweden, even if there are some differences. In general, the purchasing department is also involved in the transportation purchasing in Sweden, but when making mode selection decisions, it is only decision makers related to the supply chain departments that are involved. The results highlight that the transportation tender process in France is rather handled by two departments (purchasing and supply chain), whereas in Sweden several different departments (grouped into the category supply chain) supervise this task.

Table 11.4 Transportation purchasing organization characteristics

		French Shippers										Swedish Shippers									
		F1	F2	F3	F4	F5	F6	F7	F8	F9	F10	S1	S2	S3	S4	S5	S6	S7	S8	S9	S10
Department participating in the choice of the carrier	Supply Chain	o	o	o	o	o	o	o		o	o	●	●	●	●			●	●	●	●
	Purchasing	o	o	o				o	o		o		●			●	●		●		
Contract length	Years	5	1	1	0	0	1	0	3	3	2	2	3	2	2	2	2	3	3	3	2
Centralization of the transport tender process/purchasing	Central	o	o	o	o	o		o	o	o	o			●	●		●		●	●	●
	Local						o					●	●		●	●	●	●			●

204 *Nathalie Touratier-Muller et al.*

However, the final decision in both countries is mainly made by units that can be categorized in the supply chain department.

From the ARA lens perspective, we could then observe that the choice of the carrier in France relies on human resources and technical assets coming from two departments only (the purchasing and the supply chain departments). Swedish shippers involve a wider variety of technical and human resources from different departments to make the final decision.

All transportation contracts among the ten Swedish shippers are signed for two or three years. Moreover, even if they only had a two- or three-year contract, all the shippers had longer relationships with those service providers, handling the largest contract for each of them. One shipper even had a 30-year relationship with its carrier.

In contrast, a wide variety of responses are observed among French shippers. Six of them do not mention any length in the contracts at all or sign a "one-year contract." We could interpret these results as a desire for a very low level of dependency. It could also be an operational strategy that fixes and regulates the price for one whole year. The four remaining French shippers have contracts that last two, three or five years.

The IMP model, which explains the specificity of BtoB characteristics through long-term relationships (Håkansson, 1982), do not seem to be reflected universally among the French shippers interviewed in this study. Although they specify orally that they want to work on a long-term relationship with their carriers, their organizational and managerial process highlight that they do not want to be confined by a long-term contractual relationship. Analyzing calls for tenders, we note that contracts in France are mainly signed at a central level. In Sweden, the ten companies focusing on environmental concerns are buying a larger part of the total transport volume centrally (44% compared with 23% for companies not focusing on the environment), even if most of the volume in all cases is bought by the local unit (52% and 72%, respectively). In two of the cases (S3 and S9), 100% of the transport volume is bought centrally.

All these elements, focusing on the transportation purchasing organization, allow us to respond to research question 3.

Conclusion

The need to achieve environmental sustainability in transport is getting increasing attention, and changes related to the purchasing process are acknowledged as one way to contribute to cutting CO_2 emissions from transport. Although environmental sustainability is gaining recognition and strength and has an incentive impact during the tender process, it does not constitute a decisive criterion in carrier selection.

Both studies conducted in Sweden and France underline similar characteristics regarding the selection criteria. However, the Swedish shippers put more emphasis on the carrier's ISO certification than the French

Considerations When Purchasing Transport 205

shippers. Although the French shippers are environmentally proactive, they do not evaluate carriers according to their compliance with the legislation (decree 2011–1336) or any ISO norm. Instead, they appreciate if carriers are committed to a voluntary program, such as the CO_2 voluntary charter, even though it does not constitute a selection criterion. The proactive companies from both countries see price as an important selection criterion. However, environmental concerns are more influential in carrier selection for the Swedish shippers than for the French shippers.

From a purchasing organizational and managerial perspective, our results highlight differences between the countries. The choice of the carrier is with some variation handled by the purchasing and the supply chain departments in both Sweden and France, However, the length of the transportation contracts highlights significant differences between the countries, with French shippers being more reluctant to sign contracts for more than one year. These elements, examined through the IMP interaction model perspective, underline that Swedish shippers may devote more effort to develop a certain degree of stability with their carriers in comparison to French shippers.

In both countries, solutions that are less polluting but not more costly are favored. Nevertheless, there is however a need to encourage changes in purchasing practices, which could be facilitated through environmental rules and adapted regulations. The French regulation, through decree 2011–1336, does not have a real impact so far, as has been demonstrated in our results.

The ARA model allowed us to examine the shipper and carrier networks in terms of activity structure. In order to obtain efficiency and effectiveness regarding environmental criteria, carriers have to embrace the changes dictated by the shippers. Whether by signing the voluntary charter of commitment (from the French shippers' perspective) or initiating environmental initiatives (from the Swedish shippers' perspective), we noticed that these proactive shippers have the ability to boost their carrier's environmental effectiveness. However, a simple and accurate standard is still lacking. In this way, common European legislation using simple tools through trucks' telematics systems would help to measure and compare more accurately carriers' environmental performance. In addition to legislation, we note that purchasing decisions are also influenced by cost effects, customer demands and organizational factors. In this particular study, we have noticed both similarities and differences between France and Sweden, but it is currently not clear if this is due to context or our sampling of respondents.

As a consequence, there is a need for further research in both countries as well as in other areas to develop these initial results. Further research efforts are also needed to investigate the impact of mandatory and voluntary initiatives to decrease road freight CO_2 emissions and motivation factors to green the transportation procurement process. This is relevant

206 Nathalie Touratier-Muller et al.

to better understand how the allocation of sustainable concerns can be taken into account by shippers in order to stimulate progressively supply chain partners to improve their environmental performance. Despite their relevance, our results cannot be generalized. To spread and strengthen these first observations, complementary studies should be conducted in a coordinated way on a larger scale.

This study, confined to two countries, has some other limitations. The main limitation relates to the small number of case companies investigated. In order to achieve an empirical generalization, it would be relevant to increase the number of respondents, using the same questionnaire and methodology. Furthermore, another limitation relates to the focus on large- and medium-sized companies. To obtain more rounded results, it would be necessary to investigate shippers' behavior among small companies.

Notes

1. European Commission report: https://ec.europa.eu/clima/policies/transport_en (accessed March 2019).
2. Swedish Environmental Protection Agency. www.naturvardsverket.se/Documents/publikationer6400/978-91-620-6848-6.pdf?pid=23767 (accessed September 2019).
3. Ministère de la Transition Ecologique et Solidaire, observations et statistiques. www.ecologique-solidaire.gouv.fr/programme-objectif-co2 (accessed February 5, 2018).
4. Government offices of Sweden, 2017. www.government.se/articles/2017/06/the-climate-policy-framework/ (accessed February 11, 2018).
5. European strategies, mobility and transport. https://ec.europa.eu/transport/themes/strategies/2011_white_paper_en (accessed June 26, 2018).

References

Andersson, D., Dubois, A., Halldorsson, A., Hedvall, K., Hulthén, K., Johansson, M. I., Rogerson, S., Sundquist, V., Sthyhre, L. (2016). *25th IPSERA Conference*, Dortmund, March 20–23.

Bardi, E. (1973). "Carrier selection from one mode." *Transportation Journal*, 13, pp. 23–29.

Björklund, M. (2011). "Influences from the business environment on environmental purchasing drivers and hinders of purchasing green transportation services." *Journal of Purchasing and Supply Management*, 11–22.

Björklund, M., Forslund, H. (2013). "The inclusion of environmental performance in transport contracts." *Management of Environmental Quality: An International Journal*, 24, 214–227.

Boyer, K., Swink, M. (2008). "Empirical elephants—Why multiple methods are essential to quality research in operations and supply chain management." *Journal of Operations Management*, 26(3), pp. 338–344.

Cova, B., Salle, R. (1992). "L'évolution de la modélisation du comportement d'achat industriel: Panorama des nouveaux courants de recherche." *Recherche et Applications en Marketing*, 7, pp. 83–106.

Considerations When Purchasing Transport 207

Evangelista, P. (2014). "Environmental sustainability practices in the transport and logistics service industry: An exploratory case study investigation." *Research in Transportation Business & Management*, 12, pp. 63–72.

Govindan, K., Rajendran, S., Sarkis, J., Murugesan, P. (2013). "Multi criteria decision making approaches for green supplier evaluation and selection: A literature review." *Journal of Cleaner Production*, 66–83.

Håkansson, H. (1982). *International Marketing and Purchasing of Industrial Goods*. Hoboken, NJ: John Wiley & Sons.

Håkansson, H. (ed.). (2009). *Business in Networks*. Chichester: John Wiley.

Håkansson, H., Snehota, I. (eds.). (1995). *Developing Relationships in Business Networks*. London: Routledge.

Isaksson, K. (2012). *Logistics Service Providers Going Green: Insights From the Swedish Market*. PhD thesis, Department of Management and Engineering, Linköping University.

Jackson, R. W., Lester A. N., Dale A. L. (1995). "An empirical investigation of the differences in goods and services as perceived by organizational buyers." *Industrial Marketing Management*, 24, pp. 99–108.

Lammgård, C. (2012). "Intermodal train services: A business challenge and a measure for decarbonisation for logistics service providers." *Research in Transportation Business & Management*, 5, pp. 48–56.

Lammgård, C., Andersson, D. (2014). "Environmental considerations and trade-offs in purchasing of transportation services." *Research in Transportation Business & Management, The Marketing of Transportation Services*, 10, pp. 45–52.

Large, R. O., Kramer, N., Hartmann, R. K. (2013). "Procurement of logistics services and sustainable development in Europe: Fields of activity and empirical results." *Journal of Purchasing and Supply Management*, 19, pp. 122–133.

Marshall, D., McCarthy, L., McGrath P., Claudy, M. (2015). "Going above and beyond: How sustainability culture and entrepreneurial orientation drive social sustainability supply chain practice adoption." *Supply Chain Management: An International Journal*, 20, pp. 434–454.

Pålsson, H., Kovács, G. (2014). "Reducing transportation emissions: A reaction to stakeholder pressure or a strategy to increase competitive advantage." *International Journal of Physical Distribution & Logistics Management*, 44, pp. 283–304.

Patton, M. (2002). *Qualitative Research and Evaluation Methods* (3rd ed.). Thousand Oaks, CA: Sage.

Piecyk, M., McKinnon, A.C. (2010). "Forecasting the carbon footprint of road freight transport in 2020." *International Journal of Production Economics*, 128, pp. 31–42.

Rogerson, S. (2012). "Connecting ordering of freight transport to logistical variables related to CO_2 emissions." In *Proceedings of the LRN Conference*, Cranfield, September 5–7, 2012.

Rogerson, S. (2016). *Environmental Concerns When Purchasing Freight Transport*. Gothenburg: Chalmers University of Technology.

Rogerson, S., Andersson, D., Johansson, M. I. (2014). "Influence of context on the purchasing process for freight TRANSPORT services." *International Journal of Logistics Research and Applications*, 17, pp. 232–248.

Thornton, L., Autry C., Gligor D., Brik A. (2013). "Does socially responsible supplier selection pay off for customer firms? A cross-cultural comparison." *Journal of Supply Chain Management*, 49, pp. 66–89.

208 Nathalie Touratier-Muller et al.

Touratier-Muller, N., Jaussaud, J. (2017). "Pratiques d'achats durables dans le transport routier de marchandises: le cas du programme français FRET 21." *Logistique & Management*, 1–12.

Van den Berg, R., De Langen, P. W. (2017). "Environmental sustainability in container transport: the attitudes of shippers and forwarders." *International Journal of Logistics Research and Applications*, 20, pp. 146–162.

Walker, H., Di Sisto, L., McBain, D. (2008). "Drivers and barriers to environmental supply chain management practices: Lessons from the public and private sectors." *Journal of Purchasing and Supply Management*, 14, pp. 69–85.

Yin, R. K. (2009). *Case Study Research: Design and Methods* (4th ed.). Applied Social Research Methods, 5. Los Angeles, CA: Sage.

12 Does International Mobility Really Increase Students' Intercultural Competence?

Anne Bartel-Radic and
Marie-Estelle Binet

Introduction

In the context of growing globalization, more and more people are internationally mobile, whether professionally or in their private lives. Over the last two decades, study abroad programs have been made available to more and more students in higher education, in Europe notably thanks to the Erasmus program. International student mobility has been strongly encouraged by public education policies because of its contribution to human capital in the context of the contemporary global knowledge economy (Guruz, 2011). Overall, international student mobility receives very positive feedback from students, future employers and public institutions. However, some returning students also mention that they spent most of their time with other students from their home country, talking in their mother tongue.

Study abroad stays have been introduced in many student curricula with the objective of developing the students' intercultural competence through significant international experience. To succeed in international interaction (i.e., to understand their interlocutors and to be understood by them), intercultural competence is essential. Intercultural competence is considered as a key competence in companies and international organizations. It is seen as an important criterion for the adaptation of the international manager or foreign assignee (Black et al., 1991), as necessary for successful interactions within multinational companies (Ralston et al., 1995) and as one of the key performance factors of intercultural team leaders (Hajro and Pudelko, 2010).

An intercultural encounter is the one that connects people from different cultures, including national cultures (Davel, Dupuis and Chanlat, 2008). Each of us is a bearer of fundamental cultural behaviors, values and assumptions, shared within the groups of belonging (Geertz, 1973). Intercultural competence is partly acquired through learning (Spitzberg and Changnon, 2009) and initiated by intercultural experiences (Hofstede, 1994). Extended stays abroad, for example, during an expatriation, can be the occasion of a "maturation"—a more important apprenticeship (Cerdin and Dubouloy, 2004).

210 Anne Bartel-Radic and Marie-Estelle Binet

The aim of this study is to understand under what conditions and in what contexts international experience during international student mobility augments intercultural competence. To do so, we collected survey data among three student cohorts of a French higher education institute, measuring aspects of their international experience and their intercultural competence. Data analysis relies on a structural equation model in which observed variables describing international experiences drive intercultural competence—a latent and unobserved variable. The results contribute not only to research but also to curriculum design in higher education, specifically concerning study abroad programs' design and preparation. This chapter first reviews the extant literature and then details the method of survey data collection and analysis before presenting the results.

Literature Review

The following literature review is twofold. The first section presents the concept, approaches and measures of intercultural competence; the second section focuses on international experience as a factor enhancing intercultural competence.

Intercultural Competence

In the field of international business, intercultural competence has been defined as "an individual's effectiveness in drawing upon a set of knowledge, skills, and personal attributes to work successfully with people from different national cultural backgrounds at home or abroad" (Johnson, Lenartowicz, and Apud, 2006: 530). In other words, intercultural competence includes the ability to draw on personal resources and traits to understand the specifics of intercultural interaction and to adjust one's behavior to these specifics. Competence is an intelligence of action that mobilizes knowledge in and through action (Zarifian, 1995). As such, intercultural competence cannot be directly observed empirically, and it can be modeled by a latent variable.

Numerous contributions, including literature reviews, on intercultural competence in the field of international business have been published during the last 15 years. However, this abundance of publications suffers from ambiguous construct definitions and poor integration (Ang et al., 2007). A striking example is the lack of connections between the literature on intercultural competence, cross-cultural competence, and cultural intelligence. Spitzberg and Changnon (2009) never mentioned the term "cross-cultural competence" in their literature review, whereas Johnson et al. (2006) quote intercultural competence in only one sentence referring to Hofstede's (2001) formulation. More recent literature (e.g., Ang et al., 2007, Thomas et al., 2008) has added a third wording: "cultural intelligence." The concept is defined as the "capability to function effectively

Students' Intercultural Competence 211

in culturally diverse settings" (Ang et al., 2007: 335). We consider that the constructs of intercultural competence and cultural intelligence are very close: both involve the understanding of the specificity of cross-cultural interaction and the capacity to adapt one's behavior to this specificity. It appears that cultural intelligence largely overlaps with a fourth concept: "global mindset" (Andresen and Bergdolt, 2017). Although the definitions largely converge, scholars not only use different terms for the concept of intercultural competence but also hardly ever integrate contributions using a different terminology. In contrast, we consider that these concepts are very close. We use the term "intercultural competence" here, but we include literature on cross-cultural competence and cultural intelligence within this wording.

Spitzberg and Changnon's (2009) presentation of 22 models of intercultural competence makes it clear that conceptualizations are highly diverse in their disciplines and terminologies as well as their scholarly and practical objectives. Van de Vijver and Leung argued in2009 that the strong interest in intercultural competence has not led to a significantly better understanding of the concept. The fuzziness of the developments on intercultural competence has even led scholars to question the usefulness of the concept itself (Livian, 2011). The main categories of models are as follows: (1) compositional models listing elements/components of intercultural competence such as individuals' knowledge and behavior (e.g., Deardorff, 2006), (2) co-orientational and adaptational models focusing on communication and interaction between people from different cultures (e.g., Fantini, 1995) and (3) developmental models including successive competence levels that can be reached through learning processes (e.g., Bennett, 1986; Hammer, Bennett and Wiseman, 2003). In other words, the vast majority of contributions on intercultural competence define the concept in terms of components, interaction processes, or levels. Among these, the compositional conceptualizations predominate in the subfield of intercultural competence, and this approach has been adopted by the subfield of cultural intelligence. This chapter also adopts a componential approach to intercultural competence.

Componential definitions of intercultural competence provide lists of components that together are thought to constitute the concept. Four types of components of intercultural competence have been identified (Ruben, 1989): attitudes, personality traits, cognitive abilities and skills, and actual behavior. These types of components roughly correspond to the classification of "knowledge, skills, abilities and other personal characteristics" (Caligiuri, 2006), with the particularity that abilities are addressed through actual behavior and other personal characteristics through specific personality traits and attitudes. For each component, Spitzberg and Changnon (2009) list dozens of elements mentioned in the literature. They argue that "the more a model incorporates specific conceptualization of interactants' motivation, knowledge, skills, context, and outcomes, in the context of an ongoing relationship over time, the more advanced the model" (2009: 44) of intercultural competence. However, the authors also recognize that "there is a need to provide a more parsimonious model" (2009: 45) than the list of 300-plus terms and concepts related to intercultural competence that they provide.

Personality traits and attitudes that are most frequently quoted in the literature (e.g., Caligiuri, 2006; Johnson et al., 2006; Spitzberg and Changnon, 2009; Van der Zee and Van Oudenhoven, 2001) as being strongly linked or equivalent to intercultural competence are open-mindedness (or openness), absence of ethnocentrism, sociability (or extraversion), emotional stability, self-confidence, empathy, attributional complexity, and tolerance for ambiguity. Some of them are stable personality traits (openness and extraversion are two of the "big five" personality traits), whereas others such as ethnocentrism and empathy are more specific attitudes (Shaffer et al., 2006).

The Intercultural Development Inventory (Hammer, Bennett and Wiseman, 2003), measures "levels" reached in the intercultural learning process. It is based on Bennett's dynamic learning perspective, including six stages of intercultural sensitivity subdivided into three ethnocentric stages and three ethno-relative stages. Ethnocentrism—"a view of things in which one's own group is the center of everything, and all others are scaled and rated with reference to it" (Neuliep, 2002: 201)—means the absence or lack of intercultural competence. Ethnocentrism is also an attitude toward cultural diversity, which makes it a component of intercultural competence and can therefore be integrated as such in a component approach of intercultural competence (Bartel-Radic and Giannelloni, 2017).

The cognitive dimension of intercultural competence—intercultural knowledge—is a component that is rarely objectively measured in scholarly research. However, culture assimilators are tools that are appropriate for doing so. They are based on the critical incident technique developed by Flanagan (1954). Critical incidents are short stories of cross-cultural situations and encounters. They are considered as critical because they are likely to be interpreted differently by people from different cultures, and because they tell of misunderstandings that might result in conflict. Each critical incident is followed by several possible answers (in most tools, four) that include an interpretation of the situation, potential courses of action, or future events. "Wrong" answers reflect ethnocentric considerations from other cultures or a stereotyped worldview. Several "right" answers are proposed in order to avoid an isomorphic presentation of cultures and to place value on tolerance for ambiguity.

Culture assimilators including several critical incidents are either culture specific (all of the critical incidents concern one particular "host" culture) or culture general (including critical incidents in various cross-cultural settings). Culture-general assimilators are less common; the most frequently quoted one was developed by Brislin (1986: 218). Ideally, they are based on theory (Bhawuk, 2001), such as dimensions of culture developed by Hofstede (2001) and others. Initially developed for training purposes, culture assimilators also represent a good tool for measuring intercultural knowledge because they can capture tacit knowledge linked to intercultural competence (Johnson et al., 2006).

International Experience as a Factor Enhancing Intercultural Competence

Scholars generally consider that international experience and training enhance intercultural competence (Bartel-Radic, 2014; Caligiuri and Tarique, 2012; Deardorff, 2006; Takeuchi et al., 2005). Three categories of intercultural training are commonly proposed in the professional and higher education contexts, focusing respectively on cognitive (university lectures), emotional (cultural awareness/sensitivity seminars) and behavioral content (Waxin and Barmeyer, 2008). The last two categories are to some degree based on intercultural interaction. Scholars have raised the concern than poor intercultural training can have a negative impact on intercultural competence through the increase of inappropriate stereotypes. Less preoccupying but still important to note, some types of training might just have no impact on intercultural competence and further raise ethical dilemmas (Szkudlarek, 2009).

International experience is a concept often mentioned but rarely precisely defined. At the team level of analysis (such as top management teams), the term "international experience" corresponds to the diversity of nationalities within the team (Sommer, 2012). At the individual level, international experience corresponds to somebody's experience in other national contexts (Hambrick et al., 1998). International experience includes a confrontation with other cultures, different political, economic, social and administrative contexts, and foreign languages. Takeuchi et al. (2005) distinguish work and private experience (as well as experience in the country of destination of a foreign assignee and experience in other foreign countries). Sommer (2012) lists five elements of international experience: work experience abroad, international education, professional experience in an international context or environment, trips to one or more foreign countries and private international experience. International experience can therefore be categorized according to the place of acquisition (in an international context within the country of origin or in more or less distant countries), according to the object (professional or private life) and the mode or the period of acquisition (school, university or work) (Sommer, 2012). Due to globalization, more and more people are gaining international experience today through a variety of means that add up and overlap in many cases. Expatriation takes various forms and is in many cases self-initiated by the interested parties themselves (Suutari and Brewster, 2000). Even without moving abroad, some "international" learning is possible in a context of diversity of religious or ethnic groups or social classes (Hendry, 1996). Foreign language learning is also a factor in "confrontation" with foreign cultures and countries and can therefore be considered as an integral part of the international experience.

Practical experience is one of the key elements of the individual learning process (Kolb, 1984). Experience and competence are therefore inextricably linked. Intercultural competence as a simultaneous understanding of one's own culture and that of others, and as "the ability to recognize and use cultural differences as a resource for learning and designing effective action in specific contexts" (Friedman and Berthoin Antal, 2005: 70), is a complex and difficult skill to acquire. Only few people achieve a high level of intercultural competence, going beyond the "false pretenses of jet-setters" to "take root in the depths of many memories, many peculiarities, to claim other belongings in addition to [theirs]" (Bruckner, 1992: 80). This difficult learning is determined by many factors, but the literature considers that the most important among them are international experience and related intercultural interaction.

The link between international experience and intercultural competence has been discussed in the field of higher education (Deardorff, 2006). The ability to acquire and improve mastery of a foreign language has long been seen as the main benefit of graduate programs abroad (Chak and Makino, 2010). There is also broad agreement that executives' international experience is a necessary resource and a potential source of competitive advantage for multinational companies (Takeuchi et al., 2005). In addition according to Hendry (1996), tourist trips could lead to intercultural skills that are more important than business trips. There is broad agreement that international experience leads to intercultural competence, but empirical research remains scarce. Caligiuri and Tarique (2012) found a significant impact of between 14% and 28% of international experiences in the private setting on three personality traits associated with intercultural competence. Paradoxically, both types of international experiences have a negative impact on international leadership performance. However, Bartel-Radic (2014) demonstrates a very weak impact (5%) of international experience on intercultural competence. Bartel-Radic, Moos and Long (2015) found no impact of an international student learning experience on intercultural competence. Given the difficulty in defining and measuring intercultural competence, international experience is frequently used as a proxy of intercultural competence in the context of human resource management decisions in the professional context. The scarce empirical results show that this equivalence is not supported by research.

There is a clear research gap concerning the conditions under which international experience augments intercultural competence. It increasingly appears in contemporary research that it is not the quantity but the quality (nature and type) of international experience that increases intercultural competence (Bartel-Radic, 2014; Caligiuri and Tarique, 2012). An analogy can be made here with research on intercultural teams; the degree of diversity within the team has no clear or direct impact on team performance, and the latter strongly depends on the context of teamwork and team interaction processes (Horwitz and Horwitz, 2007; Zellmer-Bruhn and Gibson, 2014). The "contact hypothesis" (Allport, 1954) and social learning theory (Bandura, 1977) provide theoretical support for questioning the context and degree at which intercultural interaction stimulates intercultural competence (Caligiuri and Tarique, 2012). The contact hypothesis (Allport, 1954) posits that direct contact between hostile groups makes it possible to reduce negative stereotypes. The common thread of both theories lies in the idea that learning occurs through interaction with people from different cultures. These interactions (practical experience) can generate an awareness of the diversity of cultures and a critical reflection on one's own culture (Hofstede, 1994).

The intensity of the link between international experience and intercultural competence, along with the type of international experience that best promotes intercultural competence, are therefore poorly understood. This study intends to provide additional answers to these questions. The model that we will confront with the data is presented in Figure 12.1; it questions interactions between international experience and intercultural competence. We consider intercultural competence as an unobservable variable. But the higher a person's intercultural competence, the better he or she will understand cultural differences and intercultural interaction, which means the better he or she will interpret "critical incidents."

The main hypothesis of our study is that intercultural competence is determined by learning processes related to the international student mobility and social interaction with people from foreign countries and cultures. We also hypothesize that the characteristics of the international

Figure 12.1 Impact of international experience on intercultural competence: theoretical model

216 Anne Bartel-Radic and Marie-Estelle Binet

experience and the nature of the intercultural interaction experienced by the students have an impact on their intercultural competence by the end of the academic stay, thus improving their intercultural knowledge.

Method

Our empirical study is based on a unique survey dataset collected by the authors among students of a French public higher education institute. All students of this institute are required to study abroad during the second year of their bachelor's degree. The objective of the survey was to identify the impact of this one-year academic stay abroad on their intercultural competence. For this purpose, we collected information in May 2017, May 2018 and May 2019 on the students' characteristics and intercultural competence as well as information about their study stay. A total of 324 students answered the survey (carried out by email): 87 from the first cohort in 2017, 127 from the second one in 2018 and 110 from the third cohort in 2019, representing an average response rate of approximately 50%. The international mobility lasted between 4 and 14 months (10 months on average).

Measures of Intercultural Competence

As stated earlier, intercultural competence cannot be directly observed, but the higher one's intercultural competence, the better he or she understands cultural differences in intercultural interaction. To measure this intercultural knowledge, we followed guidelines provided in the literature and constructed a "culture-general assimilator" (see below). Five "critical incidents" were selected from handbooks in the field of intercultural management, student internship reports and personal experience (see Table 12.1).

Table 12.1 Cultures concerned by the critical incidents used in the survey

Critical incident number	Main national culture concerned*	Other national culture concerned**	Main cultural dimension concerned
1	India	Czech Republic	Power distance
2	United States	Finland	Private/public space
3	Argentina	Denmark	Monochronism/ polychronism
4	Singapore	United Kingdom	Individualism/ collectivism
5	Germany	France	Universalism/ particularism

* Knowledge of this culture is essential to answer the critical incident correctly.
** Knowledge of this culture is helpful but not essential to answer the critical incident correctly.

Students' Intercultural Competence   217

We tried to select critical incidents that were not too stereotyped, not "too easy to answer," but theory based (Bhawuk, 2001), which means that related cultural differences concern a dimension of culture reported by the literature (e.g., Hofstede, 2001). One critical incident is given as an example in the Appendix. For each critical incident, four possible interpretations of the situation were formulated. For most of the incidents, one answer was completely right (offering a very good interpretation of the situation) and at least one answer was completely wrong (offering a completely false interpretation of the situation). The two remaining answers were often "partly wrong." To define the "ideal grading" for the four interpretations of each of the five critical incidents on a scale from 0 to 10, a pilot study was carried out among 11 intercultural experts and then interpreted by the authors, who also took into consideration their own interpretations of the different critical incidents. The respondents to the survey were also asked to grade all the explanations on a scale from 0 to 10. The score (between 0 and 10) achieved by the respondent on each critical incident corresponds to the "grade" of the answer chosen as the best answer by the respondent. In other words, the higher the index, the higher the respondent's intercultural knowledge.

Measures of International Experience

The study includes many variables measuring aspects of the international experience. A first group of variables measures international experience that preceded the year of study abroad: we measured the degree to which students had interacted with people from different countries, namely if they had met people from other countries, if they had traveled abroad, if they had already experienced studies abroad, if they had already lived abroad, and in this case, in how many countries and the length of their stay. These variables allow an evaluation of the level of international experience yet were capitalized by the student before the academic stay abroad. Thereby, they are an indicator of their individual human capital in terms of international experience before the stay abroad. In this sense, these variables will allow identifying the long-run persistent relationship between international experience and intercultural competence.

The second group of variables describes the academic stay abroad during the year, (2016–2017, 2017–2018 and 2018–2019, respectively) and assess the conditions of the additional international experience acquired by the students during this year of studies abroad. For that purpose, the survey included questions describing the different kinds of interactions between the students and people in the host country. Students were also asked about the positive and negative emotions they experienced during their studies abroad. These variables related to international experience were grouped into seven factors through a principal component analysis. Table 12.2 shows those factors and the items that contribute to each of them.

218 *Anne Bartel-Radic and Marie-Estelle Binet*

Table 12.2 International experiences measurement

Factors	Items contributing to each factor
Factor 1: Positive emotions and learning	Q11: I have learned a lot during the study stay. Q12: I'm more open minded, more tolerant thanks to the international experience. Q13: I'm happy with this international experience. Q14: International mobility allows to learn more than staying in your home country. Q15: I wish to live again such an experience in the future. Q16: I recommend the mobility I have experienced this year.
Factor 2: International interaction at university	Q21: My classmates were mainly other international students. Q22: My classmates were mainly students from the host country. Q23: I have done group work with students from the host country. Q24: I have done group work with international students from other countries. Q25: I have attended many courses in English. Q26: I have attended many courses in the host country language.
Factor 3: Negative emotions	Q31: I felt fear during this international experience. Q32: I felt nervousness during this international experience. Q33: I felt disgust during this international experience. Q34: I felt sadness during this international experience. Q35: I felt disdain during this international experience.
Factor 4: Difficulties of integration in the host country	Q41: I stayed on the university campus most of the time. Q42: I experienced conflicts between my moral values and those of the host country. Q43: I experienced administrative difficulties. Q44: I had difficulties in understanding the mood and humor of people from the host country.
Factor 5: Interaction with French students	Q51: My classmates were mainly other French students. Q52: I have spent most of the time with people from my home country.
Factor 6: Conflict in group work	Q61: I have done group work with students from the host country. Q62: I have done group work with other international students. Q63: I have experienced conflict in group work.
Factor 7: Visits and events	Q71: I have visited local firms or organizations. Q72: I have participated in intercultural events.

Note: Scale from 1 to 5, 1 meaning "does not apply to me at all," 2 "a little," 3 "more or less," 4 "applies" and 5 "completely applies."

Data Analysis

We used structural equation modeling (SEM) to further analyze the data. SEM encompasses a broad array of models from linear regression to measurement models to simultaneous equations, all of which include latent

Students' Intercultural Competence 219

and observed variables (see, e.g., Giannelloni and Vernette, 2015). Latent variables describe abstract concepts in our study such as intelligence, satisfaction or intercultural competence (see Figure 12.1). Our model consists of two parts. First, intercultural competence was linked to the seven factors describing international experience. Second, a reflective measurement model was used to link intercultural competence with the interpretation of the critical incidents. We used the *sem* command in Stata (2015) software. Our empirical strategy includes the following steps:

- In a first step, we retained a general model without differentiating the cohorts or the gender. Our SEM methodology allows estimating direct effects of international experience on intercultural competence and of intercultural competence on intercultural knowledge (the interpretation of the five critical incidents) but also indirect effects of international experience on intercultural knowledge.
- In a second step, we conducted group comparisons to test whether results are different depending on the cohort or on gender.

Results and Discussion

In the first section, we provide analyses to identify the overall contribution of international experience to intercultural competence. In the second section, we differentiate empirical results depending on gender and on the cohort considered.

The Impact of International Experience on Intercultural Competence

We obtain very robust results measuring the positive significant impact of intercultural competence on intercultural knowledge. Indeed, a rise in intercultural competence improves the test scores for all the five critical incidents (an average of +1 point on a 10-point scale). However, the introduction of variables describing international experience from the one-year academic stay abroad poorly improves the explanation of the latent variable "intercultural competence," as only about 4% of the understanding of intercultural competence is henceforth explained by the model. This result is close to that of Bartel-Radic (2014), who found an impact of international experience on intercultural competence of 5%. Conversely, the explanatory power of the five critical incidents is high—between 15% and 39%.

When considering the direct effects of international experience on intercultural competence, our results reveal the positive influence of positive emotions on intercultural competence, namely to have learned a lot and to feel happy with the international experience and to recommend it (Factor 1, see Table 12.2). Factors 2 to 6 (Table 12.2) are statistically insignificant and do not influence intercultural competence. Variables

220   Anne Bartel-Radic and Marie-Estelle Binet

related to international experience before international student mobility have led to an insignificant improvement of the students' intercultural competence.

We then considered how the model might be improved by dealing with the individual heterogeneity of our sample. For this reason, we re-estimated direct and indirect effects in two different models. In the first one, we included in our SEM specification one specific coefficient for men and another one for women. In the second one, we differentiated parameters by cohorts. Comparison tests of the estimates show that the model is robust concerning the influence of intercultural competence on the five critical incidents. Compared to the overall model ($R^2 = 4\%$), variables describing the international mobility improve the explanatory power of the latent variable intercultural competence at least 7% and up to 18% if we introduce the cohort's heterogeneity. All in all, dealing with individual heterogeneity enhances the explanatory power of our specification and provides some new results.

A Heterogeneous Impact of International Experience on Intercultural Competence

Gender partly affects intercultural competence. Indeed, the effect of positive emotions on intercultural competence is significant for male students and is insignificant for female students. Next, interaction of female students mainly with other French students during international mobility (Factor 5) has a negative direct effect on intercultural competence and a negative indirect impact on the five critical incidents' scores. Two other factors appear to have a positive impact on intercultural competence if we focus only on women: international interaction at the university and difficulties of integration in the host country (Factors 2 and 4, respectively). However, those two results are poorly significant at the 14% risk level only.

Finally, dealing with the heterogeneity between the three cohorts confirmed previous results but also revealed a new one. Factor 3 concerning negative emotions during mobility (having felt fear, nervousness, disgust, sadness, and disdain) significantly increases intercultural competence, if we focus on the 2017–2018 academic year only.

The main theoretical contribution of this result lies in the support brought to social learning theory (Bandura, 1977) that establishes the impact of international experience on intercultural competence. Those elements somehow give support to the contact hypothesis (Allport, 1954), stating that contact between hostile groups might reduce negative stereotypes. A possible interpretation of these results is that "emotional instability" expresses the consequences of these negative emotions on the students' feelings. This result goes along with the variables explaining intercultural learning in global teams (Bartel-Radic, 2006), among which are long-term interaction and conflict among equal team members. Conflict is "one of the most important engines of change" (Deschamps and Devos, 1993: 27) because it is a particular form of interaction including de-structuration and re-structuration. Negative interpersonal emotions are often temporary and do not fundamentally modify people's thinking. Yet conflict is capable of making people conscious of something. Conflict in top management teams can have valuable consequences (Eisenhardt, Kahwaji, and Bourgeois, 1997), and conflict is even more likely in diverse teams (Kochan et al., 2003). Cultural diversity means a high variety of values, behavior and ways of working; global teams are even often established because of the diversity of points of view inside the team. In consequence, conflict appears to be a logical outcome. Empirical studies show that diversity in teams produces more conflict (cf. Kochan et al., 2003). The learning process of intercultural competence starts with the realization of the existence of cultural differences (Bennett, 1986; Hofstede, 1994), and conflict and strong negative emotions experienced during international mobility are capable of starting this learning process.

Complexity and Intercultural Learning

When considering the direct effects of international experience on intercultural competence, our results reveal that having visited local firms or organizations, and having participated in intercultural events (Factor 7), significantly reduces intercultural competence. This result leads us to the proposition that too much complexity or interaction during the international mobility might negatively influence intercultural learning. These results show that if cultural diversity encountered during the international experience is too high, and therefore the complexity of the intercultural interaction too big, students make less sense of the cultural differences they are confronted with, and display lower intercultural competence. Previous studies have shown that global teams need "requisite variety" to be effective (Bartel-Radic and Lesca, 2011), which means that the diversity of the team has to fit the complexity of the team's task. However, if the team's diversity is too substantial, even in the case of requisite variety, the team's effectiveness is low. An analogy can be made for students' intercultural competence, because if international experience is a necessary condition for intercultural learning, this is only the case if the experienced situations are not too complex, so that the students can observe cultural differences and understand them.

Conclusion

An empirical contribution of this study lies in the insights it provides for student curriculum design. A year of study abroad clearly adds to students' intercultural competence. Interaction with students from the host culture or from other cultures are to be encouraged. Intercultural teamwork is

222 Anne Bartel-Radic and Marie-Estelle Binet

helpful for their intercultural learning and, to some degree, strong negative emotions contribute to intercultural competence. However, the higher the cultural diversity experienced by the students, the lower their intercultural competence.

The limitations of this study lie in the exploratory nature of the measures used. Moreover, the results remain weak and ambiguous on some aspects. More data analysis needs to be done to understand the mutual relationships between previous international experiences, the characteristics of international student mobility and intercultural competence.

Avenues for future research are the relationship between foreign language skills and intercultural competence and their link with international experience. The role of cultural distance and of the characteristics of the host culture on intercultural learning are also worth further investigation. It might be supposed that the cultural dimensions on which home and host cultures differ have an impact on which critical incidents are better understood. The role of emotions should also be studied more in depth. Another important research perspective lies in the effects of international experience and intercultural competence in terms of university achievement (grades and diplomas), employability, career perspectives and others. Longitudinal studies over longer periods and with larger samples are necessary to collect relevant data to study these questions.

Appendix
Example of a "Critical Incident"

Tomas, a student from the Czech Republic, worked for some time behind the bar of an Indian Members Club in London, together with an Indian man named Ali. One day, the waitress got an order wrong, and the customer did not receive what he wanted. Just at the time when the customer was complaining about this, the manager of the club entered, and he started reprimanding Tomas and Ali for the mistake that had been made. Tomas replied to the manager that he had better get the full story and the facts straight before jumping to conclusions, and that it was not really their fault. Ali did not say anything to support him. After the manager had left, Ali turned to Tomas and said, "How could you talk like this to the boss?" In fact, Ali seemed to be madder with Tomas than with the way the boss had treated them. Why did Ali react like this?

Out of the following explanations, which one is the most appropriate, according to you?

- Ali did not like Tomas's excuse that it was not his fault; he believes all workers should take responsibility for the teamwork regardless of who made the mistake.
- Ali wanted Tomas to apologize so that the customer would calm down.
- Ali is not a team player; he was not supportive when Tomas discussed with the boss.
- Ali believes that Tomas will be dismissed because he has argued with the boss.

References

Allport, G. (1954). *The Nature of Prejudice*. Cambridge, MA: Addison-Wesley.

Andresen, M., Bergdolt, F. (2017). "A systematic literature review on the definitions of global mindset and cultural intelligence—merging two different research streams," *International Journal of Human Resource Management*, 28(1), pp. 170–195.

Ang, S., Van Dyne, L., Koh, C., Ng, K. Y., Templer, K. J., Tay, C., Chandrasekar, N. A. (2007). "Cultural intelligence: Its measurements and effects on cultural

224 *Anne Bartel-Radic and Marie-Estelle Binet*

judgment and decision making, cultural adaptation and task performance." *Management and Organization Review*, 3(3), pp. 335–371.

Bandura, A. (1977). *Social Learning Theory*. Englewood Cliffs, NJ: Prentice Hall.

Bartel-Radic, A. (2006). "Intercultural learning in global teams." *Management International Review*, 46(6), pp. 647–677.

Bartel-Radic, A. (2014). "La compétence interculturelle est-elle acquise grâce à l'expérience internationale?" *Management International*, 18(Special Issue), pp. 194–211.

Bartel-Radic, A., Giannelloni, J.-L. (2017). "A renewed perspective on the measurement of cross-cultural competence: An approach through personality traits and cross-cultural knowledge." *European Management Journal*, 35(5), pp. 632–644.

Bartel-Radic, A., Lesca, N. (2011). "Do intercultural teams need 'requisite variety' to be effective?" *Management international/International Management/Gestiòn Internacional*, 15(3), pp. 89–104.

Bartel-Radic, A., Moos, C., Long, S. (2015). "Cross-cultural management learning through innovative pedagogy: An exploratory study of globally distributed student teams." *Decision Sciences Journal of Innovative Education*, 13(4), pp. 539–562.

Bennett, M. J. (1986). "Towards ethnorelativism: A developmental model of intercultural sensitivity." In R. M. Paige (ed.), *Cross-Cultural Orientation: New Conceptualizations and Applications*. New York: University Press of America, pp. 27–70.

Bhawuk, D. P. (2001). "Evolution of culture assimilators: Toward theory-based assimilators." *International Journal of Intercultural Relations*, 25(2), pp. 141–163.

Black, J. S. et al. (1991). "Toward a comprehensive model of international adjustment: An integration of multiple theoretical perspectives." *Academy of Management Review*, 16(2), pp. 291–317.

Brislin, R. W. (1986). "A culture general assimilator. Preparation for various types of sojourners." *International Journal of Intercultural Relations*, 10(2), pp. 215–234.

Bruckner, P. (1992). "Faut-il être cosmopolite?" *Esprit*, décembre, pp. 80–101.

Caligiuri, P. (2006). "Developing global leaders." *Human Resource Management Review*, 16(2), pp. 219–228.

Caligiuri, P. M., Tarique, I. (2012). "Dynamic cross-cultural competencies and global leadership effectiveness." *Journal of World Business*, 47(4), pp. 612–622.

Cerdin, J.-L., Dubouloy, M. (2004). "Expatriation as a maturation opportunity: A psychoanalytical approach based on 'copy and paste.'" *Human Relations*, 57(8), pp. 957–981.

Chak, A.M.K., Makino, S. (2010). "Are we making the right choice to go for international exchange programs?" *Journal of International Business Education*, 5, pp. 145–160.

Davel, E., Dupuis, J.-P., Chanlat, J.-F. (2008). *Gestion en contexte interculturel*. Québec: Pul et Téluq.

Deardorff, D. K. (2006). "Identification and assessment of intercultural competence as a student outcome of internationalization." *Journal of Studies in International Education*, 10(3), pp. 241–266.

Deschamps, J. C., Devos, T. (1993). "Valeurs, cultures et changement." *Intercultures*, 21, pp. 17–28.

Eisenhardt, K. M., Kahwaji, J. L., Bourgeois, L. J., III. (1997). "How management teams can have a good fight." *Harvard Business Review*, 75(4), pp. 77–85.

Fantini, A. E. (1995). "Language, culture, and world view: Exploring the nexus." *International Journal of Intercultural Relations*, 19, pp. 143–153.

Flanagan, J. (1954). "The critical incident technique." *Psychological Bulletin*, 51(4), pp. 327–358.

Friedman, V. J., Antal, A. B. (2005). "Negotiating reality: A theory of action approach to intercultural competence." *Management Learning*, 36(1), pp. 69–86.

Geertz, C. (1973). *The Interpretation of Cultures.* New York: Basic Books.

Giannelloni, J. L., Vernette, E. (2015). *Etudes de marché.* 4ème édition ed. Paris: Vuibert.

Guruz, K. (2011). *Higher Education and International Student Mobility in the Global Knowledge Economy* (revised and updated 2nd ed.). New York: SUNY Press.

Hajro, A., Pudelko, M. (2010), "An analysis of core-competences of successful multinational team leaders." *International Journal of Cross-Cultural Management*, 10(2), pp. 175–194.

Hambrick, D. C. et al. (1998). "When groups consist of multiple nationalities: Towards a new understanding of the implications." *Organization Studies*, 19(2), pp. 181–205.

Hammer, M. R., Bennett, M. J., Wiseman, R. (2003). "Measuring intercultural sensitivity: The intercultural development inventory." *International Journal of Intercultural Relations*, 27(4), pp. 421–443.

Hendry, C. (1996). "Continuities in human resource processes in internationalization and domestic business management." *Journal of Management Studies*, 33(4), pp. 475–494.

Hofstede, G. (1994). *Vivre dans un monde multiculturel.* Paris: Les Editions d'Organisation.

Hofstede, G. (2001). *Culture's Consequences: International Differences in Work Related Values.* London: Sage.

Horwitz, S. K., Horwitz, I. B. (2007). "The effects of team diversity on team outcomes: A meta-analytic review of team demography." *Journal of Management*, 33(6), pp. 987–1015.

Johnson, J. P., Lenartowicz, T., Apud, S. (2006). "Cross-cultural competence in international business: toward a definition and a model." *Journal of International Business Studies*, 37(4), pp. 525–543.

Kochan, T. et al. (2003). "The effects of diversity on business performance: Report of the diversity research network." *Human Resource Management*, 42(1), pp. 3–21.

Kolb, D. (1984). *Experiential Learning.* Englewood Cliffs, NJ: Prentice Hall.

Livian, Y.-F. (2011). "Le concept de compétence interculturelle est-il un concept utile?" *Gérer et Comprendre*, 107, pp. 87–116.

Neuliep, J. W. (2002). "Assessing the reliability and validity of the generalized ethnocentrism scale." *Journal of Intercultural Communication Research*, 31, pp. 201–216.

Ralston, D. et al. (1995). "Do expatriates change their behavior to fit a foreign culture? A study of American expatriates' strategies of upward influence." *Management International Review*, 35(1), pp. 109–122.

226   Anne Bartel-Radic and Marie-Estelle Binet

Ruben, B. D. (1989). "The study of cross-cultural competence: Traditions and contemporary issues." *International Journal of Intercultural Relations*, 13(3), pp. 229–240.

Shaffer, M. A., Harrison, D. A., Gregersen, H., Black, J., Stewart, F., Lori A. (2006). "You can take it with you: Individual differences and expatriate effectiveness." *Journal of Applied Psychology*, 91(1), pp. 109–125.

Sommer, L. (2012). "The measurement of international experience as a dimension of board indices: Concept for an improvement." *International Journal of Business Administration*, 3(4), pp. 2–19.

Spitzberg, B. H., Changnon G. (2009). "Conceptualizing intercultural competence." In D. K. Deardorff (ed.), *The SAGE Handbook of Intercultural Competence*. Thousand Oaks, CA: SAGE, pp. 2–52.

Stata. (2015). *Stata Structural Equation Modelling Reference Manual*. StataCorp LP, Stata Release 13, Statistical Software, College Station, TX.

Suutari, V., Brewster C. (2000). "Making their own way: International experience through self-initiated foreign assignments." *Journal of World Business*, 35(4), pp. 417–436.

Szkudlarek, B. (2009). "Through Western eyes: Insights into the intercultural training field." *Organization Studies*, 30(9), pp. 975–986.

Takeuchi, R. et al. (2005). "An integrative view of international experience." *Academy of Management Journal*, 48(1), pp. 85–100.

Thomas, D. C., Elron, E., Stahl G., Ekelund, B., Ravlin, E., Cerdin, J.-L., Poelmans, S., Brislin, R., Pekerti, A., Aycan, Z., Maznevski, M., Au, K., Lazarova, M. (2008). "Cultural intelligence: Domain and assessment." *International Journal of Cross-Cultural Management*, 8(2), pp. 123–143.

Van de Vijver, F.J.R., Leung, K. (2009). "Methodological issues in researching intercultural competence." In D. K. Deardorff (ed.), *The SAGE Handbook of Intercultural Competence*. Thousand Oaks, CA: SAGE, pp. 404–418.

Van der Zee, K. I., Van Oudenhoven, J. P. (2001). "The Multicultural Personality Questionnaire: Reliability and validity of self- and other ratings of multicultural effectiveness." *Journal of Research in Personality*, 35(3), pp. 278–288.

Waxin, M.-F., Barmeyer, C. (2008). *Gestion des ressources humaines internationales*. Rueil-Malmaison: Editions Liaisons.

Zarifian, P. (1995). *Compétences et stratégies d'entreprise*. Paris: Editions Liaisons.

Zellmer-Bruhn, M. E., Gibson, C. (2014). "How does culture matter? A contextual view of intercultural interaction in groups." In M. Yuki and M. Brewer (eds.), *Culture and Group Processes*. New York: Oxford University Press, pp. 342–402.

13 Are Intercultural Competences at the Center of Job-Market Demands?

Sophie Wodociag, Axelle Lutz and Chiara Ghislieri

Introduction

Globalization and pressure to innovate are pushing companies to further open up to the international sector, which in turn is driving a transformation of organizational structures (Doz et al., 2001) and changing the organizational pattern (Mayrhofer, 2011). This phenomenon implies a growing need for international human resources, diversification of mobility assignment mechanisms (Petrovic et al., 2000) and development of new competences, including intercultural competences (Spitzberg and Changnon, 2009). Employees need to deal with evolution in job conceptualization, like lifetime employment, nomad careers (Cadin et al., 2000) or career promises (Dany, 2001). They need to elaborate new strategies to guarantee their employability that integrate the international job dimension. Numerous studies confirm the importance employers give to international profiles and especially employees who have experienced intercultural mobility (Fielden et al., 2007).

Many studies have examined job conditions in a traditional international environment, typically expatriation, but little research has emerged that addresses recent evolutions of international employment (Desmarais et al., 2012). In particular, only a few empirical studies have examined the link between employability and intercultural competences. Intercultural competence development has never been examined in the specific frame of new, shorter and more flexible forms of international assignments. Some studies have challenged the relationship between international experience and intercultural competences development (Bartel-Radic, 2014). Furthermore, few longitudinal studies have observed intercultural competences and employability as dynamic processes. Employers have struggled to clearly grasp the concept of intercultural competences (Busch and Ingram, 2011). Consequently, although the main players in the job market have attempted to invest in intercultural competence development, it is still an unfamiliar concept (Bartel-Radic, 2009). A key challenge today is how to match employees' perceptions regarding job market expectations in terms of competences according to their cultural filters and their job function.

228 *Sophie Wodociag et al.*

Here we set out to examine job market expectations in terms of intercultural competences. The aim pursued is twofold:

- Understand the job market expectations through a triangular approach (international territory, several stakeholders) in order to emerge critical points (divergent or convergent) for the actors involved (students, employees, employers, institutions)
- Understand what place the different actors lend to the international dimension and to intercultural competences (Deardorff, 2006).

To this end, we led an exploratory qualitative study on 47 actors (26 women and 21 men) engaged in the Upper Rhine labor market: 13 students, 14 employees, 12 employers, and 8 institutional representatives.

The chapter first introduces the theoretical framework upon which this study was based before going on to set out the methodology used and detail the main results found. The results are then discussed in the light of scientific literature on the issue and their managerial implications.

Theoretical Foundations

With the internationalization of organizational structures, the development of intercultural competences was often considered a strategic benefit. Indeed, companies are sensitive to the cultural diversity of their worldwide branches and to the international competences developed by their employees (Berthier and Roger, 2010).

However, intercultural competences correspond to a set of analytical and strategic skills that expand the range of interpretations and actions used by people during their interpersonal interactions (Barmeyer, 2007, p. 10), which is what makes intercultural competences a potentially important strategic asset. Here, without aiming to present an exhaustive review of the literature, we cover the theoretical concepts on which our contribution was founded.

Competences and Organizational Strategy

Competence means having sufficient skills, capabilities and knowledge to demonstrate an appropriate behavior, in both words and deeds, in a particular context (Deardorff, 2011). It is based on the ability to combine resources in order to implement an activity or a process of specific actions (Le Boterf, 1994). In other words, a competence is an efficient operational know-how. According to McClelland (1965), competences form a cognitive system of models and behaviors that function together and enable people to perform at work. For Igalens and Scouarnec (2001), competences are linked to actions that result in success and performance. Indeed, demonstrating the right skills at the right time is the key to success. Other scholars

Intercultural Competences at the Centre 229

challenge the linkage between competences and performance, claiming that the people with the most talent are not always the people that deliver the best performance (François and Aissani, 2003).

The literature offers numerous classifications of competences according to the area considered. As this chapter is in the scope of international strategy, we introduce the competences as follows:

- Individual competences, that is, the operational knowledge that enables people to engage action and show responsiveness (Michaux, 2009).
- Collective competences, which correspond to the capacity to coordinate and cooperate in collective action and responsivity (Michaux, 2009). These competences emerge from the synergy of the individual interactions at work and the collective apprenticeship produced by the group's adaptation in response to shifts in international and external environment, to risks and so forth (Michaux, 2009).
- Organizational competences, which are defined as the competences guaranteeing the company's competitive position (Michaux, 2009). This leads to implicit and collective knowledge and enables the organization to efficiently carry out an activity (Galbraith, 1994) by selecting the most competent employees. Mobilizing the (sometimes new) right organizational skills at the right time helps assure continued competitive advantage. There is thus an adaptation dynamic that underlines this concept and that may potentially render the firm's strategic competences obsolete (Lawler and Ledford, 1997).

The combination between levels of these competences is not always explicit (Michaux, 2009). Some scholars posit that collective competences result from the interaction of individual competences (Tywoniak, 1998; Dejoux, 2000). For others, individual competences, especially the cooperative (Richebé, 2007) and behavioral (Cavestro et al., 2007) competences, are both founders and beneficiaries of collective knowledge (Retour and Krohmer, 2006). The collective competences seem to feed on both individual and organizational dimensions.

From Competences to Intercultural Competences

Through organizational internationalization, intercultural competences become strategic resources (Livian, 2012). Although there is no consensus regarding their definition, intercultural competences may be understood as the process of cultural sensitivity development (Bennett, 1986a, 1986b) through active exposure to cultural differences (Spitzberg and Changnon, 2009). Intercultural sensitivity refers to the level of complexity induced by the perception and awareness of different cultures: higher intercultural sensitivity equates to better perception and awareness of these cultural differences. In other

230 Sophie Wodociag et al.

words, intercultural competences correspond to the individual capacity to implement an efficient behavior and act and communicate appropriately (Deardorff, 2006) in an intercultural context. Its performance resides in the successful interactions (Barmeyer and Davoine, 2006). In a behavioral approach (Barmeyer, 2007), Earley et al. (2006) add that intercultural intelligence allows people to manage and resolve different intercultural situations respecting a logic of group harmony.

The wide span of definitions of intercultural competence illustrates the complexity underpinning this concept. Faust (2015) examines intercultural competences according to five main themes, which the authors fully discussed. The empirical part of our study is based on these dimensions:

- The cognitive dimension, which concerns the comprehension and knowledge of cultural system functioning (Black et al., 1991) for others and oneself (Davel et al., 2008; Deardorff, 2009). This requires knowledge of a market, its structure and local practices, language skills, knowledge of economic, political and social factors, and the way business is done.
- The emotional dimension, through which an individual's personal characteristics favor openness to and acceptance of others (Black et al., 1991): empathy, tolerance of ambiguity, openness to difference, lack of value judgment, flexibility, patience, curiosity and so forth. This dimension articulates a profound link between the knowledge and behavior of individuals (Earley and Ang, 2003).
- The behavioral dimension, which relates to interpersonal aspects, that is, the capacity to modify the way we behave with others (Earley and Ang, 2003), interact (Black et al., 1991; Deardorff, 2006) and communicate, in a way that is specific to the role adopted during the mobility or intercultural situation to manage, and where intercultural competences are useful for managing resources, such as for communication with other employees, setting objectives or motivating staff.
- The motivational dimension and the social network (Berthoin Antal, 2000) contribute to understand the company processes. Intercultural competences can change prospects and help understand organizational activities with a global view of the organizational system's objectives, structure and processes (Kogut and Zander, 1996). Its challenge is to motivate motivating individuals to integrate the organizational dynamic.
- The identity dimension (Morace and Schulze, 2006) considers a questioning of the concept of self, and the ability to keep a coherent identity in any situation and develop self-confidence.

Thus, intercultural competences include individual (Bennett, 1986b), collective (Barmeyer and Davoine, 2012), organizational and strategic facets

Intercultural Competences at the Centre 231

according to the context in which they are used (Faust, 2015). Therefore, they are increasingly sought after by organizations present on the international scene and thus warrant consideration in any internal or external organizational mobility process.

The Intercultural Competences—Work Relationship Linkage in International Settings

The employment relationship materializes when offer meets demand. It involves three stakeholders: the employer, the employee and the territory (Saint-Germes, 2006). The fulfilment of expectations and perceptions serves to resolve to the "employment" equation. People are expected to cultivate their potential to get recruited, to evolve within their job or to change (Hillage and Pollard, 1998)—that is, to cultivate their "employability." Employability refers to theoretical and practical competences (Harvey, 2004), like knowledge, skills and capacities.

According to Anglo-Saxon trend, the employability "initiative" is the responsibility of the individual (it is up to the employee to cultivate their skills). Conversely, European researchers stress the importance of placing this dimension within organizations and institutions (Saint-Germes, 2006), as employability is based on both informal learning, in a professional context, and formal learning, during training. This is called interactive employability. Thus, employability should be shared between the three parties involved in the relationship: the employer, the employee and the territory (Saint-Germes, 2006). Employability can be conceived as a bilateral concept: for the company, it is a strategic asset in a logic of skill creation; for the employee, it is essential to cope with the constant evolution of the labor market (Baruel Bencherqui et al., 2012). In this context, studying the expectations of the labor market implies an examination of competencies according to the perceptions of the stakeholders mentioned earlier. This theoretical framework inspired the present study and was borrowed for our empirical analysis.

Different people also have different understandings of the employment relationship. Expectations can differ according to a number of factors, like socialization, national culture, organizational culture, organizational and professional socialization and so forth (Morrison and Robinson, 1997).

Therefore, the understanding of the expectations inherent to the employment relationship results from individual culture and perceptions (Thomas et al., 2003). Their subjectivity questions their trueness. What happens if the expectations are inadequate, not understood, or fail to materialize in reality? The process becomes more complex in an international and multicultural job market where stakeholders' expectations and representations become opaque due to the cultural filter.

In an international and multicultural job market, are intercultural competences perceived as a fundamental and inescapable issue? Which

Figure 13.1 Expectation of the parties in the international job market

strategies to develop intercultural competences do the parties involved deploy? (Bartel-Radic, 2009).

Figure 13.1 addresses the question of representations and expectations concerning competences and intercultural competences through the multicultural lens of the three main actors in an international job market.

Methodology

Here we detail the methodological choices made and the adapted protocol used and then present the participants in the study.

A Regional Context Marked by High Cross-Border Mobility

The territory considered in this study is the Upper-Rhine region: the cross-border territory that includes northwest Switzerland, Alsace in France, and Baden-Wurtemberg and Rhineland-Palatinate in Germany (Koukoutsaki-Monnier, 2014). This area of sub-regional economic cooperation, institutionalized by the *Regio Basiliensis* in 1962 and then by the *Regio of Upper Rhine*, is relevant for our research as it provides a multicultural context (Hall, 2008) that is rich in both divergent representations and inter-nation

Intercultural Competences at the Centre 233

flows intensified by proximity (Hamman, 2014) that, paradoxically, are based on a common cross-border identity (Koukoutsaki-Monnier, 2014). The cross-border cooperation leads to low political and social integration linked to the progressive disappearance of the administrative border but also high economic integration characterized by high technological performance and high people mobility, as reflected in a huge cross-border flow of workers. Indeed, according to INSEE (2015), 44% of active workers (159,600 workers including 40,400 individuals in the Haut-Rhin) in the ACAL region (Alsace-Champagne-Ardenne-Lorraine) hold a cross-border job, with 30% of cross-border workers employed in industry and another 30% in the tertiary sector (16% in commerce and 14% in business services). Whereas many cross-border workers are unspecialized labor (38% in 2012), a majority are qualified workers (48%). The average age of cross-border commuters is increasing (on average, cross-border commuters in the Haut-Rhin were aged 43 in 2012). Moreover, this population is mainly male (only 35% are women). To our knowledge, there is no hard data on the tri-national labor market as a whole (without distinction of borders) and on the expectations of the different actors driving it.

Protocol

This research is part of an exploratory process. In this preliminary study, we chose to mobilize a qualitative research methodology. The qualitative survey aims to observe a situation in order to highlight and analyze one or more phenomena. It allows us to examine the meaning that people give to their experiences as well as their representations (Usunier et al., 1993). It is through a variety of situations (Bertaux, 2010) and actors that we can investigate the mechanisms implemented by the individuals in our population to arrive at the situation in which they find themselves at a given point in time (Bertaux, 2010). Our way of producing knowledge pursued abductive reasoning (Peirce, 1958), as retroduction through analogical reasoning makes it possible to go from a given conception of a phenomenon to the conception of completely different mechanisms, structures and dynamics that are still related to the phenomenon initially considered (Lawson, 1997). Thus this study covers a double methodological and empirical issue:

- Describe in depth our object of research, that is, the expectations of a tri-national job market concerning competences and intercultural competences. It is the intensity of the description that gives an objectivity to the research issues identified (Bertaux, 2010).
- Produce ideas and concepts to explain any drivers of a phenomenon found (Gavard-Perret et al., 2012) through a triangular analysis—in other words, to emerge research issues from an understanding of observed system functioning according to divergent and convergent points of view.

234 Sophie Wodociag et al.

We devised a semi-directive questionnaire that was conducted on the basis of an interview guide (or thematic grid) conceived from the focal themes (De Sardan, 1995): employment relationship, competences and intercultural competences. The guide included open-ended questions as well as a section collecting socio-professional data on the participants. The semi-directive interview was not led as an interview but more as a discussion: participants were encouraged to freely express their thoughts on the studied phenomenon. The researcher was to ensure all themes got discussed and to reopen debate or guide speech if deeper conversation was necessary.

The interviews, with an average duration of 45 minutes, were led face-to-face or by phone during the period May–July 2016. All interviews were recorded and transcribed and were done in French in order to homogenize the verbatim. Although every participant was very proficient in spoken French, language factors may have introduced expressive bias in their representations.

From a horizontal and vertical inquiry, the interviews were examined through a double thematic and comparative analysis. First was an analysis of open corpora (Blanchet and Gotman, 1992), where the recurring themes are identified in each interview and then confronted. The second was an analysis to highlight a common mechanism (same logic, same actions) between the testimonies gathered. We then cross-analyzed the theoretical concepts mobilized during the review of the literature, according to:

- Role of the participant (student, employee, employer, institution)
- Nature of competences (individual, collective, organizational, strategic)
- Representation of intercultural competences (cognitive, emotional, behavioral, motivational, identity).

Participants

Our participants sample was built progressively. In order to collect a large diversity of representations concerning the studied phenomenon, we gathered participants whose representations and experiences diverged over their functional job position (role, status, etc.) despite sharing the same social reality (Bertaux, 2010). Every perception of reality contains a part of truth. Taking into consideration multiple perceptions allows to identify an objective reality. The research issues are based on the convergence of the participants' representations.

Thus, 47 people (26 women and 21 men) participated in this survey. They were all connected to the Upper Rhine region and to the area of management. In order to reflect the structure of the labor market, the participants were classified into four categories: 13 students, 13 employees, 13 employers and 8 institutional representatives. The choice of these

Intercultural Competences at the Centre 235

Table 13.1 Profile of participants by category

Category	Profiles
Students	At least a bachelor's degree in management $n = 10$ in initial training, $n = 3$ in dual training N. 7 women, N.6 men
Employees	At least a master's degree $n = 12$ women, $n = 2$ men $n = 4, < 30$ years old; $n = 7$, between 30 and 40 years old; $n = 2, > 40$ years old $n = 8$ in the private sector, $n = 5$ in the public sector An average seven years of experience with the company $n = 10$ experts, $n = 3$ managers $n = 6$ worked in a company of > 250 employees, $n = 7$ in a SME
Employers	$n = 5$ women, $n = 8$ men $n = 13$ managers $n = 10$, private-sector companies; $n = 3$, public-sector agencies $n = 7$ companies of > 250 employees, $n = 6$ SME
Institutions	$n = 3$ women, $n = 5$ men $n = 1$, German institutions; $n = 3$, French institutions; $n = 4$ Swiss institutions

categories was based on the employability model (Saint-Germes, 2006) and made possible to report the evolution of representations over the course of the career path: the student was at the beginning of professional life, the employee had consolidated some experience, and the employer was able to experience vertical mobility. Table 13.1 details the participants' profiles by category and illustrates their diversity.

Results

First we compared expectations of the main stakeholders in the Upper-Rhine job market. Then we questioned the place of intercultural competences. Finally, we evidenced the perceived opacity of the link between intercultural competences and organizations' international trajectories.

Job Market Expectations

Participants spoke very little about their representation of the labor market per se. Their reflections on expectations, in terms of employment, remained focused on skills expected, developed or yet to develop, without making the link with the job market in which they evolve. However, the job market structure carried a high degree of complexity as it is tri-territorial and open

236   *Sophie Wodociag et al.*

to the international market, with a high range of diversified companies (from SMEs to multinationals). The different representations of this market could have led to different strategies on the part of the stakeholders. However, they each focused on their own specific case without expanding their viewpoint outwards. They only distinguished internal (within the company) and external labor markets, and their expectations diverged between these two channels.

The stakeholders identified multiple competences with divergent interpretations. Indeed, every actor evolved and perceived competences according to his or her personal and cultural context:

> "How does the company perceive that the employee is going to bring something?"; "There is a subjective effect, yet for example, companies like to think that once aged over 50 years we cannot bring anything, especially if you are a woman, etc."; "it is on the subjective side."

Nevertheless, it is possible to perform an analysis by category, as follows:

- Students encountered difficulties defining who they are, what represented them, and what is expected on the labor market. They struggled to link their degree with a job offer. Only students with a deeper experiential background (through work-study programs or internships) advanced a case for more developed know-how ("we have to encourage dual training because you learn a lot, I learn more at work than in class"). Those who already have international experience were best able to detail and justify their professional integration strategy:

  > If you do an Erasmus in Germany, you are then eligible to apply for positions, and also in Germany since you have already acquired the language. Anyway, it's always a plus to say you did a year of study abroad, and I think it's really beneficial for the person who does.

  These students thus bank on their linguistic and technological skills: "language and some software are the kind of skills you can put on a CV."
- Employees, who have begun to reap experience, know better who they are, what they are interested in and what they can offer. Experience helps them build a stronger identity. The more a person goes further in their life, the more they can experience. As a result, they can build their own cultural (or intercultural), identity map if they get the opportunity. Competences are developed over years, and the competences that make a profile interesting are versatility and the ability to build relationships and give meaning. It is not about having all the required competences ("the real problem of a

Intercultural Competences at the Centre 237

recruiter is that they want the all-in-one package, and that's not good") but showing that they have the competences to learn some more ("you have to be versatile and have to want to keep learning things"). General profiles are sometimes an asset over more specialized profiles as the employee can contribute to the organization's global strategy ("I could bring interesting new ideas to the company, rather than staying boxed in my little work"). When employees step into the shoes of their managers, they get to determine the expectations of the job market, which is not realistically a reflection they gain from their own path. A lot of them, like students, understand linguistic competences as essential because more and more companies are internationalizing ("either way, going international is critical for lots of companies"). Finally, the idea of selling themselves, even if they don't possess all the required competences, emerged as important ("even if we have no experience in a given field, I think all can be learned, so we need to sell our personality, our way to do things").

- Employers tend to value transversal competences, which aligns them with representations by the employees. Technical expertise ("core of the job") and linguistic competences are non-negotiables, but it is still the candidate's personality that makes the difference. Adaptability ("I do not need someone who is going to say: 'tell me what to do'; that is not what I'm looking for"), flexibility ("That's it, we manage to our objectives, not to the work schedule"), open-mindedness and empathy, versatility and initiative-taking ("self-management by employees in service"), tolerance and understanding of others are what make the employee stand out, as it is these competences that make them capable of responding quickly to change (innovations, globalization, etc.) and also let the organization renew itself. International experience is seen as an advantage as it deepens these aspects.
- Institutions have a more ambivalent approach. Institutions put themselves in the role of intermediary and sometimes spectator. They tend to highlight actions that can be put in place to encourage employability rather than the expectations of the job market. Like the employees and the employers, these participants speak about transversal competences like linguistic competences and IT skills, but they also voice a barrier to mobility that is a central concern ("European mobility serves to reinforce capacities for dealing with and integrating the unknown, and this experience could be reused for another position").

Table 13.2 presents the convergences and divergences in competency representations by category (students, employees, employers, institutions) as emerged from our analysis:

238 *Sophie Wodociag et al.*

Table 13.2 Convergent and divergent representations of the expected competences

Principal actors	Convergences	Divergences
Students	• Linguistics competences • Theoretical competences developed via training and education • Competences via consolidated in-company practice	• International experience • General training vs. technical specialization • Tendency to mobility • Role of the institution, which encourages (or not) professional integration
Employees	• Linguistic competences • Verbal and non-verbal communication • Adaptation • Flexibility • Versatility • Identity reflection	• International experience • Different perception of interculturality depending on the considered object: collaborators vs. company's partners • Importance of hard skills/technical competences • Representations link to the organizational context • Stay on job market standby • Build social networks • Stand out from others • Development mode of competences
Employers	• Linguistic competences • Verbal and non-verbal communication and non-verbal • Adaptation • Open-mindedness • Tolerance • Self-management of responsibilities • Knowing how to take initiative	• International experience • Position's flexibility vs. candidate's flexibility • Curiosity • Experience level vs. candidate's motivation • Development mode of competences
Institutions	• Linguistic competences	• International experience • Acquisition mode of competences • Importance of the private sphere to develop professional competences • Mobility

Finally, we observe a certain misfit between expectations of the different considered actors. Divergences are principally related to the developmental modality of competences. International experience is particularly asked for. Because of the multiculturalism of the job market considered

Intercultural Competences at the Centre 239

in this study, we expected a consensus on intercultural competences as indispensable, but this was not always the case. The next part investigates this aspect further.

International Dimension of Organizations and Intercultural Competences

Participants split their thinking between what is necessary for work in a company and the value of international experience by enhancing their transversal competences and personal features. They often match to a dimension that ties into training for intercultural competences. Nevertheless, the relation between these aspects is always tangible, although the link between intercultural and international stays unclear. Also, companies focused on the international sphere take into account cultural diversity as a driver of success in international operations ("there are always things that are good to take away and adopt in other countries"). Local companies sometimes refute this dimension, even if their teams possess a high level of multiculturalism ("in big groups, international experience is increasingly important, but at our level [French SME], not at all"). Table 13.3 shows the parallel between expected competences and intercultural competences according to cognitive, emotional, behavioral, motivational and identity-based dimensions (Earley and Ang, 2003; Deardorff, 2006; Faust, 2015) and according to participants' representations, regardless of their status (student, employee, employer, institution).

This study found that certain transversal competences are not recognized as intercultural competences by the actors interviewed. Actors outside an international context struggle to link the two.

When participants speak about intercultural competences, they think first about linguistic competences ("some languages, like English, you don't even need to put it in job ads any more"). All actors agree to say that linguistic competences are the basis of intercultural competences. Some of them stop their analysis at linguistic competences whereas others go on to also cite personal features like mobility, open-mindedness, empathy and adaptability. The intercultural and cross-generational dimension seems to be very important for work in a team: "In my team, I have Alsatians, people who come from other countries or other companies, so I have a very large panel, which makes it important to be open-minded, multicultural I would say, and multi-generational too."

According to an employer, the ability to understand the other's culture enables better interaction, which is important for someone who has to lead a team. International mobility encourages open-mindedness toward others, which in turns allows to learn more the ways they think and work as well as way they live and the way they are. However, you don't need mobility to develop this kind of competence. Intercultural competences allow people to be more flexible in intercultural situations and quickly

240 *Sophie Wodociag et al.*

Table 13.3 Parallel between competences and intercultural competences

Representations of . . .	Competences	Intercultural competences
Cognitive dimension	• Market knowledge • Theoretical knowledge • Linguistics knowledge • Computing knowledge • Technical expertise, IT • Analytical mindset • Organizational knowledge • Intercultural knowledge • Capacity to put things in perspective	• Linguistics knowledge • Intercultural knowledge
Emotional dimension	• Autonomy • Initiative-taking • Flexibility • Empathy • Open-mindedness • Adaptation • Curiosity • Tendency toward mobility • Ambition • Patience • Respect • Versatility	• Open-mindedness • Curiosity • Empathy • Adaptation • Respect
Behavioral dimension	• Communication • Conflict management • Know how to compromise • Socialization • Capacity to work in groups	• Conflict management • Communication
Motivational dimension	• Motivation • Leadership	
Identity dimension	• Knowing oneself to better know others • Personal well-being	

adapt appropriately: "If I have to recruit people from other cultures, those people will know how to adapt and will find it easy to communicate and engage with other people in the group."

When you know how the other reacts, you can avoid a lot of conflicts and benefit from a more enriching experience: "It maybe demands effort from employers and employees to make a team collaborate well, but it is also enriching." This is essential when you work in an international setting. For the institutions, European mobility can be an asset to break down barriers to geographical or professional mobility:

"Mobility could be an enabler to get a job, develop competences in employability, gain knowledge of foreign languages, adaptability"; "all life experiences participate in development of employability. European mobility helps reinforce capabilities, face the unknown, adapt to and integrate unknowns, and all this experience can be reused for another position."

However, employers are unanimous in saying that the cultural diversification of their teams stays in second place behind technical competences, which still come first.

Intercultural Competences and Organizational Strategies

The results of this study do not highlight intercultural competence as strategic competences. While they may be introduced as an added value for a résumé, they are not considered strategic resources by the organizations (in the sense of the earlier literature review).

The competences mentioned by the different actors are mainly individual competences, and sometimes collective competences, but only one employee talked about the link between employees' competences and organizational competences:

> I would say that with experience, long experience in the same company, we are going to develop a stronger versatility, a history too, the ability to link things together; so there is always better potential for the company when it can keep its employees.

Only one employee touched on evolutions in the organizational structure of his company and his competences, claiming that as the structure became less hierarchical and more horizontal, interaction between employees became easier and more direct. The important competences are now the capacity to bind socially, self-manageability, self-efficiency and readiness to engage. New technologies and the wider globalization frame and erase frontiers and even jetlag ("people are more conducive to interaction, and there is a lot of networking now, we create a network").

Discussion and Conclusion

Following this analysis of our findings, we now turn to discuss the limitations of this study and suggest lines for future research.

Contrast of the Main Findings

Looking at our first objective, this study provides insight into international job market expectations by cross-comparing the perceptions of different stakeholders. We highlight how expectations fit with transversal competences, that is, a savoir-faire that a company uses daily in the frame of its team and project management (Chauvet, 2001). This representation is

242 *Sophie Wodociag et al.*

particularly strong for the employees and employers. These meta-skills are becoming more important than technical expertise (Chauvet, 2001). This joins up with the idea of dynamic employability, which means "an ability to be in the job, to stay in it, to adapt and to bounce back if necessary" (Saint-Germes, 2006, p. 2). Is it logical, in terms of competence creation, that organizations have to consider employability as a strategic asset? For the employee, it remains essential to realign to constant evolutions in the job market (Baruel Bencherqui et al., 2012). The promise of a long-term job, based on a profession-centered logic, gives way to a promise of employability (Guerrero, 2001) and to the employability network (Boltanski and Chiapello, 1999).

Looking at our second objective, this study highlights the diversity of representations of intercultural competences with divergences of opinion about their importance. The intercultural dimension is not greatly considered by the parties involved, even if they interact in a strongly intercultural context. The job market does not explicitly demand intercultural competences, but it does value linguistic competences. At this juncture, it is important to temper these conclusions according to the adopted posture. Employers, particularly those who have a managerial position, hold less decisive representations, which is linked to fact that there is no explicit managerial device for cultural competences, even in multinationals (Chevrier, 2003). Companies essentially plan out training action oriented toward the development of cognitive skills (knowledge about the country, language) (Chevrier, 2003) to the detriment of people skills, which are nevertheless essential to resolving intercultural conflicts. The urgency of international missions often prevents proper preparation of the people sent out (Chevrier, 2003). This lack of preparation is reinforced by the emergence of new, shorter and more flexible forms of mobility (Mayerhofer et al., 2011), which lead to the banalization of international careers.

Far from being considered as strategic by the study participants, intercultural competences stay individual, or at best collective when they have to work in groups or interact with people from other cultures. Is this limitation tied to the participants' mode of development, which according to Spitzberg and Changnon (2009) is the result of an individual learning process? The collective psyche tends to only associate a high level of intercultural competence with people who have experienced long stays abroad (Dubouloy and Cerdin, 2004) or strong international mobility (Franke and Nicholson, 2002). However, the scholarship has not yet gone into any depth on investigating the link between international mobility experiences and intercultural competences (Bartel-Radic, 2014). International competence is not the only determinant in the intercultural competence learning process, as immersion in an intercultural team, for example, also helps to develop intercultural competence.

The overlap between transversal competences and intercultural competences, highlighted by our first results, shows the lack of readability of the

Intercultural Competences at the Centre 243

job market (international or classical) and confirms the lack of consensus around defining and measuring intercultural competences (Bartel-Radic, 2014; Van de Vijver and Leung, 2009). The lack of permeability between academic-world research and business-world practice could be part of the reason why companies are struggling to understand the concept.

The world today is undergoing unprecedentedly intensive globalization and it is necessary for business groups to develop good competences to set up efficient internationalization strategies. Do today's strategies correctly translate in terms of recruitment by human resources management functions? During a recruitment drive for an international post, the mode of selection all too often turns to traditional practices (Moore et al., 2002) grounded in misconceptions like the idea that all international managers share common features or that intercultural competences are developed individually (Dowling and Welch, 2005; Moore, 2002). A complementary progressive approach like personality testing together with in-situation observation would nevertheless be good ways to identify a person's capacity to interact with people from other cultures, better apprehend their communication codes, and ultimately adapt in a multicultural team (Bernard, 2004).

Limitations of the Study and Lines for Future Research

This was a preliminary study that does have limitations. First, there may be biases related to the nature of this study, such as its context or the social situation of the respondents (Poupart, 1997). We focused on participants from the same region but without distinctions of their "home" territory whereas there may be administrative, cultural and linguistic frontiers too. To better identify the representations of each participant and understand their expectations and constraints, it would be wise, in future studies, to adopt a comparative approach by nation. In addition, the diversity of competences depends on the context and the people involved (Rive and Collin, 2011). Thus the choice here to categorize participants by category as students, employees, employers and institutions could be refined to allow a sharper analysis of the results. In addition, we focused on the same business field (management) in order to have the possibility to compare expectations, but surveying other professions and business fields may give a finer analysis, as the plurality of responses collected would help better identify the specific features of each category. From a methodological standpoint, this study, like any qualitative research, is exposed to a degree of subjectivity and lacks external validity (Krefting, 1990). Future work, with quantitative input, could further explore the avenues for research highlighted here.

The capacity to understand people from different origins influences the development of intercultural or international competences. Scientific studies consistently say that there are numerous classifications and analyses of competences depending on the context of focus. The study led here

244 *Sophie Wodociag et al.*

emerged signs of linkage between transversal competences and intercultural competences, and while this is not enough to prompt a rethink of the strategic aspect of intercultural competences, our findings do question the way intercultural competences are valued and developed for the wider aim of organizational sustainability.

References

Barmeyer, C. (2007). *Management interculturel et styles d'apprentissage. Etudiants et dirigeants en France, en Allemagne et au Quebec,* Quebec: Les Presses de l'Université Laval.

Barmeyer, C., Davoine, E. (2006). "Interkulturelle Zusammenarbeit und Führung in internationalen Teams. Das Beispiel Deutschland-Frankreich." *Zeitschrift Führung und Organisation,* Februar, pp. 35–39.

Barmeyer, C., Davoine, E. (2012). "Comment gérer le retour d'expatriation et utiliser les compétences acquises par les expatriés?" *Revue Internationale de Gestion,* 37(2), pp. 45–53.

Bartel-Radic, A. (2009). "La compétence interculturelle: état de l'art et perspectives." *Management International,* 13(4), pp. 11–26.

Bartel-Radic, A. (2014). "La compétence interculturelle est-elle acquise grâce à l'expérience internationale?" *Management International,* 18, pp. 194–211.

Baruel Bencherquid, D.M.K., Le Flanchec, A., Servayre, A. (2012). "L'employabilité et son rôle sur la satisfaction, la formation et les réseaux sociaux." *Recherches en Sciences de Gestion-Management Science-Ciencias de Gestión,* 92, pp. 115–132.

Bennett, M. J. (1986a). *Comprehensive Multicultural Education: Theory and Practice.* Boston: Allyn and Bacon.

Bennett, M. J. (1986b). "A developmental approach to training for intercultural sensitivity." *International Journal of Intercultural Relations,* 10(2), pp. 179–196.

Bernard, G. (2004). Les compétences interculturelles: un enjeu sous-estimé par les entreprises. *Tribune.*

Bertaux, D. (2010). *Le récit de vie.* Paris: Armand Collin, collection 128, L'enquête et ses méthodes.

Berthier, P., Roger, A. (2010, August). "Le retour de mobilité internationale: rupture et opportunité." https://halshs.archives-ouvertes.fr/halshs-00681271.

Berthoin Antal, A. (2000). "Types of knowledge gained by expatriate managers." *Journal of General Management,* 26(2), pp. 32–51.

Black, J. S., Mendenhall, M. E., Oddou, G. (1991). "Toward a comprehensive model of international adjustment: An integration of multiple theoretical perspectives." *Academy of Management Review,* 16, pp. 291–317.

Blanchet, A., Gotman, A. (1992). *L'entretien.* Paris: Nathan, p. 127.

Boltanski, L., Chiapello, E. (1999). *Le nouvel esprit du capitalisme.* Paris: Gallimard, p. 843.

Bush, V. D., Ingram, T. N. (2001). "Building and assessing cultural diversity skills: Implications for sales training." *Industrial Marketing Management,* 30, pp. 65–76.

Cadin, C., Bender, A.-F., De Saint Giniez, V., Pringle, J. (2000). "Carrières nomades et modèles nationaux." *Revue de G.R.H.,* 37, pp. 76–96.

Cavestro, W., Colin, T., Grasser, B. (2007). "La gestion des compétences à l'épreuve de la compétence collective." In W. Cavestro, C. Durieux, and S. Monchatre (dirs.), *Travail et Reconnaissance des Compétences*. Paris: Economica, pp. 15–30.

Chauvet, A. (2001). "Quels indicateurs de la compétence?" *Bulletin des bibliothèques de France* (BBF), 3, pp. 82–90.

Chevrier, S. (2003). *Le management interculturel*. Paris: PUF, p. 127.

Dany, F. (2001). Gestion de carrières des cadres: des destinées individuelles plus ou moins prometteuses. *Faire Savoirs*, pp. 25–30.

Davel, E., Dupuis, J.-P., Chanlat, J.-F. (2008). *La gestion en contexte interculturel*, Montréal: Les Presses de l'Université Laval.

De Sardan, J. P. (1995). *Anthropologie et développement. Essai en socio-anthropologie du changement social*. Marseille: Karthala Collection, Hommes et Sociétés, p. 221.

Deardorff, D. K. (2006). "Identification and assessment of intercultural competence as a student outcome of internationalization." *Journal of Studies in International Education*, 10(3), pp. 241–266.

Deardorff, D. K. (2009). "Implementing intercultural competence assessment." *The SAGE Handbook of Intercultural Competence*. Thousand Oaks, CA: Sage, London, pp. 477–491.

Deardorff, D. K. (2011). "Intercultural competence in foreign language classrooms: A framework and implications for educators.' In Witte and Harden (eds.), *Intercultural Competence: Concepts, Challenges, Evaluations*, ISFLL, vol. 10. Peter Lang International Academic Publishers, Oxford.

Dejoux, C. (2000). "Pour une approche transversale de la gestion des compétences." *Gestion*, 6, pp. 15–31.

Desmarais, C., Ghislieri, C., Wodociag, S. (2012). "Les cadres pendulaires internationaux: des conditions de travail particulièrement difficiles?" *Revue Française de Gestion*, 38(226), pp. 91–106.

Dowling, P., Welch, D. (2005). *International Human Resource Management: Managing People in an International Context* (4th ed.). Mason, OH: South-Western.

Doz, Y., Santos, J., Williamson, P. (2001). *From Global to Metanational: How Companies Win*. Boston: Harvard Business School Press.

Dubouloy, M., Cerdin, J. L. (2004). "Expatriation as a maturation opportunity: A psychoanalytical approach based on 'copy and paste.'" *Human Relations*, 57(8), pp. 957–981.

Earley, P. C., Ang, S. (2003). *Cultural Intelligence: Individual Interactions Across Cultures*. Palo Alto: Stanford University Press.

Earley, P. C., Ang, S., Tan, J. S. (2006). *CQ: Developing Cultural Intelligence at Work*. Stanford: Stanford University Press.

Faust, C. (2015). *Représentations et gestion des compétences interculturelles, le Cas de Renault*. Doctoral thesis, Paris-Est University.

Fielden, J., Middlehurst, R., Woodfield, S. (2007). *Global Horizons for UK Students: A Guide for Universities*. London: Council for Industry and Higher Education.

François, P.-H., Aissani, Y. (2003). "Représentations sociales des compétences et processus d'autorégulation des conduits." In C. Garnier and W. Doise (eds.), *Les Représentations sociales. Balisage du problème d'étude*. Montréal: Éditions Nouvelles.

246 *Sophie Wodociag et al.*

Franke, J., Nicholson, N. (2002). "Who shall we send? Cultural and other influences on the rating of selection criteria for expatriate assignments." *International Journal of Cross-Cultural Management,* 2(1), pp. 21–36.

Galbraith, J. R. (1994). *Competing with Flexible Lateral Organizations.* Reading: Addison-Wesley.

Gavard-Perret, M.-L., Gotteland, D., Haon, C., Jolibert, A. (2012). *Méthodologie de la recherche en gestion—Réussir son mémoire ou sa thèse.* Paris: Pearson Education, p. 428.

Guerrero, S. (2001). "Quelle stratégie de carrière, pour quel salaire? L'exemple des cadres français." *Gestion,* 26, pp. 12–17.

Hall, S. (2008). *Identités et cultures: Politiques des cultural studies.* Paris: Éditions Amsterdam, p. 411.

Hamman, P. (2014). *Repenser la ville à l'heure des injonctions au développement durable, dans Questions de communication.* Nancy: PUN—Editions Universitaires de Lorraine, p. 470.

Harvey, L. (2004). "Analytic quality glossary, quality research international." http://www. qualityresearchinternational. com/glossary.

Hillage, J., Pollard, E. (1998). "Employability: Developing a framework for policy analysis." *Labour Market Trends,* 107, pp. 83–84.

Igalens, J., Scouarnec, A. (2001). "La gestion par les compétences: construction d'une échelle de mesure." *Revue de Gestion des Ressources Humaines,* 40, pp. 2–16.

INSEE, Populations légales (2015). https://www.insee.fr/fr/statistiques/3292701.

Kogut, B., Zander, U. (1996). "What firms do? Coordination, identity and learning." *Organization Science,* 7(5), pp. 502–518.

Koukoutsaki-Monnier, A. (2014). *Identités (trans)frontalières au sein et autour de l'espace du Rhin supérieur.* Nancy: PUN—Editions Universitaires de Lorraine, p. 252.

Krefting, L. (1990). "Rigor in qualitative research: The assessment of truthworthiness." *American Journal of Occupation Therapy,* 45, pp. 214–222.

Lawler, E. E., Ledford, G. E. (1997). "New approaches to organizing: Competencies, capabilities and the decline of the bureaucratic model." In C. C. Cooper and S. E. Jackson (eds.), *Creating Tomorrow's Organizations: A Handbook for Future Research in Organizational Behavior.* Chichester: Wiley pp. 231–249.

Lawson, T. (1997). *Economics and Reality.* London: Routledge.

Le Boterf, G. (1994). *De la compétence, essai sur un attracteur étrange.* Paris: Les Editions d'organisation.

Livian, Y.-F. (2012). "Le concept de compétence interculturelle est-il un concept utile?" *Annales des Mines—Gérer et comprendre,* 107, pp. 87–94.

Mayerhofer, H., Schmidt, A., Hartmann, L., Bendl, R. (2011). "Recognising diversity in managing work life issues of flexpatriates." *Equality Diversity and Inclusion: An International Journal,* 30(7), pp. 589–609.

Mayrhofer, U. (2011). *Le management des firmes multinationales.* Paris: Vuibert, p. 268.

McClelland, D. C. (1965). "Toward a theory of motive acquisition." *American Psychologist,* 20, pp. 321–333.

Michaux, V. (2009). "Articuler les compétences individuelle, collective, organisationnelle et stratégique: les éclairages de la théorie des ressources et du capital social." In D. Retour, T. Picq, C. and Defélix (eds.), *Gestion des*

Intercultural Competences at the Centre 247

compétences—Nouvelles relations, nouvelles dimensions, France: Recherche AGRH: Vuibert, pp. 13–33.

Moore, R., Savall, H., Bonnet, M. (2002). "A la recherche d'une approche intégrée du management." In M. Peron (ed.), *Transdisciplinarité: fondement de la pensée managériale anglo-saxonne?* Paris: Economica.

Morace, C., Schulze, H. (2006). "Quelles compétences interculturelles pour les PME/PMI en Europe? L'exemple d'entrepreneurs en Bretagne et en Basse-Saxe." In J. Klusmeyer, U. Meyerholt, P. and Wengelowski (eds.), *Oldenburg, Beratung—Evaluation—Transfer*. Oldenburg University, Oldenburg (Deutschland), pp. 73–90.

Morrison, E. W., Robinson, S. L. (1997). "When employees feel betrayed: A model of how psychological contract violation develops." *Academy of Management Review*, 22, pp. 226–256.

Peirce, C. S. (1958). *Collected Papers*. Cambridge, MA: Harvard University Press.

Petrovic, J., Harris, H., Brewster, C. (2000). *New Forms of International Working*. Cranfield University, CReME Research Report 1/00 Cranfield School of Management.

Poupart, J. (1997). "L'entretien de type qualitatif: considérations épistémologiques, théoriques et méthodologiques." In J. Poupart, J.-P. Deslauriers, L. H. Groulx, A. Laperrière, R. Mayer, and A. P. Pires (eds.), *La recherche qualitative: Enjeux épistémologiques et méthodologiques*. Montréal: Gaëtan Morin, pp. 173–206.

Retour, D., Krohmer, C. (2006). "La compétence collective, maillon clé de la gestion des compétences." In C. Defélix, A. Klarsfeld, E. and Oiry (eds.), *Nouveaux regards sur la gestion des compétences*. Paris: Vuibert, pp. 139–173.

Richebé, N. (2007). "La rémunération des compétences est-elle un bon outil d'incitation à la coopération des salariés? Réflexions autour du paradoxe de la coopération." In *Rémunération des compétences*. Paris: Editions Economica, pp. 137–157.

Rive, J., Collin, P. M. (2011). "Evaluation des métiers à l'international: plaidoyer pour la création d'un observatoire des métiers." In U. Mayrhofer and A. Rugman (eds.), *Le management des firmes internationales*. Paris: Vuibert, p. 268.

Saint-Germes, E. (2006). *L'employabilité par ses pratiques d'évaluation lors des restructurations avec plan de sauvegarde de l'emploi*. 15th AGRH Congress, Reims Management School.

Spitzberg, B. H., Changnon, G. (2009). "Conceptualizing intercultural communication competence." In D. K. Deardorff (ed.), *The SAGE Handbook of Intercultural Competence*. Thousand Oaks, CA: Sage, pp. 2–52.

Thomas, D. C., Au, K., Ravlin, E. C. (2003). "Cultural variation and the psychological contract." *Journal of Organizational Behavior*, 24(5), pp. 451–471.

Tywoniak, S. A. (1998). "Le modèle des ressources et compétences: un nouveau paradigme pour le management stratégique?" In H. Laroch and J.-P. Nioche (eds.), *Repenser la stratégie—fondements et perspectives*. Paris: Vuibert, pp. 166–204.

Usunier, J.-C., Easterby-Smith, M., Thorpe, R. (1993). *Introduction à la recherche en gestion*. Paris: Economica, p. 233.

Van de Vijver, F.F.R., Leung, K. (2009). "Methodological issues in researching intercultural competence." In D. K. Deardorff (eds.), *The Sage Handbook of Intercultural Competence*. Thousand Oaks, CA: Sage, pp. 404–418.

14 Conclusion

Bruno Amann and Jacques Jaussaud

The contributions included in this book attempt to outline the considerable cultural and societal challenges involved in international management. The coordinators of the book wanted to organize it around three levels: at the strategic level, which is dealt mainly with in the first part of the book; at the ethical decision-making and corporate social responsibility level, which are dealt with in the second part of the book; and at the management and business practices level, which are dealt mainly with in the third part of the book.

At the level of strategic decision-making, the focus is on a number of major imbalances: imbalances arising from an unstable environment, an environment in crisis and the resilience, if any, of the organizations operating there; imbalances between organizations that resemble each other, followed by asymmetrical relationships; cultural imbalances and crises, or cultural imbalances and apprehension of the final hierarchical relationship.

In terms of ethical decision-making and corporate social responsibility, the variation takes place both at the national level (Cameroon, China) and at the organizational structural level (multinationals, including firms).

In terms of management and business practices, interculturalism is studied across certain national cultures (Turkey, India, Germany, Brazil) and through the intercultural expectations of the labor market in countries' border regions.

However, this three-tiered organization does not enable the comprehensive coverage of the cultural and societal challenges of international management to be fully addressed in such a slender book as this. The approach developed here is thus certainly partial, in certain regards possibly biased, certainly incomplete, reflecting nevertheless the choices and concerns of the coordinators as much as the ones of the different authors. Each author, in respect of sometimes sensitive issues, is solely or with co-authors collectively responsible for formatting the research and the development of ideas in their chapter.

This book is briefly a snapshot of the concerns of an academic community.

Index

Africa (n), 5, 26, 32, 99, 127
Algeria (n), 22, 25, 29
America (n), 78, 120, 141, 183, 185
Alliances
  asymmetric, 16, 9, 35, 36, 37, 41–43
  firm's, 3
  strategic, 16, 39

Bangladesh, 19
Bartlett, 98, 130
Beamish, 34, 38, 47, 163
Beijing, 148, 166
Brazil, 5, 93, 75, 76, 79
Brazilian
  German-Brazilian collaboration, 76,
    81–82, 88
  German-Brazilian context, 81, 85
  managers, 82, 83, 86
  subsidiary, 76, 79, 82
Business Ethics, 101, 119, 129, 143

Cameroon, 28, 97, 248
Canada, 21
Chairman Mao, 139, 140, 144
Child
  one-child policy, 95, 137, 150
China
  communist party, 140
  CSR, 137, 141
Chinese
  firms, 143
  population, 145
  values, 145
  students, 137, 147
Chittoor, 3, 7
Compliance, 22, 120, 130, 163, 188,
  194, 197
Confucianism, 138, 153

Control
  definition, 4
  internal tools, 106, 120
  Internalized mechanisms, 78
  systems, 4
Corporate social responsibility
  Africa, 99
  China, 137
  definition, 98
  guidelines, 98
  mechanisms, 107
  principles, 100
  transnational, 100
CSR *see* corporate social responsibility
CSR in, 137
  labor Laws, 142
  Made-in-China, 141
  Me-Generation, 144, 155
  NGO, 143
  socialist market economy, 140, 145
Culture
  Chinese, 139
  Indian, 184
  corporate, 77, 100, 119, 132, 192
  national, 62, 64, 121, 127, 177,
    210, 232
  organizational, 62, 78, 159, 177, 231

D'Iribarne, 64, 76, 101, 119, 130
Deng Xiaoping, 95, 137, 140
Diversity, 4, 64, 95, 103, 107, 118, 130,
  164, 185, 213, 221, 234, 242

Education
  generalist, 78, 88
  higher, 148, 210, 213
  public policies, 209
  quality, 89

250   *Index*

Egypt, 71
Eisenhardt, 15, 221
Emerging countries, 3, 94, 134
Environmental
   consideration, 193
   performance, 194, 197
   policies, 143
   sustainability, 204
   turbulence, 55
   regulation, 2
Entry modes, 35, 62
EPG – EPRG model, 63, 71
European union, 161, 194
Ethics, 6, 95, 99, 104, 106, 112, 118,
   143, 146, 156, 184
Ethical, 2, 4, 95, 98, 99, 106, 112,
   118, 127, 144, 154, 156,
   158–159, 184, 248
   charters, 118, 121, 130
   decision-making, 2, 248
   principles, 5, 105, 124, 146
   standards, 121, 129, 132
   tools, 95, 118, 122
   values, 5, 119, 158, 164

Fdi *see* Foreign Direct Investment
France, 2, 25, 66, 71, 95, 108, 122, 126,
   146, 148, 173, 187, 193, 216
French, 2, 26, 36, 39, 43, 63, 65, 72,
   77, 100, 105, 125, 137, 153,
   193, 210, 216, 220, 234
Foreign direct investment, 99, 114, 160

Gender, 119, 162, 219, 220
Germany
   family-owned company, 76, 81
   hidden champion, 27, 75
   multinational companies (MNCs),
   5, 75, 82
Geringer, 4, 163
Greenhouse gas emissions, 193

Hampden-Turner, 64, 91
Hebert, 181
Hofstede, 61, 65, 210, 217
Hu Jintao, 138
Huawei, 3
Human rights, 143, 146
Hymer, 21

India, 126, 173, 175, 186, 216
Indian Management, 203
Intercultural competence, 173, 209,
   212, 227

Islam, 77, 96, 156
Ivory Coast 26, 28

Japan, 84, 95, 122, 125, 138,
   146, 198
Johanson and Vahlne, 37, 47
Job-Market Demand, 227

Kindleberger, 21
Korea (n), 23, 27, 84, 146

Learning, 12, 31, 35, 77, 85, 88, 125,
   140, 179, 209, 214

Mao *see* Chairman Mao
Maoism *see* Maoist
Maoist, 137, 139
Mintzberg, 198
Mobility
Müsiad, 156

Ngos *see* non-governmental
   organizations
Non-governmental organizations, 1,
   99, 112, 143

Prahalad and Doz, 102
Perlmutter, 63, 71, 86, 132
Pettigrew, 180

Qatar, 26

Resilience, 12, 33, 247
Revolution, 5, 9, 11, 138, 178, 184

Saudi Arabia, 26
Schein, 79, 86, 177
Schwartz, 5, 64, 147, 153
SME *see* small and medium-sized
   enterprise
Small enterprise, 36
Small and medium-sized enterprise
   definition, 36
   internationalization, 45,
   60, 103
SOE *see* State-Owned Enterprises
State-owned enterprises, 141
Supply chain, 199, 206
Sustainability, 27, 179, 181, 187, 200,
   204, 244
Sweden, 122, 193

Tata, 187
Trompenaars, 64

Tunisia (n)
  context, 5, 13, 16
  jasmine revolution, 5
Turkey, 156, 160, 168

United Nation Organization, 181
United Kingdom, 118, 216
United States, 3, 84, 95, 120, 122,
  140, 175, 183, 216, 234

Weick, 11, 198
Wholly owned enterprises *see* wholly
  owned subsidiaries
Wholly owned subsidiaries, 62
World Bank, 17, 99, 124, 181

Xi Jinping, 137, 143

Yin, 60, 199

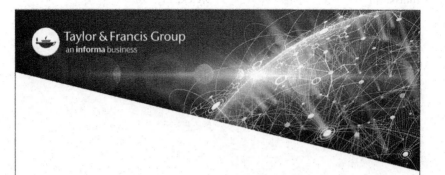